MICROSOFT®
MOUSE
PROGRAMMER'S
REFERENCE

MICROSOFT® MOUSE
PROGRAMMER'S
REFERENCE

Microsoft
P R E S S
®

PUBLISHED BY

Microsoft Press
A Division of Microsoft Corporation
16011 NE 36th Way, Box 97017, Redmond, Washington 98073-9717

Library of Congress Cataloging in Publication Data

Microsoft Mouse programmer's reference.
Includes index.
1. Microcomputers—Programming.   2. Computer interfaces.
I. Microsoft Press.
QA76.6.M516   1989   005.265   88-32395
ISBN 1-55615-191-8

Printed and bound in the United States of America.

1 2 3 4 5 6 7 8 9   MLML   3 2 1 0 9

Distributed to the book trade in the United States
by Harper & Row.

Distributed to the book trade in Canada by General
Publishing Company, Ltd.

Distributed to the book trade outside the United States
and Canada by Penguin Books Ltd.

Penguin Books Ltd., Harmondsworth, Middlesex, England
Penguin Books Australia Ltd., Ringwood, Victoria, Australia
Penguin Books N.Z. Ltd., 182-190 Wairau Road, Auckland 10, New Zealand

British Cataloging in Publication Data available

IBM®, PC/AT®, and PS/2® are registered trademarks of International Business Machines
Corporation. CodeView®, InPort®, Microsoft®, MS-DOS®, and XENIX® are registered trademarks
of Microsoft Corporation. UNIX™ is a trademark of AT&T Bell Laboratories. Microsoft Mouse
is a trademark of Microsoft Corporation.

Project Manager: David L. Rygmyr   **Project Editor:** O'Vivian Kent-Russell   **Technical Editor:** John Clark Craig

Contents

Acknowledgments

Several people made outstanding contributions to the *Microsoft Mouse Programmer's Reference*. In particular, we would like to thank the following reviewers whose technical skills and timely critiques proved invaluable to this project: Eric Fogelin, Tom Hensel, Greg Lee, and Paul Schuster. Their expertise, hard work, and dedication helped make this book a superb tool for serious programmers.

In addition, we would like to thank the following reviewers and writers who also made essential contributions: Rich Abel, Henry Burgess, Tom Button, Stew Chapin, Barbara Hubbard, Len Oorthuys, Steve Shaiman, Rick Thompson, Bill Wesse, and Nathan Williams.

Introduction

The *Microsoft Mouse Programmer's Reference* is both an overview and a technical resource for experienced programmers. The *Mouse Reference* includes a history of the Microsoft Mouse, an overview of mouse programming, detailed information on writing and using mouse menu programs, and detailed information on using the mouse programming interface to add mouse support to an application program you've written. In addition, the *Microsoft Mouse Programmer's Reference* offers a wealth of sample programs in several languages to demonstrate the topics and functions discussed in this book.

This package includes disks that contain the MOUSE.LIB and EGA.LIB libraries and all the sample mouse menu and mouse programming interface programs listed in this book. In addition, the disks include several lengthy sample programs not listed in the book.

The *Microsoft Mouse Programmer's Reference* is divided into four sections. Part I, "Introduction," provides a history of the Microsoft Mouse and an overview of mouse programming. Part II, "Mouse Menus," details the mouse menu programming language, gives a complete description of each mouse menu statement, and offers sample mouse menu programs. Part III, "Mouse Programming Interface," discusses the topics you'll need to consider when adding mouse support to a program you're writing. Part III also describes each of the mouse function calls available through MOUSE.LIB or Interrupt 33H and offers sample programs in QuickBASIC, Interpreted BASIC, C, Quick C, MASM, FORTRAN, and Pascal. In addition, Part III includes information on adding mouse support to programs that will run on an EGA and describes the EGA Register Interface functions available through the EGA.LIB library. The appendixes in Part IV cover mouse command line switches, mouse messages, and the ASCII character set.

The following notational conventions are used in this book:

Italics	Variable names, replaceable parameters in syntax lines, and function names in text
Initial Cap	Menu names, menu command names, and mouse function names
ALL CAPS	Filenames, directory names, and MS-DOS command names
Boldface	User input (what the user types)

PART I

Introduction

Chapter 1: Evolution of the Mouse

- The Early Mice
- The Microsoft Mouse
- Looking Ahead

Chapter 2: Overview of Mouse Programming

- The Mouse Driver
- Mouse Menus
- The Mouse Programming Interface

Chapter 1

Evolution of the Mouse

The mouse—a small, hand-held device that controls the movement of the cursor on a computer screen—was first developed 25 years ago. From humble beginnings as an odd-looking, one-button, wooden prototype, the mouse has evolved into a sleek, sophisticated tool that is nearly as familiar to today's computer user as the keyboard.

Spanning fewer than 10 years of the mouse's 25-year history, Microsoft's role in the evolution of the mouse is nevertheless significant. The Microsoft Mouse, first introduced in 1983, has set new standards for how people interact with the computer. Although Microsoft didn't invent the mouse, it has done much to fine-tune it. To understand Microsoft's involvement, let's look at how the mouse originated and developed.

THE EARLY MICE

We were experimenting with lots of types of devices at the time. Once the mouse proved itself to us, we tested it against several other devices, and it clearly won. I felt that until something better came along, the mouse would definitely remain the best pointing device for computer users.

—Doug Engelbart
Inventor of the mouse

When Doug Engelbart developed his wooden prototype of the mouse at Stanford Research Institute in 1963, he designed it for use with his Augment computer. Englebart's ideas later influenced the designs of the Xerox Star, Apple Lisa, and Apple Macintosh personal computers. Not even Engelbart then envisioned what occurred over the next 25 years.

Engelbart's mouse was a simple analog device that responded to each movement of the mouse by sending a signal to the software that shifted the position of the cursor on the screen. Inside the wooden mouse body were two metal wheels that were connected to the shafts of two variable resistors. Figure 1-1 shows Engelbart's mouse.

Figure 1-1. *Doug Engelbart's original wooden mouse.*

The concept of using a mouse became more widely known in the early seventies when Xerox Corporation's Palo Alto Research Center (PARC) commissioned Jack S. Hawley to build the first digital mouse. Hawley's mouse was basically a digital version of Engelbart's mouse. At the time, Xerox was developing the powerful Alto computer and wanted to include a mouse as part of the computer package. Although the Xerox Alto performed poorly in the marketplace—fewer than a hundred were sold—it paved the way for the future development of personal computers and the mouse. In 1975, Xerox asked Hawley to develop a new standard for the mouse, a standard that many manufacturers adopted and followed into the eighties. After Hawley completed his commission for Xerox, he went on to design and manufacture mice through his own company, the Mouse House, in Berkeley, California.

THE MICROSOFT MOUSE

As the Xerox mouse received more attention, Microsoft began to consider the idea of designing a mouse. A former Xerox PARC employee, Charles Simonyi, had recently joined Microsoft and wanted to add mouse support to a new product, Microsoft Word. At about the same time, Microsoft's Bill Gates, Paul Allen, and Raleigh Roark were also exploring ideas for hardware products.

From a Lump of Clay

In the early eighties, Microsoft was a small company with no in-house design resources. For most of its design needs, the company relied on a Seattle graphic designer, David Strong, who had developed the Microsoft corporate logo and color scheme. It therefore seemed natural for Microsoft to approach Strong for assistance with the mouse design.

After the Microsoft team explained precisely what it wanted—a small, easy-to-handle mouse unit just big enough to accommodate the required internal circuitry—Strong went to work. He produced a 2½-inch by 4-inch by 1¼-inch clay model with thumbtacks on the underside that simulated gliders (Figure 1-2).

Figure 1-2. *The clay model for the original Microsoft Mouse.*

As Raleigh Roark recalls, "A bunch of us sat around a conference table for hours just gliding this lump of clay back and forth, trying to decide if we liked the feel of it. Nobody could really agree. After a while, we settled on the design and dimensions we thought would work.

Then, with the clay model in hand, I got on a plane for Tokyo to meet with an electronics manufacturer to get them to build the thing.''

Roark flew to Tokyo with Kay Nishi, who was then a Microsoft vice president and president of ASCII Corporation in Japan. Nishi and Roark met with manufacturing engineers to discuss what Microsoft wanted. Discussions came to an abrupt, but temporary, halt when the engineers said it couldn't be done. They believed that the mouse encoders couldn't possibly be squeezed into the small, hand-size mouse that Microsoft wanted. As Roark remembers, ''There was a bunch of grumbling about how this was impossible—it just couldn't be done. Then suddenly the room grew quiet, and the chief of engineering said, 'Our engineers will now leave the room for exactly one hour, and when they return they will have a solution to this problem.' The engineers came back with a workable design, and a few months later Microsoft had its first mouse.''

The First Generation

Doing the serial mouse was the biggest thrill for me. It was a conceptual breakthrough; no one had been able to do anything like it before.
—Raleigh Roark
Head of the Microsoft Serial Mouse Development Team

In June 1983, Microsoft introduced a new product for the IBM Personal Computer, the Microsoft Bus Mouse. This was a two-button mechanical mouse that relied on a steel ball and a pair of rollers to register movement as the mouse glided across a flat surface. The mouse was powered by a half-size circuit board that contained an Intel 8255 Programmable Peripheral Interface and some support chips. A distinct advantage of the Microsoft mouse (shown in Figure 1-3) was that its mechanical encoders used very little power.

A year after the release of the bus mouse, Microsoft developed a serial version of the mouse. This was a major technological breakthrough because the mouse could be connected directly to an RS-232 serial port. It required neither a bus card nor a separate power supply because a CMOS processor in the mouse drew enough power from the RS-232 port for operation.

 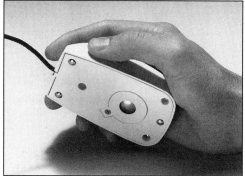

Figure 1-3. *Microsoft's first-generation mouse.*

The first-generation mice had separate, hardware-specific operating software (mouse drivers) for the bus and serial versions and a separate linkable library, MOUSE.LIB, for high-level language development. To help people become comfortable using mice, Microsoft also provided these programs in the original mouse package:

- Notepad, a mouse-oriented text editor

- Piano, an on-screen piano keyboard that users could "play" with the mouse

- Life, a graphic game in which users followed the life and death of simulated microorganisms they designed

Subsequent releases of the mouse software in 1983–1984 brought updates and enhancements to Notepad, the addition of a drawing program named Doodle, and the introduction of mouse menus. With mouse menus, Microsoft provided a way to make the mouse accessible to applications that weren't originally designed for use with a mouse. Users of VisiCalc, Multiplan, WordStar, and Lotus 1-2-3 could now install special menus that allowed use of the mouse within those applications. In addition, Microsoft provided a MENU.COM program for loading menus and a MAKEMENU.EXE compiler so that people could design and build their own mouse menus.

With the release of MS-DOS 2.0 in 1983, the mouse took advantage of a new MS-DOS feature known as installable device drivers. With installable device drivers, it became much easier to configure any computer system for use with MS-DOS and the mouse.

In 1985, two major software releases, Microsoft Mouse 3.0 and 4.0, introduced support for the IBM PC/AT and the growing number of high-resolution graphics devices. People could now install mouse software for use with most display adapters, including the Hercules Graphics Card, the IBM Color Graphics Adapter (CGA), the IBM Enhanced Graphics Adapter (EGA), and other newly introduced high-resolution display adapters and monitors. In addition, the mouse driver could now autodetect the hardware configuration it was installed on.

With software release 4.0 in May 1985, Microsoft replaced Doodle with a popular state-of-the-art graphics application, PC Paintbrush.

The Second Generation

The Microsoft gray-button mouse, with its 200 ppi, changed the nature of the way people used mice. Doubling the sensitivity meant that users didn't have to push a mouse all over a desk to move the cursor around the screen.

—Steve Shaiman
Lead Software Designer for Microsoft Mouse 5.0

In October 1985, the mouse achieved a new level of sophistication with its more streamlined, professional look and reengineered driver. Many changes were immediately visible: a gray color for the buttons, a redesigned body, larger wraparound buttons, and a rubber-covered steel ball in place of the solid steel ball. But the true significance of this release could be felt rather than seen. By doubling the resolution to 200 ppi (points per inch), Microsoft made the mouse much easier to use. Figure 1-4 shows Microsoft's second-generation mouse.

The gray-button mouse required much less surface area for movement (a circle of 4–5 inches), and most operations could be accomplished easily with simple wrist and hand movements. By contrast, the earlier mouse seemed clunky and cumbersome, requiring movement over a relatively large surface area (a circle of 8–10 inches).

Figure 1-4. *Microsoft's second-generation mouse.*

In May 1986, Microsoft released a modified version of the bus mouse interface that was powered by a custom InPort chip, which further enhanced mouse performance because the mouse driver could take advantage of the chip's programmable interrupt rate.

Improved performance of mouse hardware set the stage for what was perhaps the most important mouse software release, Microsoft Mouse 6.0. Introduced in September 1986, Microsoft Mouse 6.0 brought a major overhaul of the mouse software:

- PC Paintbrush was updated and renamed Microsoft Paintbrush.

- A mouse setup program was added, and Show Partner, a graphics presentation program, was added. (Show Partner was discontinued in version 6.1).

- Expert mouse menus were added for power users of Lotus 1-2-3, Display Write III, and Multimate 3.31.

- Computer-based tutorials became part of the package. (These were discontinued in version 6.1.)

- A mouse Control Panel let people adjust the sensitivity of the mouse for different applications.

Furthermore, in this release an optional international version of the mouse driver generated messages in any one of nine foreign languages, which let software developers readily build in mouse support for most foreign-language applications. The international driver is shipped to users outside the United States.

The Third Generation

The new Microsoft Mouse (the one that looks like a bar of Dove soap), with its repositioned ball and seemingly improved mechanism, makes all the difference in the world.

—John C. Dvorak
PC Magazine, December 22, 1987

The third-generation mouse, introduced in September 1987, had a smaller, sleeker mouse body with easy-to-use buttons that clicked when pressed.

Figure 1-5 shows Microsoft's third-generation mouse.

 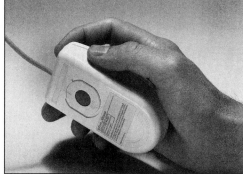

Figure 1-5. *Microsoft's third-generation mouse.*

The internal architecture of this new Microsoft Mouse remained basically the same as that of the gray-button mouse, but some major changes made the mouse easier to control—changes such as moving the traction ball to the front of the mouse and making the left button larger than the right. In July 1988, the *Wall Street Journal* published an article (shown in Figure 1-6) about the ergonomics of the third-generation mouse.

Software included in the mouse package continued to improve and offered increasingly more options. Microsoft currently offers the mouse in a variety of bus-version and serial-version hardware and software configurations. The bus version, like earlier Microsoft bus mice, uses its own card. The serial version can be connected directly to a serial port or to the mouse port on IBM PS/2 computers and other PS/2-style mouse port interfaces.

Figure 1-7 on p. 12 illustrates the milestones in Microsoft mouse history.

Tiny Mouse Holds Many Design Problems

COMPUTER MICE cram a surprising number of design issues into a tiny package, as Microsoft Corp. proved when it undertook to develop a new model of the hand-held control.

SHAPE: "Most mice on the market take their shape from the form of a computer or keyboard. They're rectilinear, with fairly hard edges," says Paul Bradley, an industrial designer at Matrix Product Design Inc., of Palo Alto, Calif., which was responsible for the new mouse's appearance. "We used a softer form that's closer to the contour of a hand."

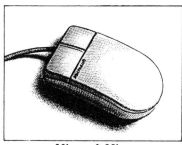

Microsoft Mice:
Old (top); New (bottom)

Matrix collaborated with human-factors specialists at ID Two in San Francisco and engineers at David Kelley Design, Palo Alto.

SIZE: "At first we thought a much smaller device, to be held in the fingertips, might give more accurate control," says Mr. Bradley. Tests proved that wrong. "Our mouse is lower, but otherwise not smaller," he says. "You can drive it with your fingertips, but still rest your hand on it."

BALANCE: A mouse rolls on a plastic ball set in its underside, usually at about the middle. The designers moved the ball forward to facilitate fingertip operation.

CONTROLS: ID Two did extensive testing on the type, size and configuration of the two buttons that execute mouse commands. It found that making one button larger than the other improved performance without troubling left-handed users, but that a ridge was needed between the buttons as a tactile landmark. Test users preferred buttons with crisply clicking feedback over a "mushier" button used earlier.

FINISH: Most mice tend to have a textured finish, often in universal humdrum computer beige. Microsoft chose to make the new mouse glossy white.

Microsoft considers the effort worthwhile. Since it introduced the model last fall, sales have already exceeded total previous Microsoft mouse sales since 1984.

Figure 1-6. *Article from the* Wall Street Journal *about the new Microsoft Mouse.*

MILESTONES IN MICROSOFT MOUSE HISTORY

HARDWARE RELEASES

Mouse 1.0
Bus Version
The Microsoft Green-button Mouse
Microsoft introduced its first mouse: a two-button, mechanical mouse designed for the IBM PC. The mouse supported Microsoft Word.

Mouse 1.0
Serial Version
The Microsoft Green-button Mouse
Designed to plug directly into an RS-232 serial port instead of a separate bus card.

Mouse 5.0
The Microsoft Gray-button Mouse
Reengineered hardware and software doubled the sensitivity and resolution (200 ppi) of the earlier mouse.

Mouse 5.03
The Inport Mouse
Introduction of the InPort Mouse. The InPort chip is a custom LSI (Large Scale Integration) Microsoft design used in the bus mouse board and as the peripheral interface on the Microsoft MACH 10 and MACH 20.

Mouse 6.10
The Microsoft Mouse for the IBM PS/2
Introduction of the Microsoft Mouse for the IBM PS/2 mouse port. Microsoft's PS/2 Mouse arrived on the market a month after the first announcement of the PS/2 line.

Mouse 1.0
The New Mouse
Microsoft redesigned the mouse body and moved the track ball to the front of the mouse. The mouse became available in three different software configurations and two hardware configurations.

MAJOR SOFTWARE RELEASES

JUNE 1983

DECEMBER 1983

FEBRUARY 1984

JANUARY 1985

MAY 1985

OCTOBER 1985

APRIL 1986

SEPTEMBER 1986

MAY 1987

SEPTEMBER 1987

Mouse Driver 1.0
Contained the mouse driver plus software that demonstrated and taught use of the mouse. This release supported Microsoft Word and contained separate drivers for bus and serial versions.

Mouse Driver 2.0
Contained updates to the driver software plus the introduction of a new graphics program, Doodle.

Mouse Driver 3.0
Provided early support for the IBM Enhanced Graphics Adapter (EGA) and MS-DOS 3.x. The disk also contained updates to Notepad.

Mouse Driver 4.0
With Mouse Driver 4.0, Doodle was replaced with Z-Soft's popular color painting program, PC Paintbrush. The mouse software was extended to two floppy disks.

Mouse Driver 5.0
Mouse Driver 5.0 was revised to install and identify the type of mouse in use. Reengineered mouse hardware enhanced software performance (resolution now 200 ppi).

Mouse Driver 6.0
Mouse Driver 6.0 was a major update. The disk contained a new mouse setup program and a new version of Microsoft Paintbrush. It also contained computer-based training and Control Panel.

Mouse Driver 6.1
Microsoft added the following support for VGA graphics: serial-interface and bus-interface versions of EasyCAD, and Microsoft Windows 2.03 with Microsoft Paintbrush.

Figure 1-7. *Major hardware and software releases of the Microsoft Mouse.*

LOOKING AHEAD

As software becomes more complex, more of us will need to adopt pointing devices to work efficiently with computers. There is probably a mouse in your future.

—Cary Lu
Author of *The Apple Macintosh Book, 3rd ed.,* Microsoft Press

Sometime in the not-too-distant future, every microcomputer will be shipped with a mouse. As the world moves to Windows and OS/2, mice will become as endemic as keyboards are.

—Steve Shaiman
Director, Microsoft Hardware Group

In the summer of 1988, 25 years after Doug Engelbart crafted his wooden prototype, Microsoft celebrated the sale of its millionth mouse.

Today, software applications with graphical user interfaces are rapidly becoming the norm rather than the exception, and with this comes wider acceptance and use of the mouse. As OS/2 and Presentation Manager, Microsoft Windows, and other graphical-user-interface software come into wider use, using a mouse makes increasingly more sense and begins to seem a necessity rather than a luxury.

Chapter 2

Overview of Mouse Programming

The mouse is an electronic device that sends signals to your computer. To your software, these signals represent cursor movements and button presses. However, the raw data sent to your computer is difficult to use in its original form. Also, different signals are generated depending on whether a bus, InPort, serial, or PS/2 mouse is used. To give programmers an easy-to-use, consistent interface, Microsoft and most other mouse manufacturers provide a mouse driver.

THE MOUSE DRIVER

A mouse driver is software that lets the operating system consistently interpret the raw data from the mouse. The Microsoft mouse driver does this by providing application programs with 35 function calls that let programs perform specific tasks, such as checking the state of a mouse button. These function calls are consistent regardless of the mouse hardware you use.

Microsoft provides three methods for interfacing with the mouse driver: mouse menus, the mouse library, and direct calls to MS-DOS Interrupt 33H. Each method has distinct advantages and disadvantages, and each method fulfills a particular need. For example, you can use mouse menus only with existing applications. However, you can use the mouse library and Interrupt 33H in programs you write yourself.

Using Mouse Menus

Mouse menus let you integrate the mouse into most preexisting text-based software packages that wouldn't otherwise support the mouse. Thus, you can bring up menus that aren't necessarily in the application, and you can emulate keystrokes. You can also assign mouse motions and button presses to tasks you would normally perform with the keyboard.

Using the Mouse Library

The mouse library lets you incorporate the mouse into an application as you write it. Because the mouse support becomes an integral part of the program, the functionality of the mouse support within the application program far exceeds that which you can obtain with mouse menus. The library lets the application take advantage of 35 mouse function calls, which are accessible from high-level languages such as interpreted BASIC, QuickBASIC, C, QuickC, FORTRAN, and Pascal. The function calls are also accessible from MASM.

Using MS-DOS Interrupt 33H

You can access the mouse driver directly through MS-DOS software Interrupt 33H, which provides you the same 35 functions that are available through the mouse library. Because the overhead of making library calls is eliminated, a program written using Interrupt 33H is smaller and faster than the same program written using the mouse library. Most professionally developed programs that use the mouse interact with it through Interrupt 33H. Any language that can make calls to the MS-DOS interrupts can use this method of interfacing with the mouse driver.

MOUSE MENUS

A mouse menu displays menus on the screen with options you can select. The selected option can feed characters into the keyboard buffer for the current application, or it can execute other menu commands.

NOTE: The only way the mouse menu programs interact with an application is by detecting mouse motion or button presses and then feeding characters into the keyboard buffer.

The keyboard buffer is a small portion of memory that holds characters you type on the keyboard. Your application program reads these characters from the buffer in the order in which they were input and acts on them accordingly. A mouse menu program can emulate the keyboard by sending characters directly to the keyboard buffer as you move the mouse or press one or more mouse buttons.

Menu software loads the keyboard buffer much faster than you can load it by typing at the keyboard. How fast the buffer is loaded by the keyboard is limited to a set rate determined by each computer's BIOS; however, the menu software doesn't have this limitation. For this reason, when the mouse emulates the direction keys, the cursor moves much faster than if you pressed the actual keys on the keyboard.

NOTE: Because certain applications access the keyboard directly, your mouse menu program might not work as you expect. In addition, mouse menu programs can't generate some keystrokes, such as Ctrl-Alt-Del. These keystrokes are listed under the TYPE statement entry in Chapter 4, "Mouse Menu Language Statements."

Keyboard Mapping

A mouse menu program recognizes seven mouse actions:

- Left button pressed
- Right button pressed
- Both buttons pressed
- Right motion
- Left motion
- Up motion
- Down motion

You can make each of these actions correspond to one or more menu commands. For example, some useful and common mappings of mouse actions to the keyboard buffer include the following:

- Right, left, up, and down motions that correspond to the right-arrow, left-arrow, up-arrow, and down-arrow keys

- A button press that corresponds to pressing Enter or Esc

- A button press that tells the menu software to display a custom menu, which you usually write to execute application program commands or MS-DOS commands

The following mouse menu program demonstrates some simple keyboard mapping:

```
BEGIN lb,rb,bb,lm,rm,um,dm,48,48
lb:      EXECUTE f1      ;Left button emulates F1 key
rb:      EXECUTE entkey  ;Right button emulates Enter key
bb:      EXECUTE escape  ;Both buttons emulate Esc key
lm:      EXECUTE left    ;Left movement emulates left-arrow key
rm:      EXECUTE right   ;Right movement emulates right-arrow key
um:      EXECUTE up      ;Up movement emulates up-arrow key
dm:      EXECUTE down    ;Down movement emulates down-arrow key

f1:      TYPE 0,59       ;These commands perform the
entkey:  TYPE enter      ;actual work when you move
escape:  TYPE 27         ;the mouse or press one or
left:    TYPE 0,75       ;both mouse buttons.  Refer
right:   TYPE 0,77       ;to Chapter 4 for detailed
up:      TYPE 0,72       ;explanations of each of
down:    TYPE 0,80       ;these commands.
```

Creating a Mouse Menu

The mouse menu programming language has commands that let you create custom pop-up menus in a variety of configurations and hierarchies. You can create simple single-function menus, or you can create elaborate multilayer menu systems in which choosing an item from one menu can call up another menu.

You follow the same basic steps to create a mouse menu as you do when developing any other software:

1. Design and write the source code

2. Compile the source file

3. Run the mouse menu program

4. Debug the program

For instructions on creating a mouse menu program, see Chapter 3, "Creating Your Own Mouse Menu."

THE MOUSE PROGRAMMING INTERFACE

Mouse menus provide mouse support for an existing application program that doesn't already support the mouse. However, the most efficient way to add mouse program support is to write the mouse support directly into the application program's code. The mouse can then become a separate user-input device of its own, not merely a keyboard emulator. The most important feature the mouse brings to the user interface is the *free-floating* cursor used in many popular products such as Microsoft Word, Microsoft Works, AutoCAD, Microsoft Paintbrush, and Microsoft Windows. This feature makes programs more intuitive, user-friendly, and easy to learn.

As the link between the mouse hardware and the application software, the mouse driver keeps constant track of mouse movement and button-press information. When an application program needs mouse information, it makes a request to the driver, which then returns the requested information to the application program.

Working with Functions

The mouse driver understands 35 input and output operations. Each operation, or function, is a specific instruction to the mouse driver that enables a program to communicate with the mouse. Some functions request information about the mouse such as button-press information, relative cursor position, and relative motion. Other functions control characteristics of the mouse interface such as regulating the sensitivity of cursor motion, defining the shape of the cursor, and limiting cursor movement to a specific area. The application program tells the mouse driver what it wants through the mouse function calls, and the driver does the rest.

Communicating with the Mouse Driver

You can use two methods to communicate with the mouse driver from within a program: You can use the MOUSE.LIB library, which allows the program to communicate with the mouse driver using the calling conventions of a particular language, or you can communicate with the driver using MS-DOS Interrupt 33H. All mouse function calls are available using library calls or using MS-DOS Interrupt 33H. Each method has its distinct advantages; however, functionality is the same in both methods.

NOTE: The mouse driver and the corresponding interface control only the mouse. You must set video modes and program interaction with the mouse within a program as required for your specific application.

Using the MOUSE.LIB Library

You can use the MOUSE.LIB library supplied with the disks in this book as a library file for several Microsoft languages. Using the libraries lets you add mouse support to a program by making procedure calls in Pascal, subprogram calls in QuickBASIC, function calls in C and QuickC, or subprogram calls in FORTRAN. The library enables all parameter passing and declarations to be consistent with the language you are using. Because of this, no special programming techniques are necessary to program the mouse. Calls to the mouse simply become another subroutine.

To use the mouse library, the language you use must support Microsoft library conventions. If the language supports the conventions, you can link the library with your program. For information about linking to various mouse programs, see Chapter 9, "Sample Mouse Programming Interface Programs."

You should also consult the documentation of the language you are using regarding the linking of external libraries. If the language doesn't support the Microsoft library conventions, you will be unable to link with the MOUSE.LIB library. However, it might be possible to program the mouse using Interrupt 33H as described in the following section.

Using Interrupt 33H

A command in the AUTOEXEC.BAT or CONFIG.SYS file usually loads the mouse driver when MS-DOS starts. The driver installs the starting address as the vector for Interrupt 33H and then attaches itself to the operating system. You can then access the mouse driver through software Interrupt 33H. When your software calls this interrupt, the system finds the address of the mouse driver in the interrupt vector table, goes to the mouse driver, and executes the requested function.

NOTE: The mouse driver (MOUSE.COM or MOUSE.SYS) must be in memory when an application or program uses mouse function calls. When the driver is loaded, programs can access the Interrupt 33H vector if they use the mouse function calls (in which the driver provides an interface for application programmers).

You can specify the different functions by loading the AX, BX, CX, and DX registers with the appropriate values. Some functions also use the ES, SI, and DI registers. The mouse driver returns values to the calling routine through these same registers. For detailed information on using registers to pass function variables, see Chapter 8, "Mouse Function Calls."

The primary advantage of using Interrupt 33H instead of the mouse libraries is improved execution speed. Interrupt 33H circumvents the overhead associated with calling subroutines by calling the interrupt directly. Also, languages that can't use the supplied mouse library can use Interrupt 33H if they can load processor registers and make calls to MS-DOS.

EGA Register Interface

Although the mouse driver supports the EGA and VGA, programmers sometimes like to program the EGA or VGA hardware directly. Because the mouse driver keeps track of the EGA and VGA registers, programmers must take some special considerations into account when programming the D, E, F, 10, 11, 12, and 13 graphics modes of the EGA and VGA adapters.

For detailed information on using the EGA Shadow Register Interface, see Chapter 10, "Writing Mouse Programs for IBM EGA Modes."

PART II

Mouse Menus

Chapter 3: Creating Your Own Mouse Menu

- Mouse Menu Language Commands
- Statement Format
- Mouse Menu Program Structures
- Creating a Mouse Menu Program

Chapter 4: Mouse Menu Language Statements

- Statement Syntax Conventions
- Statement Descriptions

Chapter 5: Sample Mouse Menu Programs

- The SIMPLE Mouse Menu Program
- DOSOVRLY Mouse Menu Program
- Other Sample Mouse Menu Programs

Chapter 3

Creating Your Own Mouse Menu

The mouse menu programming language is designed to provide mouse support for applications that don't currently support the mouse. The menu communicates to the application through the keyboard buffer by using a set of commands. This chapter describes how to use those commands to design and run your own mouse menus.

MOUSE MENU LANGUAGE COMMANDS

The mouse menu programming language consists of 13 commands. You use these commands in statements that assign different functions to the mouse, create menus, and simulate the pressing of keys.

Table 3-1 lists the commands in the mouse menu programming language:

TABLE 3-1: MOUSE MENU COMMANDS	
Command	*Purpose*
ASSIGN	Assigns new values to mouse events or changes mouse movement sensitivity.
BEGIN	Assigns initial actions taken when a mouse event occurs and sets initial mouse-movement sensitivity.
EXECUTE	Specifies the label of the statement that contains the mouse menu command or commands to be executed when you move the mouse, press a mouse button, or choose a menu item.

(continued)

TABLE 3-1: MOUSE MENU COMMANDS *(continued)*	
Command	*Purpose*
MATCH	Specifies the action taken if a certain character or string of characters is displayed at a specific location on the screen.
MENU	Begins a menu subroutine.
MEND	Ends a menu subroutine.
NOTHING	Indicates that no action will be taken. NOTHING is used as an alternative to the EXECUTE, TYPE, and MATCH statements.
OPTION	Specifies a menu item within a menu subroutine and the action taken when you select that item.
POPUP	Begins a pop-up subroutine.
PEND	Ends a pop-up subroutine.
SELECT	Defines the action taken when you select an item from a pop-up menu.
TEXT	Defines the text for a pop-up menu title or menu items.
TYPE	Specifies the key or keys ''typed'' into the keyboard buffer when you move the mouse, press a mouse button, or choose a menu item.

STATEMENT FORMAT

In the mouse menu programming language, you can enter statements in uppercase or lowercase letters. Most statements have the following format:

```
[label:] command [parameters ;comments]
```

NOTE: The BEGIN statement and statements within menu and pop-up subroutines don't use this format because they don't require labels. The BEGIN statement doesn't need a label because it's always the first statement in a program, and statements within menu or pop-up subroutines don't need labels because they run sequentially.

The components of a statement are described in the following sections.

Labels

A label is the name you give a mouse menu statement. Except for statements in menu or pop-up subroutines, all statements must have labels for the program to access them. Your program calls a statement when its label is referenced in another statement. When the labeled statement is completed, control returns to the statement that referenced the label. In other words, control doesn't fall through to the next statement. In the following statement, *mat1* is the label of the MATCH statement:

```
mat1: MATCH 23,,inverse,"Format",exec1,exec2
```

When you include a label, be sure to follow these guidelines:

- Begin a label with a letter and follow it immediately with a colon.

- Leave at least one space between the colon and the command.

- Do not use mouse menu command names or the words *backsp*, *enter*, *esc*, or *tab* for labels.

- Use any printable standard ASCII characters except a colon in a label.

- Use labels that suggest what the statement does in the program. For example, you could use *menu1* as the label for the first menu subroutine.

Parameters

A parameter is a variable that affects the action of a statement. When you use a statement, you must substitute an appropriate value for each parameter you want to use. All statements except NOTHING, MEND, and PEND have parameters.

Parameters follow the command word in a statement. When you use parameters in a statement, you must type a space between the command word and the first parameter. Commas must separate any additional parameters.

The EXECUTE and TYPE statements let you use from 1 to 15 parameters. However, other statements require a specific number of parameters. Suppose you are using one of these other statements, such as the MATCH statement, and you don't want to use a particular parameter. However, you do want to use the parameters that follow. To accomplish this, you include an additional comma to hold the place of the unused parameter. The MAKEMENU utility automatically uses the default value for any parameter that you leave out of a statement that has a required number of parameters.

For example, in the following statement, *23*, *inverse*, *Format*, *exec1*, and *exec2* are five of the six required values for MATCH statement parameters. The fact that the second comma immediately follows the first comma tells the MAKEMENU utility that the second parameter is not included and that the default value should be used:

```
mat1: MATCH 23,,inverse,"Format",exec1,exec2
```

The mouse menu programming language uses three types of parameters: *numeric* parameters, *string* parameters, and *attribute* parameters.

Numeric Parameters

You use numeric parameters for numeric data, such as screen coordinates or movement-sensitivity values for the mouse.

In the preceding example, *23*, the row coordinate for the MATCH statement, is the value for a numeric parameter.

String Parameters

Most string parameters specify text for menus or messages. A string parameter can contain digits, letters, special characters, or spaces.

You must enclose a string in double-quotation marks (" "). You cannot use a double-quotation mark as part of the string: The double-quotation marks enclosing the string are the only ones allowed.

Attribute Parameters

The attribute parameter determines the display attribute, which specifies how a menu or message box appears on the screen. This parameter can have one of four values: *normal*, *bold*, *inverse*, or, if your system uses a color display adapter and monitor, a number that designates specific foreground and background colors. Figure 3-1 shows how the normal, bold, and inverse values affect the text displayed by a pop-up menu.

| Normal | Bold | Inverse |

Figure 3-1. *Effects of display attributes applied to pop-up menu text.*

If you don't specify an attribute parameter, the default attribute is used. Default attributes are included in the description of each statement in Chapter 4, "Mouse Menu Language Statements."

Color Menus

If your system uses a color display adapter and color monitor, you can use the attribute parameter in a MATCH, MENU, or POPUP statement to specify particular colors for the background and foreground of a menu or message box. Text is displayed in the foreground color; the remainder of the box is displayed in the background color.

Table 3-2 lists the background and foreground colors available, and it gives a corresponding value for each color. The value for a particular color differs depending on whether you use the color for the foreground or the background. The display attribute that specifies a particular color combination is the sum of the values for the desired foreground and background colors. Suppose you want green text on a blue background. The value for a green foreground is 2, and the value for a blue background is 16. Therefore, the value of the attribute parameter is 18.

NOTE: Color shades can vary on different equipment. Also, if you specify a display-attribute value greater than 127, the foreground color blinks when the menu or message box is displayed. In addition, a gray background (128) looks the same as a black background (0).

TABLE 3-2: FOREGROUND AND BACKGROUND COLOR VALUES

Color	Foreground	Background
Black	0	0
Blue	1	16
Green	2	32
Cyan (blue-green)	3	48
Red	4	64
Magenta	5	80
Brown	6	96
White	7	112
Gray	8	128
Light blue	9	144
Light green	10	160
Light cyan	11	176
Light red	12	192
Light magenta	13	208
Yellow	14	224
White (high intensity)	15	240

Specifying a value of 7 is equivalent to specifying the *normal* attribute parameter. The value 7 is the sum of 0 (the value for a black background) and 7 (the value for a white foreground). Specifying a value of 15 is equivalent to specifying the *bold* attribute parameter. The value 15 is the sum of 0 (the value for a black background) and 15 (the value for a high-intensity white foreground). Specifying a value of 112 is the equivalent of specifying the *inverse* attribute parameter. The value 112 is the sum of 112 (the value for a white background) and 0 (the value for a black foreground).

Comments

Comments describe what a statement does. They are used to help you and anyone else who might read your program to understand the program, and they have no effect on how the statement is executed.

You can insert a comment at the end of a statement or on a separate line. To specify a comment, simply type a semicolon (;) followed by the comment. If you include a comment on the same line as a statement, separate the last parameter of the statement and the semicolon preceding the comment with one or more spaces. The following is an example of a TYPE statement followed by a comment:

```
F1: TYPE 0,59      ;Simulates pressing the F1 key
```

MOUSE MENU PROGRAM STRUCTURES

The following sections describe how each type of command is used in a mouse menu source program. For detailed information about commands and their parameters, see Chapter 4, "Mouse Menu Language Statements."

Mouse Event Commands

Mouse event commands, BEGIN and ASSIGN, specify which statements the program executes when you press a mouse button or move the mouse.

The BEGIN Command

Use a BEGIN command to specify the initial statements executed when particular mouse events occur and to set the initial mouse sensitivity. Always use a BEGIN command as the first statement in your program.

You can include one or more of the following parameters in the BEGIN statement:

- Button parameters: *lfbtn* (left button), *rtbtn* (right button), and/or *btbtn* (both buttons). Button parameters define the action taken when you press one or both mouse buttons.

- Movement parameters: *lfmov* (mouse left), *rtmov* (mouse right), *upmov* (mouse up), and/or *dnmov* (mouse down). Movement parameters define the action taken when you move the mouse.

- Movement-sensitivity parameters: *hsen* (horizontal movement sensitivity) and/or *vsen* (vertical movement sensitivity). Movement-sensitivity parameters define how much the mouse must move before the cursor moves. This is helpful in tailoring cursor movement to the different column and row widths found in spreadsheet programs. You specify the movement of the mouse in a unit of distance known as a mickey, which is approximately $\frac{1}{200}$ inch. For more information on the mickey, see Chapter 6, "Mouse Programming Interface."

The ASSIGN Command

Use the ASSIGN command to assign new values to mouse events and mouse sensitivity. An ASSIGN command is useful if you want your mouse menu program to execute different statements or subroutines, depending on one of the following:

- The current mode of an application program

- Other conditions that require the mouse buttons to cause different actions or the movement sensitivity to change

Menu Subroutine Commands

Menu subroutines create single-column pop-up menus, which are bordered menus with a single column of menu items (Figure 3-2).

Figure 3-2. *Single-column pop-up menu.*

To choose items in a menu, you move the mouse pointer to the desired item and then press either mouse button. If you press both mouse buttons at once, the equivalent of a NOTHING command is executed and the menu disappears.

MENU, OPTION, and MEND are menu subroutine commands. To code menu subroutines, use the following format:

```
label:  MENU ["title"],[row],[column],[attribute]
        OPTION ["text"],[label]
          .
          .
          .
        MEND
```

The MENU Command

Begin each menu subroutine with a MENU command. You can include four parameters:

- The menu's title, enclosed in double-quotation marks (" ")

- The row and column of the screen where the upper-left corner of the menu will appear

- The menu's display attribute

The OPTION Commands

Include OPTION commands within a menu subroutine to specify one or more menu items and the action taken when you choose an item. Always include at least one OPTION command that lets you exit from the menu.

The *text* parameter is the text the menu displays for that item. If you omit the *text* parameter, the menu displays a blank line. Case is significant; that is, uppercase and lowercase are displayed exactly as you type them.

The *pointer* parameter is the label of the statement that is to be executed when you choose that menu item. If you do not specify a *pointer* parameter, the equivalent of a NOTHING statement is executed when that item is chosen, and the menu disappears.

The MEND Command

Always follow the last OPTION command with a MEND (menu end) command, which ends the menu subroutine.

Sample Menu Subroutine

The following menu subroutine produces the Inverse Attribute menu shown earlier, in Figure 3-1.

In this example, the upper-left corner of the menu produced by this subroutine appears at row 5, column 20. Because an attribute is not specified in the MENU statement, the *inverse* display attribute (the default) is used. When the menu appears on the screen, the first menu item is highlighted (in this case, *Cancel Menu*).

If you select *Cancel Menu*, the menu disappears because a *pointer* parameter is not specified for that OPTION statement. If you select any other item, the statement identified by the label specified in the *pointer* parameter for that OPTION statement is executed.

```
menu1: MENU "BASIC Commands",5,20
        OPTION "Cancel Menu"
        OPTION "List",F1
        OPTION "Run",F2
        OPTION "Load",F3
        MEND
F1: TYPE 0,59    ;Simulates pressing the F1 key
F2: TYPE 0,60    ;Simulates pressing the F2 key
F3: TYPE 0,61    ;Simulates pressing the F3 key
```

Pop-up Subroutine Statements

You can use pop-up subroutines to create multiple-column menus and message boxes.

You use multiple-column menus in the same way as single-column menus: Choose an item by moving the mouse pointer to the item, and then press either mouse button. Pressing both mouse buttons at once is the equivalent of a NOTHING statement and removes the menu from the screen. When the menu first appears on the screen, the first menu item, as defined by the first SELECT statement in the POPUP subroutine, is highlighted. Figure 3-3 shows a multiple-column menu.

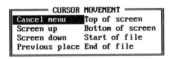

Figure 3-3. *Multiple-column menu.*

Message boxes are simply pop-up menus that display messages instead of menu items (Figure 3-4). You can combine pop-up subroutines with MATCH commands so that message boxes appear when your application program changes the display mode or when other conditions change the screen display.

```
╔══════════ MOUSE HELP ══════════╗
║                                ║
║ Left button  - Displays Edit/Block menu     ║
║ Right button - Displays Cursor Movement menu ║
║ Both buttons - Displays Edit/File menu      ║
║                                ║
║ Moving the mouse up, down, left, or right   ║
║ causes the cursor to move in that direction. ║
╚════════════════════════════════╝
```

Figure 3-4. *Message box.*

The pop-up subroutine statements are the POPUP, TEXT, SELECT, and PEND statements.

To code pop-up subroutines for multiple-column menus and message boxes, use the following format:

```
label:  POPUP [row],[column],[attribute]
        [TEXT ["text"]]
            .
            .
            .
        SELECT row,column,length,[pointer]
            .
            .
            .
        PEND
```

The POPUP Command

Begin each pop-up subroutine with a POPUP command. You can include three parameters:

- The row of the menu's upper-left corner

- The column of the menu's upper-left corner

- The menu's display attribute

The TEXT Command

Include TEXT commands within a pop-up subroutine to specify the menu title, menu items, and, optionally, menu borders. Type the title text, item text, and menu borders exactly as they'll appear on each line of the menu and enclose them in double-quotation marks (" ").

NOTE: Menus created with the MENU command and menus created with the POPUP command differ. The MENU command, which creates only single-column menus, creates a border around the displayed menu and draws a line between the menu title and the menu items. Figure 3-1 shows an example of those lines. The POPUP command doesn't draw these lines, so you must include line-drawing characters within TEXT statements. The easiest way to do this is to use equal signs (=) or hyphens (-) for the horizontal lines, and vertical-line characters (¦) for the vertical lines. Examples of this technique are shown on the following pages. To use the same line-drawing characters created by the MENU command, use the line-drawing characters of the extended ASCII character set. These are shown in Appendix G, "ASCII Character Set." To create these characters, hold down the Alt key, type the number of the character on the numeric keypad, then release the Alt key. The line-drawing character will appear on your screen.

The text generated by a TEXT command will be located on the screen relative to the coordinates you specify in the POPUP statement.

The SELECT Commands

Use SELECT commands to define the area in which you can choose each menu item. Specify the row, column, and length of the screen area you want to select, relative to the menu's upper-left corner. The coordinates of the upper-left corner of a pop-up menu are (1,1). You can also include a *pointer* parameter to specify a statement that is executed when you choose an item on the screen that is pointed to by that SELECT statement. As with the OPTION statement for a single-column menu, you simply specify the label of the statement that will be executed.

You must include at least one SELECT command in each pop-up subroutine as an exit point.

The PEND Command

Always follow the last SELECT command with a PEND (pop-up end) command, which ends the pop-up subroutine.

Sample Pop-up Subroutines

The following pop-up subroutine creates the multiple-column menu shown earlier, in Figure 3-3.

In this example, the upper-left corner of the menu is at row 2, column 1. Because an attribute parameter is not specified in the POPUP statement, the *inverse* display attribute (the default) is used.

The TEXT statements specify the menu's borders, title, and items . Their location is relative to the coordinates you specified in the POPUP statement as the upper-left corner of the menu. The first character of the first menu item starts at relative row 2, column 3 in the menu; however, its actual screen coordinates are row 3, column 3. When the pop-up menu appears on the screen, the first item is highlighted.

The SELECT statements define item-selection areas. In the first item (*Cancel menu*), 2, 3, and 15 define the row, column, and length of the selection area. Because the SELECT statement for the *Cancel menu* doesn't include a label for the *pointer* parameter, the menu disappears from the screen if you select *Cancel menu*. The other SELECT statements execute the statements named in their *pointer* parameters.

```
movemen: POPUP 2,1
         TEXT " ======== CURSOR MOVEMENT ======== "
         TEXT ": Cancel menu     Top of screen    :"
         TEXT ": Screen up        Bottom of screen :"
         TEXT ": Screen down      Start of file    :"
         TEXT ": Previous place End of file        :"
         TEXT " ================================= "
         SELECT 2,3,15
         SELECT 3,3,15,keyctrlr
         SELECT 4,3,15,keyctrlc
         SELECT 5,3,15,keyctrlqp
         SELECT 2,18,17,keyctrlqe
         SELECT 3,18,17,keyctrlqx
         SELECT 4,18,17,keyctrlqr
         SELECT 5,18,17,keyctrlqc
         PEND
```

The following pop-up subroutine creates the message box shown earlier, in Figure 3-4. Note that the message box in Figure 3-4 uses the upper-ASCII characters 186, 187, 188, 200, 201, and 205 to create the border.

In this example, the POPUP statement defines row 2, column 1 as the upper-left-corner coordinates. Because an *attribute* parameter is not specified in the POPUP statement, the *inverse* display attribute is used.

The TEXT statements define the message-box border, title, and message text. Their screen location is relative to the coordinates you specified in the POPUP statement as the upper-left corner of the menu. The single SELECT statement highlights the menu box title and defines

an exit point for the menu. Because the message box has only one
SELECT statement, you cannot move the cursor within the message box.

```
mousehlp: POPUP 2,1
  TEXT " ================= MOUSE HELP ==================== "
  TEXT ":                                                  :"
  TEXT ": Left button  - Displays Edit/Block menu          :"
  TEXT ": Right button - Displays Cursor Movement menu     :"
  TEXT ": Both buttons - Displays Edit/File menu           :"
  TEXT ":                                                  :"
  TEXT ": Moving the mouse up, down, left, or right        :"
  TEXT ": causes the cursor to move in that direction.     :"
  TEXT ":                                                  :"
  TEXT " ================================================= "
  SELECT 1,18,10
  PEND
```

Action Commands

Action commands specify the action taken when you choose a menu
item, press one or both buttons, or move the mouse. The EXECUTE,
TYPE, and NOTHING commands are action commands.

It's important to understand the flow of the actions taken by
mouse menu programs. Most programming languages follow sequentially from one statement to the next unless they encounter a branch-
ing statement or a subroutine call. You can think of mouse menu
program statements as subroutines, with an implied *return* at the end
of each statement. The only exception to this rule occurs with the
statements in the menu or pop-up subroutines, but if you think of the
MENU-MEND and POPUP-PEND blocks as single complex statements,
the rule applies to all cases.

A mouse menu program is entered when one of the actions of the
BEGIN or ASSIGN statements occurs, such as pressing a mouse button or
moving the mouse. The program then branches to the labeled statement indicated in the BEGIN or ASSIGN statement. When the program
completes that statement, it returns to the BEGIN or ASSIGN statement
and terminates. Before completing its task, however, that statement
might call out another statement, and so on.

When the program completes the action of a labeled statement, it
returns control to the statement that referenced that label. The program terminates when the nested chain of statements completes its

tasks and the program flow returns to the originating BEGIN or ASSIGN statement.

The following example shows the flow of the action when you press the right mouse button:

```
BEGIN    leftb,rightb                ;Pressing the right button calls "rightb"

leftb:   NOTHING                     ;Pressing the left button does nothing

rightb:  MATCH 1,1,,"XXX",found,nope ;If XXX is found in the upper-left
                                     ;corner, call "found" otherwise, call
                                     ;"nope"

found:   EXECUTE txt1,txt3           ;Simulates typing "Xs were found!"
nope:    EXECUTE txt1,txt2,txt3      ;Simulates typing "Xs were not found!"

txt1:    TYPE "Xs were "
txt2:    TYPE "not "
txt3:    TYPE "found!"
```

Assuming that *XXX* is currently displayed in the upper-left corner of the screen, the program takes the following actions when the right button is pressed:

Statement	Action
1. BEGIN	Program starts here when you press the right button.
2. BEGIN:rightb	The BEGIN statement calls *rightb*.
3. BEGIN:rightb:found	The MATCH statement labeled *rightb* calls *found*.
4. BEGIN:rightb:found:txt1	The EXECUTE statement labeled *found* calls *txt1*.
5. BEGIN:rightb:found	The TYPE statement labeled *txt1* is completed and control returns to *found*.
6. BEGIN:rightb:found:txt3	The EXECUTE statement labeled *found* calls *txt3*.
7. BEGIN:rightb:found	The TYPE statement labeled *txt3* is completed and control returns to *found*.
8. BEGIN:rightb	The EXECUTE statement labeled *found* is completed and control returns to *rightb*.

(continued)

continued

Statement	Action
9. BEGIN	The MATCH statement labeled *rightb* is completed and control returns to the originating BEGIN statement.
	The BEGIN statement is completed, the mouse menu program terminates, and control returns to you.

The EXECUTE Command

Use the EXECUTE command to define a series of statements that will be executed when you do the following:

- Press one or both mouse buttons.

- Choose a menu item.

- Move the mouse.

- Cause a MATCH command to be executed.

To specify statements that the EXECUTE statement calls out, you use statement labels. You can specify up to 15 labels for each EXECUTE statement. The following EXECUTE statement uses five labels. This statement executes the statement labeled *dsk*, then the statement labeled *s*, and so on. After the program executes the statement labeled *exec4*, it returns to the statement that referenced *exec1*.

```
exec1: EXECUTE dsk,s,a,s,exec4
```

It is possible for an EXECUTE command to call out another EXECUTE command. Furthermore, up to 15 EXECUTE commands can call out other EXECUTE commands. For example, the following sequence of nested EXECUTE commands simulates typing **abcdef**:

```
start:   EXECUTE abcdef
abcdef:  EXECUTE abc,def
abc:     EXECUTE ab,c
ab:      EXECUTE a,b
a:       TYPE "a"
b:       TYPE "b"
c:       TYPE "c"
def:     TYPE "def"
```

The TYPE Command

Use the TYPE command to simulate pressing keys on the keyboard. For example, the following TYPE statement simulates pressing the A key:

```
key1: TYPE "A"
```

The following TYPE statement simulates typing the *diskcopy a: b:* command and pressing the Enter key:

```
key15: TYPE "diskcopy a: b:",enter
```

Note that you can enter a series of separate keystrokes by separating each group with commas. You can indicate which key is simulated in one of three ways:

- Use the the key's name, enclosed in double-quotation marks (for example, "A").

- Use the ASCII code for the character on the key (for example, use 65 for *A*). You can use extended ASCII codes, ASCII control characters, and extended keyboard scan codes to simulate special keys or key sequences, such as the Alt, Ctrl-Q, Spacebar, and direction keys. (For a list of ASCII control characters and extended keyboard scan codes, see Appendix G, "ASCII Character Set.")

- Use the key's symbolic name if it has one. The predefined symbolic keys are enter, tab, backsp, and esc.

In the following TYPE statements, the comments indicate which key or keys each statement simulates.

Notice that the statements labeled *dir* and *a* simulate typing character strings by enclosing the characters in double-quotation marks. The statements labeled *lf, rt, up,* and *dn* define the direction keys by using extended keyboard scan codes. The statement labeled *s* simulates pressing the Spacebar by using the standard ASCII code for a space. The statement labeled *ent* simulates pressing the Enter key by using the symbolic name for the key. The statement labeled *cls* simulates typing the MS-DOS CLS command and pressing the Enter key. The statements labeled *ctrlc* and *ctrld* simulate pressing Ctrl-key combinations. The statements labeled *home* and *end* simulate pressing the Home and End keys.

Statement	Comments
`dir: TYPE "dir"`	; Types the DIR command
`a: TYPE "a:"`	; Types a:
`lf: TYPE 0,75`	; Simulates the left-arrow key
`rt: TYPE 0,77`	; Simulates the right-arrow key
`up: TYPE 0,72`	; Simulates the up-arrow key
`dn: TYPE 0,80`	; Simulates the down-arrow key
`s: TYPE 32`	; Types a space
`ent: TYPE enter`	; Simulates the Enter key
`cls: TYPE "cls",enter`	; Types CLS command, simulates Enter key
`ctrlc: TYPE 3`	; Types Ctrl-C
`ctrld: TYPE 4`	; Types Ctrl-D
`home: TYPE 0,71`	; Types Home
`end: TYPE 0,79`	; Types End

The NOTHING Command

Use the NOTHING command to specify that no action is taken.

The MATCH Command

Use a MATCH command to direct a mouse menu program to take different actions, depending on what is displayed on the screen.

A MATCH statement specifies a string of characters, a row and column on the screen, and a display attribute. If a line on the screen matches the specified string, begins at the specified row and column, and appears in the specified display attribute, then the program executes a particular statement. This feature enables a mouse menu program to respond to different operating modes of the application program or screen display.

For example, if an application program always displays the word *COMMAND* in column 1 of row 22 of the screen when it is in command mode and if it displays the word *ALPHA* in the same place when it is in alphanumeric mode, you can use a MATCH command to take a different action, depending on which mode the application program is in.

A MATCH statement uses the following format:

```
MATCH row,column,[attribute],string,match,nomatch
```

The *row* and *column* parameters describe where the *string* parameter must be located on the screen for a match. To be matched, the row and column parameters must point to the first character of a string. If the *row* and *column* parameters are blank, the default is (1,1). If the *string* parameter is blank, the match succeeds with any text.

The *attribute* parameter indicates how the string must appear on the screen for a match. This parameter can have the normal, bold, or inverse symbolic values or an integer value that denotes specific foreground and background colors. If the *attribute* parameter is left blank or if it has the value 0, all display attributes are matched.

The *match* and *nomatch* parameters are the labels of the statements executed if the match is made or not made, respectively. If the *match* or *nomatch* parameters are blank, the equivalent of a NOTHING command is executed.

Sample Program

The mouse menu source program on page 43 shows how MATCH statements are used. It also changes the active drive when you press the right mouse button. The program goes through the following procedure:

- When you press the right mouse button, the *chdriv* EXECUTE statement calls the *checka* MATCH statement and then clears the screen.

- The *checka* MATCH statement checks row 2, column 1 on the screen. If it finds a: in normal display, it executes the *tob* statement. If a: is not found, it executes the *checkb* statement, which performs a similar check for the b: characters. The program calls up to three MATCH statements, looking for the first match with a:, b:, or c:.

- The *tob* statement clears the screen, changes the active drive to B, and ends the mouse menu program. Similarly, *toc* and *toa* change the active drive to C or A.

- If the three MATCH statements fail to find a:, b:, or c: at row 2, column 1, the program clears the screen and terminates without changing the active drive. With the screen cleared, the MS-DOS prompt should put the active drive letter in row 2, column 1, ready for the next press of the right mouse button.

- Pressing the left button creates a directory listing, and pressing both buttons simulates typing Ctrl-C.

```
BEGIN dir,chdriv,ctrlc                  ;Labels for left, right, or both
                                        ;buttons
chdriv:   EXECUTE checka,cls            ;Calls "checka," then clears screen

checka:   MATCH 2,1,normal,"a:",tob,checkb  ;If a: found, change to drive B
checkb:   MATCH 2,1,normal,"b:",toc,checkc  ;If b: found, change to drive C
checkc:   MATCH 2,1,normal,"c:",toa         ;If c: found, change to drive A

toa:      EXECUTE cls,a,ent            ;Clears screen, changes to drive A
tob:      EXECUTE cls,b,ent            ;Clears screen, changes to drive B
toc:      EXECUTE cls,c,ent            ;Clears screen, changes to drive C

a:        TYPE "a:"                    ;Types a:
b:        TYPE "b:"                    ;Types b:
c:        TYPE "c:"                    ;Types c:

cls:      TYPE "cls",enter             ;Clears the screen
dir:      TYPE "dir",enter             ;Gets directory listing

ent:      TYPE enter                   ;Types the Enter key
ctrlc:    TYPE 3                       ;Types Ctrl- C
```

CREATING A MOUSE MENU PROGRAM

The following procedure lets you create a mouse menu source file. It then shows you how to create a mouse menu program from the source file by using the MAKEMENU utility.

To create a mouse menu, do the following:

1. Write the mouse menu source file by using a text editor or word processing program.

2. Save the source file with the filename extension .DEF. A file with this extension is used by the MAKEMENU utility to generate a mouse menu program (a .MNU file). When a source file is converted to a .MNU file, the resulting file must not exceed 57 KB.

3. Type **makemenu** and press the Enter key.

4. At the prompt, type the name of the source file (without the .DEF extension), and then press the Enter key.

NOTE: Be sure to save the source file as a standard ASCII text file. Most simple text editors save files in ASCII by default. In word-processing programs, such as Microsoft Word, however, you usually need to select a special unformatted option to get ASCII text. You can combine steps 3 and 4 by typing **makemenu** *followed by a space and the name of the source file (without the .DEF extension) on the same line.*

If your file contains no errors, MAKEMENU displays the following message:

Conversion completed

and returns you to MS-DOS. The mouse menu is then ready for you to test. However, if your file contains errors, MAKEMENU displays the types of errors and the statements that contain the errors. In this case, correct the source program and repeat steps 3 and 4. For more information on error messages, see Appendix B, "Domestic Mouse Driver Messages."

NOTE: The disks that come with this book include mouse menu source files for some commonly used applications that don't have built-in mouse support (such as WordStar). If you want to create a mouse menu from one of the source files included on the disks, you can copy the source file and edit the copy to meet your specific needs. You can then use the preceding procedure to create mouse menus from these source files.

Testing the Mouse Menu Program

When the mouse menu source file has been successfully translated into an executable menu file, it is ready for you to test.

NOTE: If you did not specify that the mouse driver should be loaded every time you start MS-DOS when you ran the Mouse Setup program, be sure you type **mouse** *to install the mouse driver before you start your menu file. The menu will load before you type* **mouse***; however, it will not work.*

To test the mouse menu, do the following:

1. Type **menu** *filename* at the MS-DOS prompt and press the Enter key to start your mouse menu program. In this command, *filename* is the name of the .MNU file generated by MAKEMENU with or without the .MNU extension. When the mouse menu file is loaded, the following message appears:

   Menu installed

2. Start your application program and try out the menu to ensure that it works under all conditions in your program.

3. If your application program doesn't work the way you want it to, quit the application program, then end the mouse menu program by typing **menu off** at the MS-DOS prompt and pressing the Enter key. The following message is displayed:

Keyboard emulation off

4. Correct the source file, and then run the MAKEMENU utility again.

Running a Mouse Menu Program

Follow the steps below to run a mouse menu program.

1. Use the MS-DOS COPY command to copy the mouse menu (.MNU) file and the MENU.COM file onto the disk that contains the application program with which you want to use the menu.

2. Type **menu** *filename* to run the mouse menu program for the application. In this command, *filename* is the name of the mouse menu program. When the mouse menu file is loaded, the following message appears:

Menu installed

NOTE: To start a mouse menu program that is not in the current directory, include the pathname of the directory that contains the mouse menu file as part of filename.

3. Run the application program according to the instructions in the program's documentation.

A mouse menu program runs independently of the corresponding application program. You should end the mouse menu program you're running and begin another whenever you end one application and begin another.

Ending a Mouse Menu Program

To end the mouse menu program, you simply type **menu off** and press the Enter key. The following message is displayed:

Keyboard emulation off

You can then load and run another mouse menu program.

Allocating Memory for Mouse Menus

MENU.COM can allocate up to 57 KB of memory for a mouse menu program. (The size of MENU.COM [7 KB] plus the size of the .MNU file cannot exceed 64 KB.) If the menu file is smaller than 6 KB, MENU.COM allocates 6 KB of memory. If the menu file is greater than 6 KB, MENU.COM allocates the exact size of the file.

Every time you start MS-DOS, the first menu file you load determines the amount of memory reserved for a menu file. If you plan to use more than one mouse menu before restarting your system, first load the .MNU file that requires the greatest amount of memory so that MENU.COM will allocate enough memory to hold each menu file.

Note that a mouse menu will work only if the application it is working with allows memory-resident programs to run with it. In addition, a mouse menu will not work with an application that intercepts the keyboard interrupt and bypasses the keyboard buffer.

If you type **menu off** to disable a mouse menu, note that the memory allocated by MENU.COM will not be released for use by other programs.

Chapter 4

Mouse Menu Language Statements

This chapter describes in detail each statement used by the mouse menu programming language. Each statement description includes the statement syntax, a description of each parameter, and one or more examples of how to use the statement.

STATEMENT SYNTAX CONVENTIONS

The following syntax conventions apply for each statement:

- The command word appears in uppercase.

- Labels appear in lowercase. A colon (:) and a space must separate each label from the command word.

- Parameters appear in lowercase italic. A comma (,) must separate each parameter from other parameters. If you don't include a parameter, you must include an additional comma where the parameter would have appeared.

- A parameter in brackets ([]) is optional. A parameter that doesn't appear in brackets is required.

- If a parameter appears in double-quotation marks (" "), you must include the double-quotation marks.

- If a parameter appears more than once in a statement, the second occurrence of the parameter is enclosed in brackets and followed by an ellipsis (...).

THE ASSIGN STATEMENT

The ASSIGN statement has the following format:

label: ASSIGN [*lfbtn*],[*rtbtn*],[*btbtn*],[*lfmov*],[*rtmov*], [*upmov*],[*dnmov*],[*hsen*],[*vsen*]

Description

The ASSIGN statement redefines one or more of the mouse parameters in the BEGIN statement or in the most recent ASSIGN statement. If you don't specify a parameter value in an ASSIGN statement, the last parameter value given (in either the BEGIN statement or another ASSIGN statement) is used. Statement labels are the values you use for all parameters except *hsen* and *vsen*.

Parameters

The parameters for the ASSIGN statement are as follows:

Parameter	Description
lfbtn	Label of the first statement to be executed when you press the left mouse button
rtbtn	Label of the first statement to be executed when you press the right mouse button
btbtn	Label of the first statement to be executed when you press both mouse buttons at once
lfmov	Label of the first statement to be executed when you move the mouse to the left
rtmov	Label of the first statement to be executed when you move the mouse to the right
upmov	Label of the first statement to be executed when you move the mouse forward
dnmov	Label of the first statement to be executed when you move the mouse backward
hsen	Value of the horizontal-movement-sensitivity parameter
vsen	Value of the vertical-movement-sensitivity parameter

Example

In the following example, the BEGIN statement assigns initial values to all button and movement parameters. Because values are not specified for the sensitivity parameters (*vsen* and *hsen*), the default values of 4 and 8 are used.

The ASSIGN statement changes the values of the left button, right button, and up-and-down-movement parameters. It also changes the value of *hsen* to 16 and the value of *vsen* to 18. Commas indicate which values aren't being changed.

```
BEGIN esc,ent,mm1,lf,rt,up,dn
 .
 .
 .
reassign: ASSIGN y,not,,,,not,not,16,18
```

THE BEGIN STATEMENT

The BEGIN statement has the following format:

```
BEGIN [lfbtn],[rtbtn],[btbtn],[lfmov],[rtmov],
[upmov],[dnmov],[hsen],[vsen]
```

Description

The BEGIN statement defines the actions taken when the mouse is used.

The parameters for BEGIN define the statements executed when you move the mouse or press the mouse buttons. They also define the movement sensitivity for the mouse. All parameters for the BEGIN statement are optional. If you don't provide a value for a button or mouse-movement parameter (all parameters except *hsen* and *vsen*), nothing happens when you press a mouse button or move the mouse. If you don't provide a value for *hsen* or *vsen*, the default values of 4 and 8 are used. Statement labels are the values you use for all parameters used with the BEGIN statement except *hsen* and *vsen*.

NOTE: When a mouse menu subroutine (see MENU and POPUP) is executed, the parameters for the BEGIN statement do not affect the mouse functions within that subroutine. You can use either mouse button to choose an item in a menu, and all mouse-movement functions are active.

The movement-sensitivity parameters, *hsen* and *vsen*, control the horizontal-movement and vertical-movement sensitivity of the mouse. Movement sensitivity is the distance the mouse must move (measured in mickeys) before the on-screen pointer moves. (For more information on the mickey, see Chapter 6, ''Mouse Programming Interface.'')

Parameters

Because the BEGIN statement is always the first statement in a menu source file, it doesn't require a label. The parameters for the BEGIN statement follow.

Parameter	Description
lfbtn	Label of the first statement executed when you press the left mouse button.
rtbtn	Label of the first statement executed when you press the right mouse button.
btbtn	Label of the first statement executed when you press both mouse buttons.
lfmov	Label of the first statement executed when you move the mouse to the left.
rtmov	Label of the first statement executed when you move the mouse to the right.
upmov	Label of the first statement executed when you move the mouse forward.
dnmov	Label of the first statement executed when you move the mouse backward.
hsen	Number between 0 and 32,767 that defines how many mickeys the mouse must move horizontally before the on-screen pointer moves. If you specify 0, the mouse is disabled horizontally. If you do not specify a value, the default value of 4 mickeys is used.
vsen	Number between 0 and 32,767 that defines how many mickeys the mouse must move vertically before the on-screen pointer moves. If you specify 0, the mouse is disabled vertically. If you do not specify a value, the default value of 8 mickeys is used.

Example

The BEGIN statement in this example defines initial values for all parameters except *btbtn*, *hsen*, and *vsen*. Because *btbtn* isn't specified, nothing happens when you press both mouse buttons. Because values are not given for *hsen* and *vsen*, the default values of 4 and 8 mickeys are used.

```
BEGIN ent,es,,lf,rt,up,dn
 lf:  TYPE 0,75   ;Simulates pressing the left-arrow key
 rt:  TYPE 0,77   ;Simulates pressing the right-arrow key
 up:  TYPE 0,72   ;Simulates pressing the up-arrow key
 dn:  TYPE 0,80   ;Simulates pressing the down-arrow key
 es:  TYPE esc    ;Simulates pressing the Esc key
ent: TYPE enter   ;Simulates pressing the Enter key
```

THE EXECUTE STATEMENT

The Execute statement has the following format:

```
label: EXECUTE label [,label ... ]
```

Description

The EXECUTE statement carries out other statements when you

- Select a menu and pop-up item
- Move the mouse
- Press one or both mouse buttons
- Execute a MATCH statement

Each EXECUTE statement can specify up to 15 other statements to execute. An EXECUTE statement can call other EXECUTE statements; you can link up to 15 EXECUTE statements in this manner. Statements within an EXECUTE statement are executed sequentially, starting with the first statement.

Parameters

The parameters for the EXECUTE statement are as follows:

Parameter	Description
label	Name of the EXECUTE statement. All EXECUTE statements must be labeled.
label	Name(s) of the label(s) to execute. Each EXECUTE statement begins with a label. However, you should not use that label as a parameter within that EXECUTE statement or in a nested EXECUTE statement—if you do, you will create an endless loop.

Examples

In this example, the EXECUTE statement labeled *exec4* executes the statements labeled *dir, s, a,* and *ent,* which simulate typing *dir a:* and then pressing Enter.

```
dir:    TYPE "dir"          ;Types the DIR command
s:      TYPE 32             ;Simulates pressing the Spacebar
                            ;TYPE " " can also be used
a:      TYPE "a:"           ;Types a:
ent:    TYPE enter          ;Simulates pressing the Enter key
exec4:  EXECUTE dir,s,a,ent
```

In the following example, two EXECUTE statements are nested, and the first EXECUTE statement calls the second. The comments describe the flow of the program when the *exec1* statement is activated.

```
exec1:  EXECUTE a,ent       ;Executes statements labeled a and ent
                            ;and then returns to wherever exec1 was called

a:      EXECUTE a1,a2       ;Executes a1 and a2 and then returns to the second
                            ;part of the EXECUTE statement labeled exec1

a1:     TYPE "a"            ;Simulates typing a lowercase a and then returns
                            ;to the middle of the a: statement

a2:     TYPE "AA"           ;Simulates typing uppercase AA and then returns
                            ;to the end of the a: statement

ent:    TYPE enter          ;Simulates pressing the Enter key and then returns to
                            ;the end of the statement labeled exec1
```

The following examples cause infinite loops, which you should avoid. EXECUTE statements must not call themselves.

```
bad1:   EXECUTE bad1        ;Infinite loop
```

Also, a nested EXECUTE statement must not call any EXECUTE statement that leads to its own activation.

```
bad2:   EXECUTE bad3        ;Executes statement labeled bad3
bad3:   EXECUTE bad2        ;Infinite loop
```

THE MATCH STATEMENT

The MATCH statement has the following format:

label: MATCH [*row*],[*column*],[*attribute*],"*string*",*match*,*nomatch*

Description

The MATCH statement executes other statements or subroutines, depending on whether it finds a specified string at a given screen location. You must provide values for the *row* and *column* parameters in absolute screen coordinates. The starting coordinates for the screen are at row 1, column 1.

Parameters

The parameters for the MATCH statement are as follows:

Parameter	Description
label	Name of the MATCH statement. All MATCH statements must be labeled.
row	Number that specifies the row of the first character of the match string. If you do not specify a value, row 1 is assigned.
column	Number that specifies the column of the first character of the match string. If you do not specify a value, column 1 is assigned.
attribute	Value that specifies how the match string must appear on the screen for a match to occur. This can be the normal, bold, or inverse symbolic values, or it can be a decimal value that denotes specific foreground and background colors. (This value is the sum of the foreground and background colors you want to use.) If you leave the *attribute* parameter blank or give it the value of 0, the MATCH statement matches any attribute. For more information on the *attribute* parameter, see Chapter 3, "Creating Your Own Mouse Menu."
string	String you want to match. The string can contain up to 255 ASCII characters. You must specify the *string* parameter, and you must enclose it in double-quotation marks (" ").

(continued)

continued

Parameter	Description
match	Label of a statement or subroutine executed if the string is matched. This label must exist in the program. If you do not specify a label, nothing happens when the match is made.
nomatch	Label of a statement or subroutine executed if the string is not matched. This label must exist in the program. If you do not specify a label, nothing happens when the match is not made.

Example

The following example from the WS.DEF menu source file, included on the disks in this book, checks whether WordStar is displaying the Beginning menu or the Main menu.

When you press the left mouse button, the following occurs:

- The MATCH statement labeled *leftb* looks for an *e* at row 1, column 12. This is the first character in the string *editing no file*, which appears on the screen in that position if WordStar version 3.2 is displaying the Beginning menu. If *leftb* finds the *e* in that position, it executes the statement labeled *imen*. (In WS.DEF, the *imen* statement displays the No-File pop-up menu for WordStar.) If *leftb* doesn't find the *e* in that position, it executes the statement labeled *chk33*.

- The *chk33* statement looks for the letter *n* at row 1, column 12. This is the first character in the string *not editing*, which is on the screen in that position if WordStar version 3.3 is displaying the Beginning menu. If the *chk33* statement finds the *n* in that position, it executes the statement labeled *imen*. (In WS.DEF, the *imen* statement displays the No-File pop-up menu for WordStar.) If *chk33* doesn't find the *n* in that position, it executes the *chkl* statement.

- The *chkl* statement looks for a colon (:) after the disk drive identifier in the first line of the WordStar Main menu display. If *chkl* finds a colon, it executes the statement labeled *emen*. (In WS.DEF, the *emen* statement displays the Edit/Block pop-up menu.) If *chkl* doesn't find a colon, the menu program does nothing.

```
BEGIN   leftb,rightb,bothb,mousel,mouser,mouseu,moused,16,40
leftb:  MATCH 1,12,normal,"e",imen,chk33
chk33:  MATCH 1,12,,"n",imen,chk1
chk1:   MATCH 1,11,,":",emen,not
imen:   POPUP 2,1
          .
          .
          .
        PEND
emen:   POPUP 2,1
          .
          .
          .
        PEND
not:    NOTHING
```

THE MENU...MEND STATEMENTS

MENU statements have the following format:

```
label: MENU ["title"],[row],[column],[attribute]
       .
       .
       .
       MEND
```

Description

The MENU statement is the first statement in a menu subroutine that creates a bordered, single-column pop-up menu. The specific dimensions of a menu are determined by the number of items in a menu. The dimensions are also determined by the largest number of characters in the longest menu item or in the menu title.

When the menu is displayed, the first menu item is highlighted. You can choose any menu item by moving the mouse until that item is highlighted and then pressing either mouse button. If you press both mouse buttons, the equivalent of a NOTHING statement is executed and the menu disappears. Any movement or button actions defined in a BEGIN or ASSIGN statement are ignored within the MENU subroutine.

Each menu subroutine must have a MEND (menu end) statement, which indicates the end of a menu subroutine. The MEND statement has no parameters.

NOTE: The MENU statement automatically generates a border around the entire menu and draws a line between the menu title and the menu items.

Parameters

The MENU statement has the following parameters:

Parameter	Description
label	Name of the menu subroutine. All menu subroutines must be labeled.
title	Text of the menu title, enclosed in double-quotation marks (" "). The menu title is limited to one line. If you don't specify a title, MENU generates a blank line.

(continued)

continued

Parameter	Description
row	Number that specifies the row where the upper-left corner of the menu border appears. Be sure to specify a value that displays the entire menu. (For example, if the menu contains 20 items and you choose a row value greater than 3, some of the screen items will not appear on a 25-row screen.) If you don't specify a row, the upper-left corner is assigned row 1.
column	Number that specifies the column where the upper-left corner of the menu appears. If you don't specify a column, the upper-left corner is assigned column 1.
attribute	Value that specifies how the menu is displayed on the screen. This can be normal, bold, or inverse, or it can be a decimal value that specifies particular foreground and background colors. (For more information on the *attribute* parameter, see Chapter 3, "Creating Your Own Mouse Menu.") If you don't specify a value, MENU uses the inverse value. The colors of the mouse pointer depend on the display-attribute value for the menu. For detailed information on how the interaction between the mouse pointer and menu display determines the colors of the pointer, see Chapter 6, "Mouse Programming Interface."

Example

In the following example, the MENU statement contains all four parameters. The menu title is *Display Directory*. The upper-left corner of the menu border is at row 5, column 5. The menu is displayed with a normal screen attribute.

The OPTION statements specify which statements execute when you choose items from the menu. OPTION statements are described in greater detail later in this chapter.

NOTE: You should always include a provision for the user to make the menu disappear without causing an action to occur. This example includes a Cancel *option that, because it doesn't have a label in the line, executes the equivalent of a NOTHING statement.*

```
menu1: MENU     "Display Directory",5,5,normal
       OPTION   "Cancel"
       OPTION   "a:",ex1
       OPTION   "b:",ex2
       OPTION   "c:",ex3
       MEND
ex1:   EXECUTE dir,s,a,ent    ;DIR a:
ex2:   EXECUTE dir,s,b,ent    ;DIR b:
ex3:   EXECUTE dir,s,c,ent    ;DIR c:
ent:   TYPE enter             ;Simulates pressing the Enter key
dir:   TYPE "dir"             ;Types the DIR command
a:     TYPE "a:"              ;Types a:
b:     TYPE "b:"              ;Types b:
c:     TYPE "c:"              ;Types c:
s:     TYPE 32                ;Types a space
```

THE NOTHING STATEMENT

The NOTHING statement has the following format:

label: NOTHING

Description

The NOTHING statement specifies that no action occur when you press a mouse button, move the mouse, or choose a menu option. You can also use the NOTHING statement to specify that no action occur when a MATCH statement is executed.

Parameters

The NOTHING statement has no parameters.

Example

This example from the WS.DEF mouse menu program, which is included on the disks in this book, determines which pop-up menu is displayed when you press the right mouse button.

The WS.DEF program does the following:

- If the MATCH statement finds the specified character, it executes the statement labeled *movemenu*, which displays the CURSOR MOVEMENT pop-up menu.

- If the MATCH statement doesn't find the specified character, it executes the NOTHING statement, labeled *nul*, and the mouse menu program does nothing.

```
rightb:  MATCH 1,11,NORMAL, ":",movemenu,nul
   .
   .
   .
movemenu:  POPUP 2,1
TEXT "======= CURSOR MOVEMENT ======="
   .
   .
   .
nul:     NOTHING
```

THE OPTION STATEMENT

The OPTION statement has the following format:

`[label:] OPTION [text],[pointer]`

Description

OPTION statements define each menu item in a menu subroutine: the text of the menu item and the action taken when you choose the item.

You usually don't label OPTION statements, although you can if you want to. If you do label them, the MAKEMENU program ignores the labels when it assembles the source program.

Parameters

The parameters for OPTION statements are as follows:

Parameter	Description
text	Text for the menu item. You must enclose the text in double-quotation marks (" "). If you don't specify text for a menu item, OPTION displays a blank line for that item.
pointer	Label of the statement that is executed when you choose the menu item. If you don't include a *pointer* parameter, the menu clears from the screen when you choose the menu item. (The equivalent of a NOTHING statement is executed.) For example, you'd leave out the *pointer* parameter for a *Cancel Menu* item.

Example

The following example shows OPTION statements that define four menu items. If you choose the first menu item, the menu disappears from the screen because the OPTION statement doesn't have a *pointer* parameter. If you choose any other menu item, the specified statement is executed.

```
menu5:  MENU     "Display Directory",5,5,normal
        OPTION   "Cancel"
        OPTION   "a:",ex1
        OPTION   "b:",ex2
        OPTION   "c:",ex3
        MEND
ex1:    EXECUTE dir,s,a,ent    ;DIR a:
ex2:    EXECUTE dir,s,b,ent    ;DIR b:
ex3:    EXECUTE dir,s,c,ent    ;DIR c:
ent:    TYPE enter             ;Simulates pressing the Enter key
dir:    TYPE "dir"             ;Types the DIR command
a:      TYPE "a:"              ;Types a:
b:      TYPE "b:"              ;Types b:
c:      TYPE "c:"              ;Types c:
s:      TYPE 32                ;Types a space
```

THE POPUP...PEND STATEMENTS

POPUP statements have the following format:

```
label: POPUP [row],[column],[attribute]
       .
       .
       .
       PEND
```

Description

The POPUP statement is the first statement in a pop-up subroutine that creates a multiple-column menu or a message box.

Each pop-up subroutine must have a PEND (pop-up end) statement, which indicates the end of a pop-up subroutine.

Parameters

The parameters for the POPUP statement are as follows:

Parameter	Description
label	Name of the pop-up subroutine. All POPUP statements must be labeled. Do not label the PEND statement.
row	Number that specifies the row where the upper-left corner of the first row of the menu or message box appears. Be sure to specify a value that displays the entire menu or message box. (For example, if the menu or message box contains 20 lines and you choose a row value greater than 5, some of the screen items will not appear on the 25-row screen.) If you don't specify a row, the upper-left corner is assigned row 1. (Note: Subsequent menu items in a pop-up menu are created with the TEXT statement.)
column	Number that specifies the column where the upper-left corner of the menu or message box appears. If you don't specify a column, the upper-left corner is assigned column 1.

(continued)

continued

Parameter	Description
attribute	Value that specifies how the menu is displayed on the screen. This can be normal, bold, or inverse, or it can be a decimal value that specifies particular foreground and background colors. (For more information on the *attribute* parameter, see Chapter 3, "Creating Your Own Mouse Menu.") If you don't specify a value, POPUP uses the inverse value. The colors of the mouse pointer depend on the display-attribute value for the menu. For detailed information on how the interaction between the mouse pointer and menu display determines the colors of the pointer, see Chapter 6, "Mouse Programming Interface."

NOTE: Unlike the MENU statement, which generates a border around the entire menu and draws a line between the menu title and the menu items, a POPUP statement doesn't draw any lines. You must, therefore, include line-drawing characters within the TEXT statements that are part of the pop-up subroutine. The easiest characters to use are the equal sign (=) or the minus sign (−) for horizontal lines, the vertical line character (¦) for vertical lines, and the plus sign (+) for the corners. You can also use the upper-ASCII line-drawing characters, which are listed in Appendix G, "ASCII Character Set."

In addition, the POPUP statement provides a greater degree of control when you define menu choices than does the MENU statement. Your pop-up subroutine must include SELECT statements to select and act upon the menu choices presented with TEXT statements.

Examples

The following example is a simple pop-up menu. When you press the left mouse button, the pop-up menu lets you select one of two MS-DOS commands. The POPUP statement defines the upper-left corner of the menu as row 5, column 20. The menu border is created using plus signs (+), pipes (¦), and equal signs (=). The second line of the menu displays the title. In addition, three menu selections are presented in the fourth and fifth lines, as defined by the SELECT statements. SELECT statements are discussed in further detail later in this chapter.

```
BEGIN leftb

leftb: POPUP 5,20,inverse
       TEXT  "+====================+"
       TEXT  ":  POPUP - DOS helper :"
       TEXT  "+--------------------+"
       TEXT  ":     CLS     DIR     :"
       TEXT  ":    Exit POPUP menu  :"
       TEXT  "+====================+"
       SELECT 5,4,17
       SELECT 4,6,5,cls
       SELECT 4,14,5,dir
       PEND

cls:   TYPE "cls",enter
dir:   TYPE "dir",enter
```

The following example from the WS.DEF mouse menu program, included on the disks in this book, is a pop-up subroutine for a message box.

ASCII graphics characters create solid double borders for the menu. Also, the single SELECT statement clears the message box from the screen because it does not include a *pointer* parameter. Therefore, pressing either mouse button clears the message box from the screen.

```
mousehlp: POPUP 2,1
  TEXT " ============== MOUSE HELP ================= "
  TEXT ":                                           :"
  TEXT ": Left button  - Displays Edit/Block menu    :"
  TEXT ": Right button - Displays Cursor Movement menu :"
  TEXT ": Both buttons - Displays Edit/File menu     :"
  TEXT ":                                           :"
  TEXT ": Moving the mouse up, down, left, or right  :"
  TEXT ": causes the cursor to move in that direction. :"
  TEXT ":                                           :"
  TEXT " ========================================== "
  SELECT 1,18,10
  PEND
```

THE SELECT STATEMENT

The SELECT statement has the following format:

```
SELECT row,column,length[,pointer]
```

Description

The SELECT statement in pop-up subroutines defines selection areas for items on the menu. It also specifies which statement executes if the cursor is in the defined area. The defined area doesn't have to contain any text.

NOTE: The highlight in a menu or message box moves from one defined selection area to another when you move the mouse. It's a good idea to define each part of a menu with a SELECT statement so that the movement of the highlight and the movement of the mouse are visually coordinated; however, be sure you don't define the same screen position with more than one SELECT statement.

Parameters

The parameters for the SELECT statement are as follows:

Parameter	Description
row	Number that defines the horizontal starting point (row) of the item-selection area relative to the *row* and *column* coordinates you specified in the POPUP statement.
column	Number that defines the vertical starting point (column) of the item-selection area relative to the *row* and *column* coordinates you specified in the POPUP statement.
length	Number of characters in the item-selection area. If you don't specify a number, the SELECT statement assumes one character.
pointer	Label of the statement executed when you choose the menu item. If you don't include a *pointer* parameter, the menu disappears from the screen. (You can press either button to select the item; however, if you press both buttons, the item is not selected and the menu merely disappears from the screen.)

Example

The SELECT statements in the following example let you select *CLS* to clear the screen, *DIR* to get a directory listing, or *Exit pop-up menu* to clear the menu from the screen.

Notice that the first SELECT statement in a pop-up subroutine defines which selection will be highlighted when the menu appears.

```
BEGIN leftb

leftb: POPUP 5,20,inverse
       TEXT "+====================+"
       TEXT ":  POPUP - DOS helper :"
       TEXT "+--------------------+"
       TEXT ":    CLS      DIR    :"
       TEXT ":   Exit pop-up menu :"
       TEXT "+====================+"
       SELECT 5,4,17
       SELECT 4,6,5,cls
       SELECT 4,14,5,dir
       PEND
cls:   TYPE "cls",enter
dir:   TYPE "dir",enter
```

THE TEXT STATEMENT

The TEXT statement has the following format:

```
TEXT "string"
```

Description

The TEXT statement in pop-up subroutines defines the menu title, the text for menu items, and the characters used to draw lines and borders. It is similar to the *title* and *text* parameters in the MENU and OPTION statements, but it lets you place text anywhere on the screen (as long as the text is below and to the right of the upper-left corner of the pop-up menu).

Parameter

The parameter for the TEXT statement is as follows:

Parameter	Description
string	The pop-up menu title or the text of a menu item. Text can include ASCII graphics characters for lines and borders, and you must enclose all text in double-quotation marks (" "). The location of text on the screen is relative to the upper-left corner set by the POPUP statement. Also, text display attributes are determined by the *attribute* parameter in the POPUP statement.

Example

The TEXT statements in the following example define the appearance of the pop-up menu. The statements completely define the borders, title, and all menu selections.

```
BEGIN leftb

leftb: POPUP 5,20,inverse
       TEXT "+====================+"
       TEXT ":  POPUP - DOS helper :"
       TEXT "+--------------------+"
       TEXT ":    CLS      DIR    :"
       TEXT ":   Exit pop-up menu :"
       TEXT "+====================+"
       SELECT 5,4,17
       SELECT 4,6,5,cls
       SELECT 4,14,5,dir
       PEND


cls:   TYPE "cls",enter
dir:   TYPE "dir",enter
```

THE TYPE STATEMENT

The TYPE statement has the following format:

label: TYPE *key* [*,key*...]

Description

A TYPE statement simulates typing one or more keys.

NOTE: All keys you specify in the TYPE statement are inserted into a keyboard buffer when the menu program is running. They are not output as keystrokes until the menu program becomes inactive.

Parameters

The parameters for the TYPE statement are as follows:

Parameter	Description
label	Name of the TYPE statement. Every TYPE statement must be labeled.
key	Name of the key.

The name of the key can be:

- One or more letters or numbers enclosed in double-quotation marks (such as "X" or "dir").

- A standard ASCII code (characters 0 through 127) or an extended ASCII code (characters 128 through 255). The ASCII control characters (0 through 31) that you can use with the TYPE statement are listed in Appendix G, "ASCII Character Set."

- An extended-keyboard-scan code. (These are listed in Appendix G, "ASCII Character Set.")

- Any of the following predefined symbolic keys: enter, tab, backsp, esc.

NOTE: If you want to simulate typing a double-quotation mark ("), use ASCII code 34.

Examples

The following TYPE statements use character strings to define the keys:

```
dir:    TYPE "dir"  ;Types the DIR command
a:      TYPE "a:"   ;Types a:
```

The following TYPE statement uses an ASCII code to simulate typing a space:

```
s:      TYPE 32     ;Types a space
```

The following TYPE statements use extended-keyboard-scan codes to simulate the arrow keys:

```
lf:     TYPE 0,75   ;Simulates pressing the left-arrow key
rt:     TYPE 0,77   ;Simulates pressing the right-arrow key
up:     TYPE 0,72   ;Simulates pressing the up-arrow key
dn:     TYPE 0,80   ;Simulates pressing the down-arrow key
```

Key Sequences That Can't Be Simulated

Some key sequences can't be simulated by using the TYPE statement because they are suppressed in the ROM (Read-Only Memory) BIOS (Basic Input/Output System) keyboard routine. These include the following key combinations:

- Alt-Backspace

- Alt-Esc

- Alt plus one of the direction keys

- Alt plus one of the following characters: [ ] ; ' – , . / *

- Alt plus one of the following keys: Enter, Ctrl, Shift, Caps Lock, Num Lock, Scroll Lock

- Ctrl-Alt-Del

- Ctrl-Break

- Ctrl-Ins

- Ctrl plus one of the direction keys

- Ctrl plus one of the following characters: 1 3 4 5 7 8 9 0 = ; ' – , . /

- Ctrl plus one of the following keys: Tab, Shift, Caps Lock, Num Lock
- Shift-PrtSc

Chapter 5

Sample Mouse Menu Programs

This chapter discusses the source program listings for two simple
mouse menu programs that simplify some tasks commonly performed
on an IBM personal computer or compatible.

Use your word processor or text editor to create the source file for
either mouse menu, run the MAKEMENU utility to generate a mouse
menu file, and then start using the mouse menu immediately. You can
also use these listings as a basis for designing similar mouse menus that
include features specific to your needs.

THE SIMPLE MOUSE MENU PROGRAM

The SIMPLE mouse menu program lets you use the mouse instead of
commonly used keys. It is most helpful when used with applications
that require frequent use of the direction keys. For example, in many
spreadsheet applications you must press the direction keys to move the
cursor. If the SIMPLE mouse menu is installed, you can move the cursor
by simply moving the mouse. In addition, pressing the left mouse button is equivalent to pressing the Enter key, pressing the right mouse
button simulates pressing the Esc key, and pressing both buttons
at once is the same as pressing the Ins key. If your application doesn't
use one of these keys and you press the corresponding mouse button(s)
by accident, the application responds as if you had typed a key on the
keyboard. You can then correct the mistake as you would correct any
typing error.

The source program for the SIMPLE mouse menu is as follows:

```
; A menu that simulates direction, Enter, Esc,
; and Ins keys
;
;
BEGIN ent,es,ins,lf,rt,up,dn,32,16
;
ent:    TYPE enter        ; Enter key
es:     TYPE esc          ; Esc key
ins:    TYPE 0,82         ; Ins key
;
lf:     TYPE 0,75         ; Left-arrow key
rt:     TYPE 0,77         ; Right-arrow key
up:     TYPE 0,72         ; Up-arrrow key
dn:     TYPE 0,801        ; Down-arrow key
```

THE DOSOVRLY MOUSE MENU PROGRAM

The DOSOVRLY (DOS overlay) mouse menu lets you choose several MS-DOS commands at the MS-DOS command level by pointing to a menu option and pressing the mouse. In other words, this mouse menu "overlays" MS-DOS.

In addition to a main menu, the DOSOVRLY mouse menu program has two submenus, Directory and Change Directory, which list additional MS-DOS commands. The source listing for DOSOVRLY is a good example of how to create a hierarchy of menus and submenus in one of your own mouse menu programs.

The DOSOVRLY mouse menu program provides several features that are useful at the MS-DOS command level:

- Moving the mouse left and right simulates pressing the left-arrow and right-arrow keys. This lets you edit your MS-DOS commands by simply moving the mouse.

- Pressing the right mouse button simulates pressing Enter.

- Pressing both mouse buttons at once simulates typing CLS, the MS-DOS command for clearing the screen.

- Pressing the left mouse button displays the DOSOVRLY main menu. Options on this menu let you clear the screen, execute the MS-DOS DATE or TIME command, or choose the Directory or Change Directory submenu. To select a menu option, move the highlight to the option and then press either mouse button. From within a submenu, you can choose an option to move to the other submenu or to return to the main menu.

NOTE: In the DOSOVRLY source program, the lb, rb, bb, lm, *and* rm *parameters specified in the BEGIN statement are labels for EXECUTE statements. These EXECUTE statements branch to the appropriate MENU or TYPE statements.*

If you want to simplify the following program, branch directly from the BEGIN statement to the *mnu1* menu subroutine and to the TYPE statements by using the following statement:

```
BEGIN mnu1,ent,cls,left,right
```

The source program for the DOSOVRLY mouse menu is as follows:

```
BEGIN lb,rb,bb,lm,rm
  lb:   EXECUTE mnu1    ; Select Main Menu if left button
  rb:   EXECUTE ent     ; Type Enter if right button
  bb:   EXECUTE cls     ; Type CLS command if both buttons
  lm:   EXECUTE left    ; Press left-arrow key if left motion
  rm:   EXECUTE right   ; Press right-arrow key if right motion
  ;
mnu1: MENU "Main Menu",2,55,NORMAL
    OPTION "cancel           ",none
    OPTION "clear the screen ",cls
    OPTION "date             ",date
    OPTION "time             ",time
    OPTION "Directory        ",mnu3
    OPTION "Change Directory ",mnu2
    MEND
  ;
mnu2: MENU "Change Directory",2,55,NORMAL
    OPTION "cancel           ",none
    OPTION "cd ..            ",cd1
    OPTION "cd               ",cd2
    OPTION "Directory        ",mnu3
    OPTION "Main menu        ",mnu1
    MEND
  ;
mnu3: MENU "Directory",2,55,NORMAL
    OPTION "cancel           ",none
    OPTION "dir              ",dir
    OPTION "dir *.exe        ",dire
```

(continued)

continued

```
    OPTION "dir *.bat        ",dirb
    OPTION "dir *.bak        ",dirx
    OPTION "dir *.sys        ",dirs
    OPTION "dir *.doc        ",dird
    OPTION "dir *.           ",dirz
    OPTION "Change Directory ",mnu2
    OPTION "Main menu        ",mnu1
    MEND
;
none:      NOTHING           ; Do nothing
;
ent:       TYPE enter
cls:       TYPE "cls",enter
left:      TYPE 0,75         ; Left-arrow key
right:     TYPE 0,77         ; Right-arrow key
date:      TYPE "date",enter
time:      TYPE "time",enter
cd1:       TYPE "cd ..",enter
cd2:       TYPE "cd "
dir:       TYPE "dir",enter
dire:      TYPE "dir *.exe",enter
dirb:      TYPE "dir *.bat",enter
dirx:      TYPE "dir *.bak",enter
dirs:      TYPE "dir *.sys",enter
dird:      TYPE "dir *.doc",enter
dirz:      TYPE "dir *."
```

OTHER SAMPLE MOUSE MENU PROGRAMS

The disks that accompany this book contain ten sample mouse menu programs, which you can recognize by the .DEF filename extension. Of the ten .DEF files, five are demonstration programs and five are fully operational mouse menu programs designed for use with early versions of IBM Multiplan, Microsoft Multiplan, Symphony, VisiCalc, and WordStar. These files are located in the \MENUS directory on disk 2.

Demonstration Programs

The five demonstration programs on the disks are designed to show various elements of mouse menu programming. The source files for these programs are the COLOR.DEF, DROP.DEF, EXECUTE1.DEF, EXECUTE2.DEF, and KBD.DEF files. Each of these files contains comments that explain how the demonstration program works. For an overview of each demonstration program, read the following sections.

The COLOR Program

When you run the COLOR program, it displays a menu of all possible color choices for mouse menus:

```
┌QUIT─────────────────────────────────────────────────────────────┐
│ 000 016 032 048 064 080 096 112 128 144 160 176 192 208 224 240 │
│ 001 017 033 049 065 081 097 113 129 145 161 177 193 209 225 241 │
│ 002 018 034 050 066 082 098 114 130 146 162 178 194 210 226 242 │
│ 003 019 035 051 067 083 099 115 131 147 163 179 195 211 227 243 │
│ 004 020 036 052 068 084 100 116 132 148 164 180 196 212 228 244 │
│ 005 021 037 053 069 085 101 117 133 149 165 181 197 213 229 245 │
│ 006 022 038 054 070 086 102 118 134 150 166 182 198 214 230 246 │
│ 007 023 039 055 071 087 103 119 135 151 167 183 199 215 231 247 │
│ 008 024 040 056 072 088 104 120 136 152 168 184 200 216 232 248 │
│ 009 025 041 057 073 089 105 121 137 153 169 185 201 217 233 249 │
│ 010 026 042 058 074 090 106 122 138 154 170 186 202 218 234 250 │
│ 011 027 043 059 075 091 107 123 139 155 171 187 203 219 235 251 │
│ 012 028 044 060 076 092 108 124 140 156 172 188 204 220 236 252 │
│ 013 029 045 061 077 093 109 125 141 157 173 189 205 221 237 253 │
│ 014 030 046 062 078 094 110 126 142 158 174 190 206 222 238 254 │
│ 015 031 047 063 079 095 111 127 143 159 175 191 207 223 239 255 │
└──────────────────────────────────────────────────────────────────┘
```

The numbers in the menu are the sums of the various foreground and background color combinations listed in Table 3-2 in Chapter 3. The COLOR program can help you choose color combinations for MENU or POPUP statements.

The DROP Program

The DROP program demonstrates how you can create drop-down menus. When you run the program and press the left mouse button, the following main menu appears:

```
┌─────────┬──────────┬───────────┐
│ CLR SCRN │ LIST DIR │ CH DRIVE │
└─────────┴──────────┴───────────┘
```

If you choose the leftmost menu item, CLR SCRN, the DROP program clears the screen and causes the main menu to disappear. If you choose the middle menu item, LIST DIR, a second pop-up menu appears in place of the main menu, giving the appearance of a drop-down menu:

```
┌─────────┬──────────┬───────────┐
│ CLR SCRN │ LIST DIR │ CH DRIVE │
└─────────┼──────────┼───────────┘
          │   dir    │
          │  *.bat   │
          │  *.com   │
          │  *.doc   │
          │  *.exe   │
          │  *.sys   │
          │  CANCEL  │
          └──────────┘
```

The selection rectangle is restricted to the items within the newly displayed column, letting you list a directory of the current drive in one of several ways.

If you choose the rightmost main menu item, CH DRIVE, a third pop-up menu appears in place of the main menu. Like the second menu, the third menu also gives the appearance of a menu "pulled down" from the main menu.

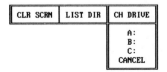

The EXECUTE1 Program

The EXECUTE1 demonstration program is designed to show the EXECUTE mouse menu command.

When you press the left mouse button, a menu with a single option appears on the screen. The option leads to a second menu, and then it clears the screen. Although the string *cls <enter>* is sent to the keyboard buffer before the second menu is displayed, the screen doesn't clear until after the second menu disappears because the contents of the keyboard buffer are not processed until the mouse menu returns control to MS-DOS.

The EXECUTE2 Program

The EXECUTE2 demonstration program is designed to show how to create a multi-level menu.

The program relies on mouse event trapping to determine whether or not a second menu is displayed. When you press the left mouse button, a menu is displayed in the upper-right corner of your screen. If you press either mouse button, the program clears the screen and the menu disappears. If you press both buttons, the menu disappears and the program does not clear the screen. If, however, you move the mouse horizontally before pressing the left or right mouse button, a second menu is displayed. The horizontal mouse movement is the event trapped by the mouse menu program—unless it detects horizontal mouse movement, the mouse menu program will not display the second menu.

Note: The EXECUTE2 program is well commented; we recommend that you read the source file before you compile and run the program.

The KBD Program

The KBD program is designed to provide partial keyboard emulation
with the mouse. Most, but not all, the keystrokes that the mouse can
emulate are included in the program.

When you press a mouse button, the following pop-up menu is
displayed:

```
┌────┬────┬────┬───────┬───┬───┐
│quit│Ctrl│Symb│ Enter │Ins│Del│
├─┬──┴┬─┬─┬┴┬─┬─┴┬─┬─┬─┬─┴┬─┬─┴┬┤
│@│A│B│C│D│E│F│G│H│I│J│K│L│M│N│O│
│P│Q│R│S│T│U│V│W│X│Y│Z│[│\│^│]│^│
│`│a│b│c│d│e│f│g│h│i│j│k│l│m│n│o│
│p│q│r│s│t│u│v│w│x│y│z│{│|│}│~│·│
├─┴─┴─┴─┴─┴──┴─┴─┴─┴─┴─┴─┴─┴─┬─┤
│           spacebar          │BS│
├─┬─┬─┬─┬─┬─┬─┬─┬─┬─┬─┬─┬─┬─┬─┬─┤
│ │!│ │#│$│%│&│'│(│)│*│+│,│-│.│/│
│0│1│2│3│4│5│6│7│8│9│:│;│<│=│>│?│
├─┬─┬─┬──┬──┬──┬──┬──┬──┬─────┤
│h│↑│p│ f1 f2 f3 f4 f5        │
│◄│·│►│ f6 f8 f8 f9 f10       │
│e│↓│d│                       │
└─┴─┴─┴─────────────────────────┘
```

To select a character, move the mouse pointer to that character and
double-click the left mouse button. The KBD program then sends that
character to the keyboard buffer and the menu is reactivated. To make
the menu disappear and cause the KBD program to act upon the "keystrokes" you sent to the keyboard buffer, click the Enter box at the top
of the menu.

Alternately, you can click the Ctrl box at the top of the menu,
which causes the following menu to appear:

```
┌────┬────┬────┐
│quit│Kybd│Symb│
├─┬──┴┬───┼────┤
│0│NUL│DLE│ 10 │
│1│SOH│DC1│ 11 │
│2│STX│DC2│ 12 │
│3│ETX│DC3│ 13 │
│4│EOT│DC4│ 14 │
│5│ENQ│NAK│ 15 │
│6│ACK│SYN│ 16 │
│7│BEL│ETB│ 17 │
│8│ BS│CAN│ 18 │
│9│ HT│ EM│ 19 │
│A│ LF│SUB│ 1A │
│B│ VT│ESC│ 1B │
│C│ FF│ FS│ 1C │
│D│ CR│ GS│ 1D │
│E│ SO│ RS│ 1E │
│F│ SI│ US│ 1F │
└─┴───┴───┴────┘
```

Double-clicking one of the characters in the menu causes the KBD
program to send that character to the keyboard buffer. You can also
click the Quit option to return to the MS-DOS prompt, or you can click

the Kybd option to return to the first menu. Note that this second menu has no Enter option. To select Enter, you must return to the first menu and choose the Enter option, or click the Symb option and choose the Enter option.

Clicking the Symb option on either the first or second menu causes the following menu to appear:

Double-clicking one of the characters in this menu causes the KBD program to send that character to the keyboard buffer. You can then choose the Enter option, which clears this menu and causes the KBD program to act upon the keystrokes you sent to the keyboard buffer. You can also choose the Keyboard option to activate the first menu, or you can choose the Control option to activate the second menu.

Application Mouse Menus

The five mouse menu programs on the disks are designed to work with earlier versions of five applications that didn't offer mouse support. The following table lists the names of the source files and the application programs for which they are designed:

Source File	Application Program
MPIBM.DEF	Multiplan (IBM)
MPMS.DEF	Multiplan (Microsoft)
SYM.DEF	Symphony
VC.DEF	VisiCalc
WS.DEF	WordStar

To create a mouse menu file, use the MAKEMENU utility. To load and start the mouse menu file, use the MENU program.

PART III

Mouse Programming Interface

Chapter 6: Mouse Programming Interface

- **The Mouse Driver Software**
- **Video Adapters and Displays**
- **The Virtual Screen**
- **Graphics and Text Cursors**
- **The Internal Cursor Flag**
- **Reading the Mouse**

Chapter 7: Mouse Programming Considerations

- **Setting Up Your System**
- **Advanced Topics**
- **Mouse Functions**

Chapter 8: Mouse Function Calls

- **Introduction to Mouse Functions**
- **Function Descriptions**

Chapter 9: Sample Mouse Programming Interface Programs

- **Interpreted BASIC Programs**
- **QuickBASIC Programs**
- **C and QuickC Programs**
- **MASM Programs**
- **FORTRAN Programs**
- **Pascal Programs**

Chapter 10: Writing Mouse Programs for IBM EGA Modes

- **The EGA Register Interface Library**
- **Restrictions on Using the EGA Register Interface Library**
- **EGA Register Interface Functions**

Chapter 6

Mouse Programming Interface

This chapter describes the interface between the mouse software and IBM PC or IBM-compatible computers. It discusses how your program uses mouse function calls to select the type of cursor displayed, how the cursor interacts with information on the screen, and how your actions with the mouse influence the cursor.

THE MOUSE DRIVER SOFTWARE

The following sections describe the interface issues you must consider when programming for the mouse: how your particular display adapter affects the type of mouse cursor displayed, how your program must manipulate the cursor, and how your program can acquire information about mouse activities. It discusses information you will need in order to provide the appropriate mouse support in your program—such as information on the difference between text mode and graphics mode and between graphics cursors and text cursors.

The sections also cover the concept of a virtual screen—an important concept for ensuring that the mouse driver interacts properly with the video display.

VIDEO ADAPTERS AND DISPLAYS

Many types of video adapters and video displays are available for the IBM family of personal computers. Their unique display capabilities and characteristics affect how the mouse cursor appears and moves on the screen.

Screen Modes

The screen mode defines the number of pixels and the types of objects that appear on the screen. A pixel is a point of light or a block of light made up of individual points. The screen modes available to you depend on the video adapter installed in your computer. Some adapters display both points of light and blocks of light; others display only blocks of light.

The screen modes and the video adapters that support them are listed in Figure 6-1.

Screen Mode (Hex)	Display Adapter	Text/ Graphics	Virtual Screen (x,y)	Cell Size	Bits per Pixel
0	CGA, EGA, MCGA, VGA, 3270	Text	640×200	16×8	–
1	CGA, EGA, MCGA, VGA, 3270	Text	640×200	16×8	–
2	CGA, EGA, MCGA, VGA, 3270	Text	640×200	8×8	–
3	CGA, EGA, MCGA, VGA, 3270	Text	640×200	8×8	–
4	CGA, EGA, MCGA, VGA, 3270	Graphics	640×200	2×1	2
5	CGA, EGA, MCGA, VGA, 3270	Graphics	640×200	2×1	2
6	CGA, EGA, MCGA, VGA, 3270	Graphics	640×200	1×1	1
7	MDA, EGA, VGA, 3270	Text	640×200	8×8	–
D	EGA, VGA	Graphics	640×200	2×1	2
E	EGA, VGA	Graphics	640×200	1×1	1
F	EGA, VGA	Graphics	640×350	1×1	1

Figure 6-1. *Screen-mode characteristics of the IBM PC family of video-display adapters.*

(continued)

Figure 6-1. *continued*

Screen Mode (Hex)	Display Adapter	Text/ Graphics	Virtual Screen (x,y)	Cell Size	Bits per Pixel
10	EGA, VGA	Graphics	640×350	1×1	1
11	MCGA, VGA	Graphics	640×480	1×1	1
12	VGA	Graphics	640×480	1×1	1
13	MCGA, VGA	Graphics	640×200	2×1	2

MDA = Monochrome Display Adapter
CGA = Color/Graphics Adapter
EGA = Enhanced Graphics Adapter
MCGA = Multi-Color Graphics Array
VGA = Video Graphics Array
3270 = IBM 3270 All-Points-Addressable Graphics Adapter

NOTE: For Hercules Monochrome Graphics Cards, the current convention is to use screen mode 5 for page 1 and screen mode 6 for page 0. See Appendix F for more information.

Text Mode *vs* Graphics Mode

Some adapters display only text mode, and others display both text mode and graphics mode. Each mode has its own characteristics; however, the modes share similar programming considerations for the mouse.

In graphics mode, you can access individual points of light. Some graphics modes display these points in only one color; others give you a choice of colors.

In text mode, you can access only character-cell-sized blocks of light made up of individual points. Common text modes on IBM PCs include 80 columns by 25 rows or 40 columns by 25 rows. Text mode uses less memory and is generally faster than graphics mode. The disadvantages are that color combinations apply to entire character cells, not to individual points within each character cell, and that any graphics must consist of ASCII characters.

Testing for Screen Modes

Suppose you want to write programs that can run on a variety of machines. Because you don't know what types of video adapters are installed in the other machines, and because your program might use graphics or color, your program must test each video adapter to see if the desired screen modes are available. In addition, your program should be able to compensate if only text mode is available.

In C programming the _setvideomode_ function returns a value that lets you check availability of specified video modes. The following program demonstrates this by attempting to set a medium-resolution graphics mode with as many colors as possible:

```
/*
 *  SETVID.C
 *  Short QuickC program that sets a graphics video
 *  mode based on the available graphics adapter.
 *
 *  Program list: setvid
 */

#include <stdio.h>
#include <graph.h>

main()
{
    if (_setvideomode(_MRES256COLOR))
        printf("VGA medium resolution, 256 colors\n");
    else if (_setvideomode(_MRES16COLOR))
        printf("EGA medium resolution, 16 colors\n");
    else if (_setvideomode(_MRES4COLOR))
        printf("CGA medium resolution, 4 colors\n");
    else
        printf("No medium-resolution graphics mode available\n");
}
```

In QuickBASIC, you can use the ON ERROR statement to test for valid video modes and available video adapters. The SETVID.BAS program demonstrates one way to do this:

```
'  SETVID.BAS
'  Short QuickBASIC program that sets a graphics video
'  mode based on the available graphics adapter.

    ON ERROR GOTO ErrorTrap

'  Try VGA medium resolution, 256 colors
    videoMode = 13
    SCREEN videoMode
```

(continued)

continued

```
' Try EGA medium resolution, 16 colors
  IF videoMode = 0 THEN
      videoMode = 7
      SCREEN videoMode
  END IF

' Try CGA medium resolution, 4 colors
  IF videoMode = 0 THEN
      videoMode = 1
      SCREEN videoMode
  END IF

' Clear the error trapping
  ON ERROR GOTO 0

' Did we find a valid video mode?
  IF videoMode THEN
      PRINT "Video mode number"; videoMode
  ELSE
      PRINT "No medium-resolution graphics mode available"
  END IF

' All done
  END

ErrorTrap:
  videoMode = 0
  RESUME NEXT
```

Following is a similar program in interpreted BASIC. Notice that BASICA may not support all available modes.

```
100 ' Short BASICA program that sets a graphics video
110 ' mode based on the available graphics adapter.
120 '
130 ON ERROR GOTO 270
140 VIDEOMODE = 13
150 SCREEN VIDEOMODE
160 IF VIDEOMODE THEN GOTO 230
170 VIDEOMODE = 7
180 SCREEN VIDEOMODE
190 IF VIDEOMODE THEN GOTO 230
200 VIDEOMODE = 1
```

(continued)

continued

```
210 SCREEN VIDEOMODE
220 '
230 IF VIDEOMODE THEN PRINT "Video mode number"; VIDEOMODE
240 IF VIDEOMODE = 0 THEN PRINT "No medium-resolution mode available"
250 END
260 '
270 VIDEOMODE = 0
280 RESUME NEXT
```

THE VIRTUAL SCREEN

To understand how the mouse interacts with the normal display of your program, you must understand the concept of a virtual screen.

A virtual screen simplifies programming for the screen resolutions that are available with the various video adapters. A virtual screen can be thought of as a grid that overlays the physical screen. As a programmer, you need to work only with the grid coordinates on the virtual screen. The mouse software translates the virtual-screen coordinates into the physical-screen coordinates for the current screen mode.

The mouse software operates on the computer screen as if it were a virtual screen composed of a matrix of horizontal and vertical points. In Figure 6-1 on pages 84 and 85, the Virtual Screen column shows the number of horizontal and vertical points in the matrix for each screen mode.

NOTE: The minimum size of a virtual screen is 640 pixels by 200 pixels.

Notice that most of the text and graphics modes have virtual-screen dimensions of 640 by 200 pixels. This often simplifies the task of programming the mouse in several graphics modes.

You can set or change the screen mode by issuing an Interrupt 10H instruction, which invokes a built-in routine in the computer's ROM BIOS. When issuing an Interrupt 10H, you must specify a function number and (optionally) a subfunction number that specify the work you want Interrupt 10H to perform.

Whenever your program calls Interrupt 10H to change the screen mode, the mouse software intercepts the call and determines which virtual screen to use. The mouse software also reads the screen mode and chooses the appropriate virtual screen whenever your program calls Mouse Function 0 (Mouse Reset and Status) to reset default parameter values in the mouse software.

In the following C program, the mouse driver intercepts Interrupt 10H during the second call to the _setvideomode function and then hides the mouse cursor. After you press a key, the mouse cursor reappears.

```c
#include <stdio.h>
#include <graph.h>
#include <dos.h>

void mouse(int *, int *, int *, int *);

main()
{
    int m1,m2,m3,m4;

    if (_setvideomode(_MRES256COLOR))
        {
        printf("320 x 200\n");
        m1 = 0;                     /* Reset mouse */
        mouse(&m1,&m2,&m3,&m4);
        m1 = 1;                     /* Show cursor */
        mouse(&m1,&m2,&m3,&m4);
        }
    getch();
    if (_setvideomode(_VRES16COLOR))
        {
        printf("640 x 480\n");
        getch();                    /* Cursor is now hidden */
        m1 = 1;                     /* Show cursor */
        mouse(&m1,&m2,&m3,&m4);
        }
    getch();
}

void mouse(m1, m2, m3, m4)
int *m1, *m2, *m3, *m4;
{
    union REGS reg;

    reg.x.ax = *m1;
    reg.x.bx = *m2;
    reg.x.cx = *m3;
    reg.x.dx = *m4;
```

(continued)

continued

```
    int86(0x33, &reg, &reg);
    *m1 = reg.x.ax;
    *m2 = reg.x.bx;
    *m3 = reg.x.cx;
    *m4 = reg.x.dx;
}
```

Regardless of the screen mode, the mouse software uses a pair of virtual-screen coordinates to locate an object on the screen. Each pair of coordinates defines a point on the virtual screen. The horizontal coordinate is given first.

Many mouse functions take virtual-screen coordinates as input or return them as output. Whenever you refer to a virtual-screen coordinate for a pixel or character in a mouse function, be sure the values are correct for the current screen mode. When you first program mouse functions, a common error is confusing physical-screen coordinates and virtual-screen coordinates. For example, in a medium-resolution mode (320 by 200 pixels) a horizontal mouse position of 320 pixels is at the center of the screen rather than at the right edge. In this case, even though there are 320 physical pixels across the screen, the virtual screen has 640 pixels. Remember that mouse functions always refer to virtual-screen coordinates.

The Cell Size column in Figure 6-1 shows the minimum resolution of mouse motion in terms of the virtual screen for each mode. Consider, for example, the 8-by-8 cell size shown for mode 3 (the 80-characters-by-25-lines text mode). In this mode, as the mouse cursor moves from character to character, the returned position of the mouse changes by 8 virtual-screen units. The character cell at the upper-left corner of the screen is at mouse coordinates (0,0), but as soon as the mouse cursor moves to the second character cell on that line the coordinates are (8,0). At the bottom-right character cell of the screen, the coordinates are (632,192).

Graphics Modes

In graphics modes 6, E, F, 10, 11, and 12, and in graphics modes 5 and 6 with an HGC, each pixel on the virtual screen has a one-to-one correspondence with each pixel on the physical screen. In these modes, the full range of coordinates in the Virtual Screen column of Figure 6-1 is permitted.

In graphics modes 4, 5, D, and 13, the physical screen is 320 by 200 pixels. The virtual screen for these modes is 640 by 200 pixels, which makes the modes consistent with the other CGA graphics modes. Notice that the horizontal coordinates for the mouse cursor are evenly numbered. Each horizontal pixel position on the screen represents a change of two virtual-screen units. In this way, the horizontal pixel positions numbered 0 through 319 on the physical screen map to positions 0 through 638 on the virtual screen. The vertical coordinates are unaffected because both the physical-screen and virtual-screen coordinates are numbered from 0 through 199.

Text Modes

Text modes 2, 3, and 7 display only characters on the screen, and each character is an 8-by-8-pixel group. (See the Cell Size column in Figure 6-1.)

When you are in text mode, you can't access the individual pixels in a character, so the mouse software uses the coordinates of the pixel in the cell's upper-left corner as the character's location. Because each character is an 8-by-8-pixel group, both the horizontal and the vertical coordinates are multiples of 8.

For example, the character in the upper-left corner of the screen has the coordinates (0,0), and the character immediately to the right of that character has the coordinates (8,0).

In text modes 0 and 1, as in text modes 2, 3, and 7, only characters can appear on the screen; however, in modes 0 and 1, each character is a 16-by-8-pixel block. (See the Cell Size column in Figure 6-1.)

As in text modes 2, 3, and 7, the mouse software uses the coordinates of the pixel in the cell's upper-left corner as the character's location. But because modes 0 and 1 have only half as many pixels as modes 2, 3, and 7, the mouse software uses horizontal coordinates that are multiples of 16.

For example, the character in the upper-left corner of the screen has the coordinates (0,0), and the character immediately to the right of the first character has the coordinates (16,0).

In all these text modes, whether they use 40 or 80 columns, the character cells are 8 pixels in height. This means that the vertical coordinates change by 8 virtual-screen units for each vertical-character-cell movement of the mouse cursor. For example, the first character in the second row of the screen has the coordinates (0,8).

GRAPHICS AND TEXT CURSORS

The mouse has one of three cursors:

- The graphics cursor, a shape that moves over images on the screen (for example, an arrow)

- The software text cursor, a character attribute that moves from character to character on the screen (for example, an underscore, reversed type, or a blinking square)

- The hardware text cursor, a flashing square, half-square, or underscore that moves from character to character on the screen

The mouse software supports only one cursor on the screen at a time. In the graphics modes, the graphics cursor is the only cursor available. The mouse software can display either of the two types of text cursors in the text modes. Your application program might change the cursor type, shape, or other attributes "on the fly," so it's a good idea to hide the cursor temporarily while changes are made. Hiding the cursor during changes lets the mouse driver detect any changes made by an Interrupt 10H call. Mouse Functions 1 (Show Cursor) and 2 (Hide Cursor) can help you with this. For more information on these functions, see Chapter 8, "Mouse Function Calls."

Mouse Functions 9 (Set Graphics Cursor Block) and 10 (Set Text Cursor) let you define the characteristics of the cursors in your application programs. You can define the characteristics yourself, or you can use the characteristics of the sample cursors provided in this book. For more information about the sample cursors, see Chapter 8, "Mouse Function Calls."

The Graphics Cursor

The graphics cursor, which is used when the video adapter is in one of the graphics modes, is a block of individual pixels. In modes 6, D, E, F, 10, 11, and 12, and modes 5 and 6 on an HGC, the cursor is a 16-by-16 square that contains 256 pixels. In modes 4 and 5, the cursor is an 8-by-16 square that contains 128 pixels.

As you move the mouse, the graphics cursor moves over the screen and interacts with the pixels directly under it. This interaction creates the cursor shape and background.

Screen Mask and Cursor Mask

For each graphics mode, the interaction between the screen pixels and cursor pixels is defined by two 16-by-16-bit arrays: the screen mask and the cursor mask. The screen mask determines whether the cursor pixels are part of the shape or part of the background. The cursor mask determines how the pixels under the cursor contribute to the color of the cursor when the video adapter is in text mode.

In your application programs, you can specify the shapes of the screen mask and cursor mask by defining the shapes as arrays and passing these arrays as parameters in a call to Mouse Function 9. For more information on Mouse Function 9, see Chapter 8, "Mouse Function Calls."

Mask interaction in modes 4 and 5 The interaction between the screen mask and the cursor mask differs somewhat between modes 4 and 5 and the rest of the graphics modes. In modes 4 and 5, each pair of bits in the masks represents one pixel on the screen. The graphics cursor masks are always defined as 16-by-16-bit squares; however, in modes 4 and 5 the cursor appears as an 8-by-16 rectangle of screen pixels. This two-to-one mapping causes each 2-bit pair of the masks to represent one screen pixel. In all other graphics modes, one mask bit represents one pixel on the screen.

To create the cursor, the mouse software operates on the data in the computer's screen memory that defines the color of each pixel on the screen. First, each bit in the masks expands to match the number of bits in video memory that are required for each pixel's color information. For example, in mode D each screen pixel requires 4 bits to indicate one of 16 possible colors. In this case, each *1* in the masks expands to *1111* and each *0* expands to *0000*. Other graphics modes result in different amounts of this bit expansion. Mode 4 (2 colors) doesn't require expansion; whereas mode 13H (256 colors) requires that each mask bit expand to 8 bits.

The mouse software then logically ANDs each of these bit groups with the bit group for the associated screen pixel. This allows the pixel color to remain unaltered wherever the screen-mask bit is 1. It also allows a new color setting wherever the screen-mask bit is 0. The pixel is blocked by a 0 and allowed through by a 1.

Finally, the pixel bits are XORed with the expanded bit groups from the cursor mask. Where the cursor mask is 0, the pixel is unaltered. Where the mask is 1, the color bits are inverted. This results in an inversion of the color information for the pixel. Most commonly, the screen mask is 0 and the cursor mask is 1 wherever the cursor image is shown, resulting in a solid, bright white image. Careful manipulation of the screen and cursor masks, and of the color palette information, lets you create transparent or colorful graphics cursors.

Figure 6-2 shows how these operations affect each individual screen bit.

If the screen mask bit is	And the cursor mask bit is	The resulting screen bit is
0	0	0
0	1	1
1	0	Unchanged
1	1	Inverted

Figure 6-2. *This table shows how the screen-mask bit and the cursor-mask bit affect the screen bit.*

In modes 4 and 5, each pair of mask bits maps to one screen pixel, resulting in a slightly different cursor creation. Each screen pixel requires 2 bits of color information. These 2 bits logically AND and XOR with the screen-mask-bit and cursor-mask-bit pairs to create the cursor. The most important consequence of this is that you should set each pair of mask bits to the same value to prevent the cursor image from *bleeding* around the edges. You can see this bleeding effect as a magenta or cyan (blue) fringe on the default-cursor arrow when you are in mode 4 or 5.

The illustration on page 95 depicts the screen and cursor masks for the default graphics cursor. The 1s in the screen mask let the background show through; the 0s hide the background pixels. The 1s in the cursor mask indicate bright white pixels composing the cursor image; the 0s let the background show through unaltered.

Mask interaction in modes E and 10 In modes E and 10, as in modes 6 and F, each bit in the screen mask and cursor mask corresponds to a pixel in the cursor block.

Screen Mask	Cursor Mask	Hot Spot
1001111111111111	0000000000000000	X = 0
1000111111111111	0010000000000000	Y = -1
1000011111111111	0011000000000000	
1000001111111111	0011100000000000	
1000000111111111	0011110000000000	
1000000011111111	0011111000000000	
1000000001111111	0011111100000000	
1000000000111111	0011111110000000	
1000000000011111	0011111111000000	
1000000000001111	0011111000000000	
1000000011111111	0011011000000000	
1000100001111111	0010001100000000	
1001100001111111	0000001100000000	
1111110000111111	0000000110000000	
1111110000111111	0000000110000000	
1111111000111111	0000000000000000	

The default graphics mode screen and cursor masks.

The cursor mask and screen mask are stored in off-screen memory. Each plane has its own identical copy of the cursor mask and screen mask; therefore, for each plane, the resulting screen bit in Figure 6-2 is actually the bit used in the color look-up table on the EGA.

In EGA and VGA graphics modes, the color information is kept in look-up tables. This means that the pixel-color information bits represent an index to a table of predefined colors. By changing the colors in this table, you can change the color of the mouse cursor. For more information about changing colors, see the BASIC PALETTE statement or the C _remappalette_ function in your product's language reference manual.

The Graphics-Cursor Hot Spot

Whenever a mouse function refers to the graphics-cursor location, it gives the point on the virtual screen that coincides with the cursor's *hot spot*. You can set the hot spot at any virtual-screen coordinates up to ±127 units from the upper-left corner of the screen-mask and cursor-mask definitions. This means that you can set the hot spot at a visible cursor pixel location or at an *invisible* pixel location where the background is visible. The cursor image appears on the screen relative to the hot spot.

You define the hot spot in the cursor block by passing the horizontal and vertical coordinates of the point to Mouse Function 9. For all graphics modes, the coordinates are relative to the upper-left corner of the cursor block. In most cases, the hot spot is set in the range 0 through 16, the area where the cursor pixel masks are defined; however, you can define the hot spot anywhere in the range −128 through 127.

Text Cursors

Two types of text cursors are used with the mouse. The software text cursor affects the appearance of the entire character cell, altering the character's attributes. The hardware text cursor comes with the computer hardware; it usually contains a block of scan lines in part of the character cell. Picking one type of text cursor instead of the other is largely a matter of preference. Both are fast and efficient.

The Software Text Cursor

You use the software text cursor when the video adapter is in one of the text-screen modes.

The software text cursor affects how characters appear on the screen. Unlike the graphics cursor, the software text cursor usually doesn't have a shape of its own. Instead, it changes the character attributes (such as foreground and background colors, intensity, and underscoring) of the character directly under it; however, if the cursor has a shape of its own, it is shaped as one of the 256 characters in the ASCII character set.

The screen and cursor masks control which attributes are altered and whether the ASCII code for the character itself is modified.

Screen mask and cursor mask Earlier in this chapter, you read about the relationships of screen and cursor masks to the graphics cursor. Software text cursors also use screen and cursor masks. In fact, the effect of the software text cursor on the character under it is defined by the screen mask and the cursor mask. The screen mask is a 16-bit value that determines which of the character's attributes are preserved, and the cursor mask is a 16-bit value that determines how these attributes change to yield the cursor.

To create the cursor, the mouse software operates on the data that defines each character on the screen. The mouse software first logically ANDs the screen mask and the 16 bits of screen data for the character currently under the cursor. The mouse software then logically XORs the cursor mask with the result of the AND operation, causing the cursor's appearance on the screen.

The format of the screen data for each character is shown in Figure 6-3. Each of the 16 bits shown in Figure 6-3 has a purpose as follows:

Bit(s)	Purpose
15	Sets blinking or nonblinking character
12–14	Sets the background color
11	Sets high intensity or medium intensity
8–10	Sets the foreground color
0–7	ASCII value of the character

The range of values for each field depends on the characteristics of the display adapter in your computer. (See the documentation that came with your display adapter for details.)

Bit: 15 14   12 11 10   8 7   0

Odd address   Even address

Figure 6-3. *Data format for each screen character in text mode.*

The screen mask and cursor mask are identical in structure to the character structure shown in Figure 6-3. The value contained in each field of the screen mask and cursor mask defines a character's new attributes when the cursor is over that character.

For example, to invert the foreground and background colors, be sure the screen mask and cursor mask have the values shown in Figure 6-4. (The software text cursor defined in this figure is the default cursor before Mouse Function 10 (Set Text Cursor) is called to redefine it.)

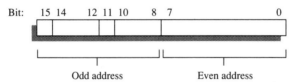

Figure 6-4. *Sample screen-mask and cursor-mask values.*

In your application programs, you can define the values of the screen mask and cursor mask by passing their values as parameters to Mouse Function 10. For more information on Function 10, see Chapter 8, "Mouse Function Calls."

Whenever a mouse function refers to the text cursor location, it gives the virtual-screen coordinates of the character under the cursor. The text cursor doesn't have a hot spot.

The Hardware Text Cursor

The hardware text cursor is another cursor that is used when the computer is in one of the text modes. This type of cursor is also set using Function 10.

The hardware text cursor is the computer's cursor—the one you see on the screen after the MS-DOS system-level prompt. The mouse software lets you adapt this cursor to your needs.

Scan lines The hardware cursor is 8 pixels long and 8 to 14 pixels high. Each horizontal set of pixels forms a line called a scan line. There are 8 to 14 scan lines.

Your program turns scan lines on or off. If a scan line is on, it appears as a flashing bar on the screen. If a scan line is off, it has no effect on the screen. Your program defines which lines are on and which are off by passing the numbers of the first and last lines in the cursor to Mouse Function 10.

The number of lines in the cursor depends on the display adapter in your computer. For example:

- If your computer has a Color/Graphics Adapter, the cursor has 8 lines, numbered 0 through 7.

- If your computer has a Monochrome Display Adapter, the cursor has 14 lines, numbered 0 through 13.

- If your computer has an Enhanced Graphics Adapter and a Color Display, the cursor has 8 lines, numbered 0 through 7.

- If your computer has an Enhanced Graphics Adapter and an Enhanced Color Display, the cursor has 8 lines, numbered 0 through 7.

THE INTERNAL CURSOR FLAG

Regardless of the type of cursor displayed, the mouse software maintains an internal flag that determines whether or not the cursor appears on the screen. The value of this flag is always 0 or less. When the value of the flag is 0, the mouse software displays the cursor. When the value of the flag is less than 0, the mouse software hides the cursor.

Application programs cannot access this flag directly. To change the flag's value, your program must call Mouse Functions 1 (Show Cursor) and 2 (Hide Cursor). Function 1 increments the flag; Function 2 decrements it. Initially, the flag's value is −1, so a call to Function 1 displays the cursor.

Your program can call Mouse Function 1 or Function 2 any number of times, but if it calls Function 2, it must subsequently call Function 1 to restore the flag's previous value. For example, if the cursor is on the screen and your program calls Function 2 five times, it must also call Function 1 five times to return the cursor to the screen.

If your program calls Function 1 to display the cursor, any additional calls to Function 1 have no effect on the internal cursor flag; therefore, one call to Function 2 always hides the cursor. In addition, your program can call Mouse Function 0 (Mouse Reset and Status), or it can change screen modes to reset the flag to −1 and hide the cursor.

READING THE MOUSE

To obtain input from the mouse, you can read the status of the mouse buttons, and you can check to see if (and how far) you have moved the mouse. In addition, your program can check how many times you pressed or released a particular button, and it can adjust the mouse-movement sensitivity.

Mouse Buttons

Mouse Function 5 (Get Button Press Information) and Function 6 (Get Button Release Information) read the state of the mouse buttons. They return a count of the number of times the buttons are pressed and released. The count that Mouse Functions 5 and 6 return is an integer value in which the first 2 bits are set or cleared. Bit 0 represents the state of the left button, and bit 1 represents the state of the right button. If a bit is set (equal to 1), the button is down. If a bit is clear (equal to 0), the button is up.

The mouse software increments a counter each time the corresponding button is pressed or released. Functions 5 and 6 can read the contents of these counters. The software sets the counter to 0 after you reset the mouse (Mouse Function 0) or after you read a counter's contents.

Mouse Unit of Distance: The Mickey

The motion of the mouse track ball translates into values that express the direction and duration of the motion. These values are given in a unit of distance called a *mickey,* which is approximately $1/200$ inch.

When you move the mouse across a desktop, the mouse hardware passes a horizontal and vertical mickey count—that is, the number of mickeys the mouse ball rolled in the horizontal and vertical directions—to the mouse software. The mouse software uses the mickey count to move the cursor a certain number of pixels on the screen.

You can use Mouse Function 11 (Read Mouse Motion Counters) to read the relative motion counters kept by the mouse software. After the counters are read, they are reset to 0. You can also obtain the absolute position of the mouse as maintained by the mouse software by calling Mouse Function 3 (Get Button Status and Mouse Position).

Mouse Sensitivity

The number of pixels that the cursor moves doesn't need to correspond one-to-one with the number of mickeys the track ball rolls. The mouse software defines a sensitivity for the mouse, which is the number of mickeys required to move the cursor 8 pixels on the screen. The sensitivity determines the rate at which the cursor moves on the screen.

In your application programs, you can define the mouse's sensitivity by passing a mickey count to Mouse Function 15 (Set Mickey/Pixel Ratio) or by calling Mouse Function 26 (Set Mouse Sensitivity). The default mickey count is 8 mickeys to 8 pixels, but the mickey count can be any value from 1 through 32,767.

For example, if you pass a count of 32, the sensitivity is 32 mickeys per 8 pixels. In this case, the cursor moves at one-fourth the speed of the default setting.

Chapter 7

Mouse Programming Considerations

The Microsoft mouse driver provides you with 35 functions to add mouse support to your application program. After you load the mouse driver—either by loading MOUSE.COM from the MS-DOS command prompt or from AUTOEXEC.BAT or by loading MOUSE.SYS with a DEVICE directive in CONFIG.SYS—you can include these functions in your application program by calling Interrupt 33H with the appropriate parameters or by using the mouse library, MOUSE.LIB.

Although using these functions is fairly straightforward, you must consider several aspects of the system on which your application is running. The most important considerations are the type of video hardware installed and what modes it is capable of displaying—mouse functions that draw, display, and move the mouse cursor are heavily dependent on the current video display mode. Other considerations include the version of the mouse driver, the country in which the application program is being used, and whether or not the application program using the mouse is a terminate-and-stay-resident (TSR) program.

SETTING UP YOUR SYSTEM

Although there are no hard-and-fast rules about where you must place mouse support within your program, you should include certain mouse functions early in your program to ensure that you properly installed the mouse driver and that its version number is high enough to support the mouse functions you plan to use in your application. In addition, because the mouse driver works closely with the video adapter, your application program must be well behaved in terms of how it uses the video adapter. For example, you should be sure your program communicates with the video adapter using the BIOS. You should not try to program the video hardware directly.

You must use four variables to make a mouse function call. The first variable identifies the function number; the other three indicate any additional information required by that function. The mouse functions return information in these same variables. You should declare these variables as you would any other integer-value variables within your program.

You make mouse function calls either by using Interrupt 33H or by calling the MOUSE.LIB library. Both offer identical functionality and differ only in how you call them. See Chapter 2, "Overview of Mouse Programming," for more information; however, note that application programs using MOUSE.LIB must treat the functions as external.

Testing for the Mouse Driver

After declaring any necessary variables and functions, you should check to see that the mouse driver was installed correctly by verifying that the vector for Interrupt 33H does not point to 0:0 or an IRET instruction. You should then include Mouse Function 0 (Mouse Reset and Status) in your program to reset the mouse driver. Optionally, you can then include a call to Mouse Function 36 (Get Driver Version, Mouse Type, and IRQ Number) to check the version of the mouse driver that is installed and to verify that the mouse functions you will use later in the application program are supported.

Be sure your program issues an error message that sends a warning if the mouse driver is not installed properly or (assuming you used Mouse Function 36) if the version of the mouse driver is not high enough to support the mouse functions you will use later.

In most cases, you can now call Mouse Function 1 in your application program to display a cursor. The cursor that appears reflects the current mode of the video adapter: The mouse driver displays a square if the video adapter is in text mode or a solid arrow if the video adapter is in graphics mode. If your video adapter is in a mode that is not supported by the mouse driver, the results can be unpredictable at this point. For example, the mouse cursor might not display, but your application might continue to run normally; or your system could lock up. (See the section on unsupported video modes later in this chapter.)

Instead of calling Mouse Function 1 (Show Cursor) to display the cursor, you can first call other mouse functions to perform such tasks as modifying the shape of the cursor or defining an area to which cursor movement will be restricted. Although you can include these calls at any point later in the program, you may want to take care of these tasks now so that you do not need to make such changes later.

Controlling the Mouse Cursor

As explained in Chapter 6, you can include in your program Function 9 (Set Graphics Cursor Block) and Function 10 (Set Text Cursor) to modify the shape of any graphics or text cursor. In addition, you can use Function 7 (Set Minimum and Maximum Horizontal Cursor Position) and Function 8 (Set Minimum and Maximum Vertical Cursor Position) to define a boundary for cursor movement on the screen. You can also use Function 16 (Conditional Off) to define an area of the screen in which the cursor will disappear if the user moves the cursor into that area.

To turn off the cursor completely, without losing any of the cursor attributes you've set in your program, you can use Function 2 (Hide Cursor). Note that after your program hides the cursor, the mouse driver still keeps track of mouse movements and button presses. If you include mouse functions in your program that continue to track mouse movements and button presses when the cursor is turned off, a call to Function 1 (Show Cursor) causes the mouse cursor to appear in the updated position. You can also use Function 4 (Set Mouse Cursor Position) to position the cursor before you display it.

Other functions let you control the relationship between mouse movements and mouse cursor movements. Function 15 (Set Mickey/Pixel Ratio) adjusts the ratio of mouse movement to mouse cursor movement, and Function 19 (Set Double-Speed Threshold) defines the speed of mouse movement that causes mouse sensitivity to double.

A single call to Function 26 (Set Mouse Sensitivity) is equivalent to separate calls to Functions 15 and 19. In most cases, you'll find it's easier to use Function 26 than to use the two separate functions. Calling Function 27 (Get Mouse Sensitivity) lets your program check the current values of the mickey-per-pixel ratio and double-speed threshold, allowing your program to use Function 26 to set them to new values if necessary.

Obtaining Button and Position Feedback

To use the mouse as more than a pointing device, you need to request feedback from the mouse driver about mouse position and button presses. Your program can then use this information to control program flow by augmenting the user interface.

You can use Function 3 (Get Button Status and Mouse Position) to determine whether the user pressed a mouse button and, if so, what the position of the cursor was when the button was pressed. This information lets your program perform such tasks as highlighting text, selecting on-screen menu items, and creating shapes.

Function 5 (Get Button Press Information) and Function 6 (Get Button Release Information) obtain mouse movement and button press status. Functions 5 and 6 are similar to Function 3 except that they maintain a buffer to keep a cumulative count of button presses or releases since those functions were last called. Function 3 checks the mouse buttons only when the function is called. Functions 5 and 6 let you build a "click-ahead" buffer into your program, much as the keyboard buffer lets you use a type-ahead buffer.

Use of Function 11 (Read Mouse Motion Counters) lets your program keep track of *relative* mouse motion, as opposed to absolute screen position. In other words, Function 11 can indicate how far the user moved the mouse since the last call to Function 11.

ADVANCED TOPICS

Several mouse functions address specific programming issues not normally encountered in the average program.

Due to the close interaction between the mouse driver and the video adapter, you need to take special steps if your program is performing advanced video techniques. (For EGA programming considerations, see Chapter 10, "Writing Mouse Programs for IBM EGA Modes.")

Video Modes

When your program changes video modes, the way the system uses video memory can change substantially. To ensure that the mouse cursor does not interfere with other portions of memory, you first include Function 2 (Hide Cursor) in your program to hide the cursor. You can then change the video mode within the program and use Function 1 (Show Cursor) to display the cursor again. Following these steps reduces the possibility that problems will occur in video memory.

NOTE: We also recommend hiding the cursor if you want to draw an object in graphics mode under the cursor. This technique prevents garbage from appearing on the screen.

Video Paging

Many video adapters have several pages available for programs to use. To accommodate this feature, your program can include Function 29 (Set CRT Page Number) and Function 30 (Get CRT Page Number), which can let the mouse driver know which video page is the active video page so that it can display the mouse cursor there.

User-Installed Mouse Interrupt Subroutines

Any mouse action that occurs as the application is running, such as moving the mouse or pressing a button, generates a hardware interrupt. The operating system senses the interrupt, suspends processing of the currently running program, and looks in the interrupt vector table for the address of the interrupt routine, which in this case is an address installed by the mouse driver when it was loaded. The operating system then transfers control to the interrupt routine, which executes and returns control to the operating system. Finally, the operating system "cleans up" the interrupt and returns control to the program that was running.

When it executes, the interrupt routine installed by the mouse driver first checks the call mask, a built-in table of bits that corresponds to each type of mouse action, such as movement, a button press, a button release, and so on. If the bit corresponding to the mouse action that caused the interrupt is set to zero, the interrupt handler simply executes as it normally would. If the corresponding bit is set to one, the interrupt handler also executes the user-written interrupt handler for that event.

Specifying Interrupt Handlers

You specify the location of an interrupt handler that you wrote, as well as changes to the call mask, by using any of three mouse functions provided for that purpose: Function 12 (Set Interrupt Subroutine Call Mask and Address), Function 20 (Swap Interrupt Subroutines), and Function 24 (Set Alternate Subroutine Call Mask and Address). You can use an additional function, Function 25 (Get User Alternate Interrupt Address), before calling Function 20 or Function 24 to determine what subroutine mask and address were set by a previous call to Function 20 or Function 24.

Writing and Installing Interrupt Handlers

You write and install custom interrupt handlers for one or more mouse actions if you want an alternate set of events to occur as the result of an action. Doing this supplements the steps the mouse driver would normally take for a mouse event.

Your first step is to write the interrupt subroutine. The interrupt subroutine needs to be a FAR assembly language program because the subroutine must be able to do an intersegment return to the mouse driver. Next, you must determine which mouse event(s) will cause your subroutine to be used in addition to the mouse driver's subroutine, and then set the appropriate call mask bit(s). A table corresponding to all mouse actions is kept by the mouse driver. For each mouse event, such as a right button press, the driver checks the portion of the table that represents that event to see if that event will cause the interrupt subroutine you have written to be executed. If so, the system will also execute your interrupt routine. Interrupt routines cannot call any MS-DOS or BIOS interrupts because MS-DOS and the BIOS are not reentrant; that is, they can't be suspended to call other instances of themselves.

To install your custom interrupt subroutine, you can use one of three functions: Function 12 (Set Interrupt Subroutine Call Mask and Address), Function 20 (Swap Interrupt Subroutines), or Function 24 (Set Alternate Subroutine Call Mask and Address). Avoid using Function 12 because Functions 20 and 24 have superseded the older call and provide more flexibility and functionality.

Mouse Function 12 Function 12 (Set Interrupt Subroutine Call Mask and Address) replaces an existing interrupt subroutine address and call mask with a new address and call mask. When the mask condition specified by Function 12 is matched, the specified subroutine is executed. The disadvantage of using Function 12 is that it doesn't offer a method for the calling program to get the existing subroutine address and call mask so that they can be restored after the subroutine specified by Function 12 is finished. For example, suppose you are writing a terminate-and-stay-resident program for the mouse and you need to install your own interrupt subroutine. Function 12 replaces the existing interrupt address in the mouse driver with its own interrupt address; consequently, the program you are running is unable to call its interrupt subroutine. We therefore strongly recommend that you use Function 20 or Function 24 instead of Function 12.

Mouse Function 20 Like Function 12, Function 20 (Swap Interrupt Subroutines) replaces an existing subroutine address and call mask with a new address and call mask. Function 20 also returns the previous address and call mask to the program so that your program can restore them after it is finished with the new subroutine and call mask.

Mouse Function 24 Function 24 (Set Alternate Subroutine Call Mask and Address) sets up to three unique interrupt addresses and call masks. This allows you to create up to three separate interrupt subroutines, each of which has its own call mask, so that your program can take a different action depending on which event specified by the call mask occurs. You do not need to create all three subroutines. For example, you can create only one interrupt subroutine and have the addresses associated with all three call masks point to it; then any of three unique events will cause that interrupt subroutine to be executed.

Alternate subroutines set by Function 24 are always activated by a combination of a Shift, Alt, or Ctrl key press combined with mouse motion or button presses. The call mask for each call to Function 24 must include one or more of the bits for the shift keys as well as one or more of the bits for mouse activity.

Light Pen Emulation

When you use Function 13 (Light Pen Emulation Mode On), the mouse emulates a light pen. You use this function primarily to include mouse support for programs that have been developed for a light pen. With light pen emulation on, the mouse loads its cursor-position values into the area of the system where a light pen would load its position values.

NOTE: You cannot use a light pen and a mouse at the same time. If your system has a light pen as well as a mouse installed, you must use Function 14 (Light Pen Emulation Mode Off) to prevent the mouse's position values from conflicting with those of the light pen. By default, light pen emulation is on.

Supported and Unsupported Video Modes

The mouse supports the following video modes:

Video Mode	Display Adapter	Mode	Screen Resolution
0	CGA, EGA, MCGA, VGA, 3270	text	640×200
1	CGA, EGA, MCGA, VGA, 3270	text	640×200
2	CGA, EGA, MCGA, VGA, 3270	text	640×200
3	CGA, EGA, MCGA, VGA, 3270	text	640×200
4	CGA, EGA, MCGA, VGA, 3270	graphics	640×200
5	CGA, EGA, MCGA, VGA, 3270	graphics	640×200
6	CGA, EGA, MCGA, VGA, 3270	graphics	640×200
7	MDA, EGA, VGA, 3270	text	640×200
D	EGA, VGA	graphics	640×200
E	EGA, VGA	graphics	640×200
F	EGA, VGA	graphics	640×350
10	EGA, VGA	graphics	640×350
11	MCGA, VGA	graphics	640×480
12	VGA	graphics	640×480
13	MCGA, VGA	graphics	640×200

MDA = Monochrome Display Adapter
CGA = Color/Graphics Adapter
EGA = Enhanced Graphics Adapter
MCGA = Multi-Color Graphics Array
VGA = Video Graphics Array
3270 = IBM 3270 All-Points-Addressable Graphics Adapter

NOTE: For Hercules Monochrome Graphics cards, the current convention is to use screen mode 5 for page 1 and screen mode 6 for page 0. See Appendix F, "Using the Mouse with the Hercules Graphics Card."

The mouse driver might not draw the cursor correctly or return correct screen coordinates in unsupported screen modes. If you want to use the mouse with an unsupported screen mode, contact Microsoft Product Support or the manufacturer of your video adapter. (Instructions for contacting Microsoft Product Support can be found in the documentation that came with your Microsoft Mouse.)

Language Support

The following table shows the languages supported by the international version of the mouse driver, the language numbers, and the language switch designators.

Language	Language Number	Switch Designator
English	0	None (default)
French	1	F
Dutch	2	NL
German	3	D
Swedish	4	S
Finnish	5	SF
Spanish	6	E
Portuguese	7	P
Italian	8	I

The /L command line switch sets the language when the mouse driver is loaded. Load-time messages are displayed in the selected language, and there are no run-time messages in the mouse driver. Messages used by the nonselected languages are not loaded into memory.

Function 34 (Set Language for Messages) is a special-case function that lets the mouse reset the language being used. This function can be used only by the mouse driver, not by your program. Using Function 34 on the domestic (English only) version of the mouse has no effect; the domestic version ignores the /L command line switch.

There may be times when you want to know the installed language. Function 35 (Get Language Number) returns the number of the currently installed language.

MOUSE FUNCTIONS

The following list shows the mouse functions by functional category:

Driver Control and Feedback
Function 0: Mouse Reset and Status
Function 21: Get Mouse Driver State Storage Requirements
Function 22: Save Mouse Driver State
Function 23: Restore Mouse Driver State
Function 28: Set Mouse Interrupt Rate
Function 31: Disable Mouse Driver

Function 32: Enable Mouse Driver
Function 33: Software Reset
Function 36: Get Driver Version, Mouse Type, and IRQ Number

Cursor Control

Function 1: Show Cursor
Function 2: Hide Cursor
Function 4: Set Mouse Cursor Position
Function 7: Set Minimum and Maximum Horizontal Cursor Positions
Function 8: Set Minimum and Maximum Vertical Cursor Positions
Function 9: Set Graphics Cursor Block
Function 10: Set Text Cursor
Function 15: Set Mickey/Pixel Ratio
Function 16: Conditional Off
Function 19: Set Double-Speed Threshold
Function 26: Set Mouse Sensitivity
Function 27: Get Mouse Sensitivity

Button and Position Feedback

Function 3: Get Button Status and Mouse Position
Function 5: Get Button Press Information
Function 6: Get Button Release Information
Function 11: Read Mouse Motion Counters

Video Control and Feedback

Function 29: Set CRT Page Number
Function 30: Get CRT Page Number

Connecting to Additional Subroutines

Function 12: Set Interrupt Subroutine Call Mask and Address
Function 20: Swap Interrupt Subroutines

Connecting to Alternate Subroutine

Function 24: Set Alternate Subroutine Call Mask and Address
Function 25: Get User Alternate Interrupt Address

Light Pen Emulation

Function 13: Light Pen Emulation Mode On
Function 14: Light Pen Emulation Mode Off

Language Support (International Version Only)
Function 34: Set Language for Messages
Function 35: Get Language Number

For more information on programming with mouse functions and for specific programming examples, see Chapter 8, "Mouse Function Calls," and Chapter 9, "Sample Mouse Programming Interface Programs."

Chapter 8

Mouse Function Calls

This chapter describes the input, output, and operation of each mouse function call. The actual statements required to make the function calls depend on the programming language you use; therefore, this chapter also provides examples showing how you can call each function in interpreted BASIC, QuickBASIC, C and QuickC, and MASM (Microsoft Macro Assembler). For further instructions on making function calls from these languages, see Chapter 9, "Sample Mouse Programming Interface Programs."

NOTE: If you design a mouse-supported application program that uses a graphics mode on the IBM EGA (or on a graphics adapter emulating an EGA) that is not supported by the mouse driver or you program the EGA hardware directly, your program must interact with the adapter through the Microsoft EGA Register Interface. For instructions on using the EGA Register Interface, see Chapter 10, "Writing Mouse Programs for IBM EGA Mode."

INTRODUCTION TO MOUSE FUNCTIONS

The table on the following page shows the number and name of each mouse function described in this chapter.

Function Number	Function Name
0	Mouse Reset and Status
1	Show Cursor
2	Hide Cursor
3	Get Button Status and Mouse Position
4	Set Mouse Cursor Position
5	Get Button Press Information
6	Get Button Release Information
7	Set Minimum and Maximum Horizontal Cursor Position
8	Set Minimum and Maximum Vertical Cursor Position
9	Set Graphics Cursor Block
10	Set Text Cursor
11	Read Mouse Motion Counters
12	Set Interrupt Subroutine Call Mask and Address
13	Light Pen Emulation Mode On
14	Light Pen Emulation Mode Off
15	Set Mickey/Pixel Ratio
16	Conditional Off
19	Set Double-Speed Threshold
20	Swap Interrupt Subroutines
21	Get Mouse Driver State Storage Requirements
22	Save Mouse Driver State
23	Restore Mouse Driver State
24	Set Alternate Subroutine Call Mask and Address
25	Get User Alternate Interrupt Address
26	Set Mouse Sensitivity
27	Get Mouse Sensitivity
28	Set Mouse Interrupt Rate
29	Set CRT Page Number
30	Get CRT Page Number
31	Disable Mouse Driver
32	Enable Mouse Driver
33	Software Reset
34	Set Language for Messages
35	Get Language Number
36	Get Driver Version, Mouse Type, and IRQ Number

Each function contains the following:

- The parameters required to make the function call (input) and the expected return values (output)

- Any special considerations regarding the function

- Sample program fragments that illustrate how to use the function call

The mouse function parameter names $M1\%$, $M2\%$, $M3\%$, and $M4\%$ are placeholders. When you make a function call, use the actual values that you want to pass. Be sure the values are appropriate for the language you are using.

Use the percent sign ($\%$) to emphasize that the passed parameters are all 16-bit integers. This is standard notation for interpreted BASIC and QuickBASIC. When you use C or QuickC, pass the addresses of short integer variables. When you use MASM, the AX, BX, CX, and DX registers correspond to the $M1\%$, $M2\%$, $M3\%$, and $M4\%$. Note that in a few special cases, ES is used for $M2\%$.

If the function description doesn't specify an input value for a parameter, you don't need to supply a value for that parameter before making the function call. If the function description doesn't specify an output value for a parameter, the parameter's value is the same before and after the function call.

NOTE: All mouse function calls require four parameters. The mouse software doesn't check input values, so be sure the values you assign to the parameters are correct for the given function and screen mode. If you pass the wrong number of parameters or assign incorrect values, you will get unpredictable results.

MOUSE FUNCTION 0: MOUSE RESET AND STATUS

Call with   M1% = 0

Returns   M1% = mouse status (if mouse found and reset = −1, otherwise = 0)
M2% = number of buttons (if mouse found and reset = 2)

Description   Mouse Function 0 returns the current status of the mouse hardware
and software. If you installed the mouse hardware and software correctly, the mouse status is = −1. (With mouse version 6.25 or later, if the
driver is installed correctly but you later disconnect a serial or PS/2
mouse, subsequent calls to Function 0 will return M1%= 0.)
If you didn't install the hardware and software, the mouse status is = 0.
Also, if the mouse pointer is currently visible, Function 0 hides it as part
of the reset process. In addition, Function 0 disables any interrupt handlers previously installed by the user for mouse events except those installed using Function 24.

Function 0 resets the mouse driver to the following default values:

Parameter	Value
Cursor position	Center of screen
Internal cursor flag	−1 (cursor hidden)
Graphics cursor	Arrow
Text cursor	Reverse video block
Interrupt call mask	All 0 (no interrupt subroutine specified)*
Light pen emulation mode	Enabled
Horizontal mickey-per-pixel ratio	8 to 8
Vertical mickey-per-pixel ratio	16 to 8
Double-speed threshold	64 mickeys per second
Minimum horizontal cursor position	0
Maximum horizontal cursor position	Current display-mode virtual screen x-value minus 1
Minimum vertical cursor position	0
Maximum vertical cursor position	Current display-mode virtual screen y-value minus 1
CRT page number	0

*This is true only for interrupt subroutines that weren't installed using Function 24.

Examples   Each of the following program fragments verifies mouse installation. If
the mouse is installed correctly, the programs reset it. The programs
also display a message stating whether the mouse was found.

*NOTE: The QuickBASIC and C/QuickC examples show how to use structure
variables that represent the AX, BX, CX, and DX registers. They also demonstrate
how to directly call the mouse interrupt. A simpler way to call the mouse functions
is to use calls to routines provided in the MOUSE.LIB library. For more information
on this alternate method, see Chapter 7, "Mouse Programming Considerations."
The method presented here also works well and shows the correlation between the
M1%, M2%, M3%, and M4% parameters and the AX, BX, CX, and DX registers.*

Interpreted BASIC

```
100 ' Mouse Reset and Status
110 '
120 ' Determine mouse interrupt address
130 DEF SEG = 0
140 MOUSEG = 256 * PEEK(207) + PEEK(206)
150 MOUSE = 256 * PEEK(205) + PEEK(204) + 2
160 DEF SEG = MOUSEG
170 '
180 M1% = 0
190 ' Check if interrupt code loaded
200 IF (MOUSEG% OR (MOUSE% - 2)) AND (PEEK(MOUSE - 2) <> 207) THEN GOTO 260
210 PRINT "Mouse driver not found"
220 DEF SEG    ' Restore BASIC data segment
230 END
240 '
250 ' Mouse Reset and Status
260 CALL MOUSE(M1%, M2%, M3%, M4%)
270 DEF SEG    ' Restore BASIC data segment
280 '
290 ' Was mouse found?
300 IF M1% = -1 THEN 340
310 PRINT "Mouse not found"
320 END
330 '
340 PRINT "Mouse found and reset"
350 END
```

QuickBASIC

```
' Mouse Reset and Status

DEFINT A-Z

TYPE RegType
     ax    AS INTEGER
     bx    AS INTEGER
     cx    AS INTEGER
     dx    AS INTEGER
     bp    AS INTEGER
     si    AS INTEGER
     di    AS INTEGER
     flags AS INTEGER
END TYPE

DECLARE SUB Interrupt (intnum%, iReg AS RegType, oReg AS RegType)

DIM iReg AS RegType
DIM oReg AS RegType

' Check for valid interrupt
DEF SEG = 0
mouseseg = 256 * PEEK(207) + PEEK(206)
mouseofs = 256 * PEEK(205) + PEEK(204) + 2
DEF SEG = mouseseg
IF (mouseseg = 0 AND mouseofs = 0) OR PEEK(mouseofs) = 207 THEN
    PRINT "Mouse driver not found"
    SYSTEM
END IF

' Mouse Reset and Status
iReg.ax = 0
Interrupt &H33, iReg, oReg

IF oReg.ax = -1 THEN
    PRINT "Mouse found and reset"
ELSE
    PRINT "Mouse not found"
    SYSTEM
END IF
```

C/QuickC

```
/*  Mouse Reset and Status */

#include <stdio.h>
#include <stdlib.h>
#include <dos.h>

main()
{
    union REGS iReg,oReg;
    void (interrupt far *int_handler)();
    long vector;
    unsigned char first_byte;

    /* Get interrupt vector and first instruction of interrupt */
    int_handler = _dos_getvect(0x33);
    first_byte = * (unsigned char far *) int_handler;
    vector = (long) int_handler;

    /* Vector shouldn't be 0, and first instruction shouldn't be iret */
    if ((vector == 0) || (first_byte == 0xcf))
        {
        printf("Mouse driver NOT installed");
        exit(1);
        }

    /* Mouse Reset and Status */
    iReg.x.ax = 0;
    int86(0x33, &iReg, &oReg);

    /* Was the mouse found? */
    if (oReg.x.ax == -1)
        printf("Mouse found and reset\n");
    else
        {
        printf("Mouse not found\n");
        exit(1);
        }
}
```

MASM

```
; Mouse Reset and Status
print   MACRO   string
        mov dx, OFFSET string
        mov ah,9
        int 21h
        ENDM

        DOSSEG
        .MODEL SMALL
        .STACK 100h
        .DATA

mesg0   db "Mouse driver not found", 13, 10, "$"
mesg1   db "Mouse not found", 13, 10, "$"
mesg2   db "Mouse found and reset", 13, 10, "$"

        .CODE

        ; Set up DS for the data segment
start:  mov ax, @DATA
        mov ds,ax

        ; Check for valid interrupt
        mov ax, 3533h            ; Get Interrupt 33H vector
        int 21h
        mov ax, es
        or  ax, bx
        jz  no_driver            ; es and bx both 0 ?
        cmp byte ptr es:[bx], 207
        jne reset

no_driver:
        print mesg0

        ; Exit with a code of 1
        mov al, 1
        jmp short exit

reset:  ; Mouse Reset and Status
        xor ax,ax                ; M1% = 0
        int 33h
```

(continued)

continued

```
              ; Was mouse found?
              or ax, ax
              jne found

              ; Mouse not found
              print mesg1

              ; Exit with a code of 1
              mov al, 1
              jmp short exit

found:    ; Mouse was found
          print mesg2

              ; Exit with a code of 0
              xor al, al

              ; Exit to MS-DOS
exit:     mov ah, 4Ch
          int 21h

END       start
```

MOUSE FUNCTION 1: SHOW CURSOR

Call with   M1% = 1

Returns   Nothing

Description   Mouse Function 1 increments the internal cursor flag and, if the value of the flag is 0, displays the cursor on the screen. The mouse driver then tracks the motion of the mouse, changing the cursor's position as the mouse changes position.

NOTE: If your program used Function 7 or Function 8 to establish a display area, Function 1 displays the cursor within that area. Also, Function 1 will disable a conditional-off region established using Function 16 (Conditional Off).

The current value of the internal cursor flag depends on the number of calls your program makes to Functions 1 and 2. The default flag value is −1. Therefore, when you start up your computer or reset the mouse driver using Mouse Function 0 or Function 33, your program must call Function 1 to redisplay the cursor. For more information on the internal cursor flag, see Chapter 6, "Mouse Programming Interface."

If the internal cursor flag is already 0, Function 1 does nothing.

Examples   Each of the following program fragments shows how you can make the mouse cursor visible after you reset the mouse driver with Function 0:

Interpreted BASIC

```
110 ' Show Cursor
120 M1% = 1
130 CALL MOUSE(M1%, M2%, M3%, M4%)
```

QuickBASIC

```
' Show Cursor
iReg.ax = 1
Interrupt &H33, iReg, oReg
```

C/QuickC

```
/* Show Cursor */
iReg.x.ax = 1;
int86(0x33, &iReg, &oReg);
```

MASM

```
; Show Cursor
mov ax,1
int 33h
```

MOUSE FUNCTION 2: HIDE CURSOR

Call with   M1% = 2

Returns   Nothing

Description Mouse Function 2 removes the cursor from the screen and decrements the internal cursor flag. After Function 2 hides the cursor, the mouse driver continues to track the motion of the mouse, changing the cursor's position as the mouse changes position.

Use this function before you change any area of the screen that contains the cursor. This ensures that the cursor won't affect the data you write to the screen.

NOTE: If your program changes the screen mode, it should call Function 2 prior to changing the screen mode and then call Function 1 so that the cursor will be drawn correctly the next time it appears on the screen.

Each time your program calls Function 2, it must subsequently call Function 1 to restore the internal cursor flag to its previous value. Alternately, your program can call Function 0 or Function 33 to force the value of the internal cursor flag to −1 and then call Function 1 to display the cursor again. For more information on the internal cursor flag, see Chapter 6, "Mouse Programming Interface."

At the end of your program, call Function 2, Function 0, or Function 33 to hide the mouse cursor; otherwise, if the internal cursor flag is 0 when the program ends, the mouse cursor remains on the screen.

Examples Each of the following program fragments shows how you can make the mouse cursor invisible:

Interpreted BASIC

```
110 ' Hide Cursor
120 M1% = 2
130 CALL MOUSE(M1%, M2%, M3%, M4%)
```

QuickBASIC

```
' Hide Cursor
iReg.ax = 2
Interrupt &H33, iReg, oReg
```

C/QuickC

```
/* Hide Cursor */
iReg.x.ax = 2;
int86(0x33, &iReg, &oReg);          .
```

MASM

```
; Hide Cursor
mov ax,2
int 33h
```

MOUSE FUNCTION 3:
GET BUTTON STATUS AND MOUSE POSITION

Call with   M1% = 3

Returns   M2% = button status
M3% = horizontal cursor coordinates
M4% = vertical cursor coordinates

Description Mouse Function 3 returns the state of the left and right mouse buttons. It also returns the state of the cursor's horizontal and vertical virtual-screen coordinates.

The button status is a single-integer value. Bit 0 represents the left button; bit 1 represents the right button. The value of a bit is 1 if the corresponding button is down and 0 if it is up.

The cursor coordinates that Function 3 returns are always within the range of minimum and maximum values for the virtual screen or within the range set with Function 7 and Function 8. For more information on the virtual screen, see Chapter 6, "Mouse Programming Interface."

Examples Each of the following program fragments returns the mouse button status and the current mouse coordinates (in virtual-screen coordinates).

Interpreted BASIC

```
300 ' Get Button Status and Mouse Position
310 '
320 M1% = 3
330 CALL MOUSE(M1%, M2%, M3%, M4%)
340 '
350 PRINT "Mouse virtual-screen coordinates: "; M3%, M4%
360 IF M2% = 0 THEN PRINT "Neither button pressed"
370 IF M2% = 1 THEN PRINT "Left button pressed    "
380 IF M2% = 2 THEN PRINT "Right button pressed   "
390 IF M2% = 3 THEN PRINT "Both buttons pressed   "
400 IF M2% > 3 THEN PRINT "Unexpected number of buttons pressed"
```

QuickBASIC

```
' Get Button Status and Mouse Position
iReg.ax = 3
Interrupt &H33, iReg, oReg

PRINT "Mouse virtual-screen coordinates: "; oReg.cx, oReg.dx

SELECT CASE oReg.bx
CASE 0
    PRINT "Neither button pressed"
CASE 1
    PRINT "Left button pressed    "
CASE 2
    PRINT "Right button pressed   "
CASE 3
    PRINT "Both buttons pressed   "
CASE ELSE
    PRINT "Unexpected number of buttons pressed"
END SELECT
```

C/QuickC

```c
/* Get Button Status and Mouse Position */
iReg.x.ax = 3;
int86(0x33, &iReg, &oReg);

printf("Mouse virtual-screen coordinates: %d,%d\n",
       oReg.x.cx, oReg.x.dx);

switch (oReg.x.bx)
    {
    case 0:
        printf("Neither button pressed\n");
        break;
    case 1:
        printf("Left button pressed  \n");
        break;
    case 2:
        printf("Right button pressed  \n");
        break;
    case 3:
        printf("Both buttons pressed  \n");
        break;
    default:
        printf("Unexpected number of buttons pressed\n");
        break;
    }
```

MASM

```asm
; Get Button Status and Mouse Position
mov ax,3                    ; M1% = 3
int 33h

mov mouse_x,cx              ; Mouse x-coordinate = M3%
mov mouse_y,dx              ; Mouse y-coordinate = M4%
mov ax,bx
and ax,1
mov left_button,ax         ; Left button = M2%, bit 0
shr bx,1
mov right_button,bx        ; Right button = M2%, bit 1
```

MOUSE FUNCTION 4: SET MOUSE CURSOR POSITION

Call with   M1% = 4
M3% = new horizontal cursor coordinate
M4% = new vertical cursor coordinate

Returns   Nothing

Description   Mouse Function 4 sets the cursor to the specified horizontal and vertical virtual-screen coordinates. The parameter values must be within the range of minimum and maximum values for the virtual screen or within the range set with Function 7 and Function 8.

The cursor appears at the new location unless one of the following conditions is true:

- Function 1 hasn't yet displayed the cursor.

- Function 2 hid the cursor.

- Function 0 or 33 hid the cursor during the reset process.

- The cursor was set to appear in a conditional-off region previously established using Function 16.

If your program set a minimum and maximum vertical and horizontal cursor position using Functions 7 and 8, Function 4 adjusts the values you specified in the function call, placing the cursor within the maximum boundaries. For example, assume you used Function 7 to set the minimum horizontal cursor position to 50 and the maximum horizontal cursor position to 90, and you used Function 8 to set the minimum vertical cursor position to 100 and the maximum horizontal cursor position to 150. If you then use Function 4 with a value of (0,0), the cursor appears at (50,100). If you use Function 4 with a value of (150, 200), the cursor would appear at (90,150). Therefore, if the horizontal cursor position or vertical cursor position you specify in Function 4 is less than the minimum or greater than the maximum values established using Functions 7 and 8, Function 4 places the cursor at the nearest corresponding edge inside the boundaries established by Functions 7 and 8.

If the virtual screen is not in a graphics mode with a cell size of 1 by 1, Function 4 rounds the parameter values to the nearest horizontal-coordinate or vertical-coordinate values permitted for the current screen mode. For more information, see Chapter 6, ''Mouse Programming Interface.''

Examples   Each of the following program fragments sets the mouse cursor to the middle of the screen. Assume that the *HMAX%* and *VMAX%* variables are the maximum virtual-screen coordinates.

Interpreted BASIC

```
110 ' Set Mouse Cursor Position
120 M1% = 4
130 M3% = HMAX% \ 2
140 M4% = VMAX% \ 2
150 CALL MOUSE(M1%, M2%, M3%, M4%)
```

QuickBASIC

```
' Set Mouse Cursor Position
iReg.ax = 4
iReg.cx = HMAX% \ 2
iReg.dx = VMAX% \ 2
Interrupt &H33, iReg, oReg
```

C/QuickC

```
/* Set Mouse Cursor Position */
iReg.x.ax = 4;
iReg.x.cx = hmax >> 1;          ; hmax / 2
iReg.x.dx = vmax >> 1;          ; vmax / 2
int86(0x33, &iReg, &oReg);
```

MASM

```
; Set Mouse Cursor Position
mov ax,4
mov cx,hmax
shr cx,1          ; hmax / 2
mov dx,vmax
shr dx,1          ; vmax / 2
int 33h
```

MOUSE FUNCTION 5: GET BUTTON PRESS INFORMATION

Call with   M1% = 5
                M2% = button

Returns   M1% = button status
               M2% = number of button presses
               M3% = horizontal cursor coordinate at last press
               M4% = vertical cursor coordinate at last press

Description Mouse Function 5 returns the following:

- The current status of both buttons

- The number of times you pressed the specified button since the last call to this function

- The cursor's horizontal and vertical coordinates the last time you pressed the specified button

The *M2%* parameter specifies which button Function 5 checks. If this parameter is 0, Function 5 checks the left button. If this parameter is 1, Function 5 checks the right button.

The button status is a single-integer value. Bit 0 represents the left button, and bit 1 represents the right button. The value of a bit is 1 if the corresponding button is down and 0 if it is up.

The number of button presses always ranges from 0 through 65535. Function 5 doesn't detect overflow, and it sets the count to 0 after the call.

The values for the horizontal and vertical coordinates are in the ranges defined by the virtual screen. These values represent the cursor position when you last pressed the button, not the cursor's current position.

Examples Each of the following program fragments returns button press information for the left mouse button accumulated since your program last called this function.

Interpreted BASIC

```
110 ' Get Button Press Information
120 '
130 M1% = 5
140 M2% = 0                        'Check left button
150 CALL MOUSE(M1%, M2%, M3%, M4%)
160 '
170 PRINT "Left button presses: "; M2%
180 PRINT "Horizontal position at last press: "; M3%
190 PRINT "Vertical position at last press:  "; M4%
```

QuickBASIC

```
' Get Button Press Information
iReg.ax = 5
iReg.bx = 0                        'Check left button
Interrupt &H33, iReg, oReg

PRINT "Left button presses: "; oReg.bx
PRINT "Horizontal position at last press: "; oReg.cx
PRINT "Vertical position at last press:  "; oReg.dx
```

C/QuickC

```
/* Get Button Press Information */
iReg.x.ax = 5;
iReg.x.bx = 0;                     /* Check left button */
int86(0x33, &iReg, &oReg);

printf("Left button presses: %d\n", oReg.x.bx);
printf("Horizontal position at last press: %d\n", oReg.x.cx);
printf("Vertical position at last press:  %d\n", oReg.x.dx);
```

MASM

```
; Get Button Press Information
mov ax,5
xor bx,bx                    ; Check left button
int 33h

mov left_presses,bx          ; Number of left button presses = M2%
mov mouse_x,cx               ; Mouse x-coordinate at last press = M3%
mov mouse_y,dx               ; Mouse y-coordinate at last press = M4%
```

MOUSE FUNCTION 6: GET BUTTON RELEASE INFORMATION

Call with
M1% = 6
M2% = button

Returns
M1% = button status
M2% = number of button releases
M3% = horizontal cursor coordinate at last release
M4% = vertical cursor coordinate at last release

Description Mouse Function 6 returns the following:

- The current status of both buttons

- The number of times you released the specified button since the last call to this function

- The cursor's horizontal and vertical coordinates the last time you released the specified button

The *M2%* parameter specifies which button Function 6 checks. If this parameter is 0, Function 6 checks the left button. If this parameter is 1, Function 6 checks the right button.

The button status is a single-integer value. Bit 0 represents the left button, and bit 1 represents the right button. The value of a bit is 1 if the corresponding button is down and 0 if it is up.

The number of button releases always ranges from 0 through 65535. Function 6 doesn't detect overflow, and it sets the count to 0 after the call.

The values for the horizontal and vertical coordinates are in the ranges defined by the virtual screen. These values represent the cursor position when you last released the button, not the cursor's current position.

Examples Each of the following program fragments returns button release information for the left mouse button accumulated since your program last called this function.

Interpreted BASIC

```
410 ' Get Button Release Information
420 '
430 M1% = 6
440 M2% = 0                         'Check left button
450 CALL MOUSE(M1%, M2%, M3%, M4%)
460 '
470 PRINT "Left button releases: "; M2%
480 PRINT "Horizontal position at last release: "; M3%
490 PRINT "Vertical position at last release:   "; M4%
```

QuickBASIC

```
' Get Button Release Information
iReg.ax = 6
iReg.bx = 0                         'Check left button
Interrupt &H33, iReg, oReg

PRINT "Left button releases: "; oReg.bx
PRINT "Horizontal position at last release: "; oReg.cx
PRINT "Vertical position at last release:   "; oReg.dx
```

C/QuickC

```
/* Get Button Release Information */
iReg.x.ax = 6;
iReg.x.bx = 0;                      /* Check left button */
int86(0x33, &iReg, &oReg);

printf("Left button releases: %d\n", oReg.x.bx);
printf("Horizontal position at last release: %d\n", oReg.x.cx);
printf("Vertical position at last release:   %d\n", oReg.x.dx);
```

MASM

```
; Get Button Release Information
mov ax,6
xor bx,bx               ; Check left button
int 33h

mov left_releases,bx    ; Number of left button releases = M2%
mov mouse_x,cx          ; Mouse x-coordinate at last release = M3%
mov mouse_y,dx          ; Mouse y-coordinate at last release = M4%
```

MOUSE FUNCTION 7: SET MINIMUM AND MAXIMUM HORIZONTAL CURSOR POSITION

Call with
M1% = 7
M3% = minimum position
M4% = maximum position

Returns
Nothing

Description Mouse Function 7 sets the minimum and maximum horizontal cursor coordinates on the screen. Thus, a call to Function 7 restricts all cursor movement to the specified area. The resolution of the current virtual screen defines the minimum and maximum values. For more information on the virtual screen, see Chapter 6, "Mouse Programming Interface."

NOTE: If the minimum value is greater than the maximum value, Function 7 interchanges the two values.

Examples Each of the following program fragments limits cursor movement to the middle half of the screen (see Figure 8-1). Assume that the *HMAX%* variable is the maximum virtual-screen horizontal coordinate.

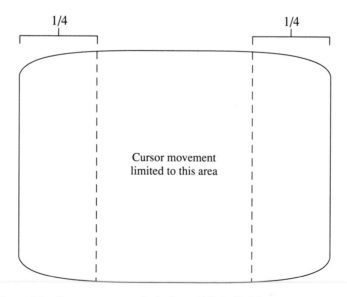

1/4   1/4

Cursor movement
limited to this area

Figure 8-1. *Cursor movement limited to middle half of the screen.*

Interpreted BASIC

```
110 ' Set Minimum and Maximum Horizontal Cursor Position
120 M1% = 7
130 M3% = HMAX% \ 4
140 M4% = 3 * HMAX% \ 4
150 CALL MOUSE(M1%, M2%, M3%, M4%)
```

QuickBASIC

```
' Set Minimum and Maximum Horizontal Cursor Position
iReg.ax = 7
iReg.cx = hmax% \ 4
iReg.dx = 3 * hmax% \ 4
Interrupt &H33, iReg, oReg
```

C/QuickC

```
/* Set Minimum and Maximum Horizontal Cursor Position */
iReg.x.ax = 7;
iReg.x.cx = hmax / 4;
iReg.x.dx = 3 * hmax / 4;
int86(0x33, &iReg, &oReg);
```

MASM

```
; Set Minimum and Maximum Horizontal Cursor Position
mov ax, 7
mov cx, hmax
shr cx, 1                 ; hmax / 2
mov dx, cx                ; 2 * hmax / 4
shr cx, 1                 ; hmax / 4
add dx, cx                ; 3 * hmax / 4
int 33h
```

MOUSE FUNCTION 8: SET MINIMUM AND MAXIMUM VERTICAL CURSOR POSITION

Call with
M1% = 8
M3% = minimum position
M4% = maximum position

Returns Nothing

Description Mouse Function 8 sets the minimum and maximum vertical cursor coordinates on the screen. Thus, a call to Function 8 restricts cursor movement to the specified area. The resolution of the current virtual screen defines the minimum and maximum values. For more information on the virtual screen, see Chapter 6, "Mouse Programming Interface."

NOTE: If the minimum value is greater than the maximum value, Function 8 interchanges the two values.

Examples Each of the following program fragments limits cursor movement to the middle half of the screen (see Figure 8-2). Assume that the *VMAX%* variable is the maximum virtual-screen vertical coordinate.

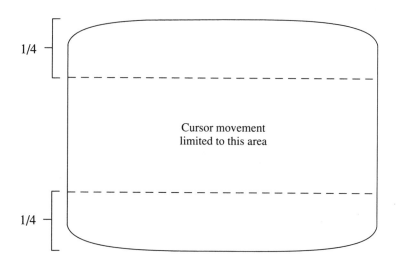

Figure 8-2. *Cursor movement limited to middle half of the screen.*

Interpreted BASIC

```
110 ' Set Minimum and Maximum Vertical Cursor Position
120 M1% = 8
130 M3% = VMAX% \ 4
140 M4% = 3 * VMAX% \ 4
150 CALL MOUSE(M1%, M2%, M3%, M4%)
```

QuickBASIC

```
' Set Minimum and Maximum Vertical Cursor Position
iReg.ax = 8
iReg.cx = VMAX% \ 4
iReg.dx = 3 * VMAX% \ 4
Interrupt &H33, iReg, oReg
```

C/QuickC

```
/* Set Minimum and Maximum Vertical Cursor Position */
iReg.x.ax = 8;
iReg.x.cx = vmax / 4;
iReg.x.dx = 3 * vmax / 4;
int86(0x33, &iReg, &oReg);
```

MASM

```
; Set Minimum and Maximum Vertical Cursor Position
mov ax, 8
mov cx, vmax
shr cx, 1              ; vmax / 2
mov dx, cx            ; 2 * vmax / 4
shr cx, 1              ; vmax / 4
add dx, cx           ; 3 * vmax / 4
int 33h
```

MOUSE FUNCTION 9: SET GRAPHICS CURSOR BLOCK

Call with   M1% = 9
M2% = horizontal cursor hot spot
M3% = vertical cursor hot spot
M4% = pointer to screen and cursor masks

Returns   Nothing

Description Mouse Function 9 defines the shape, color, and center of the graphics cursor (the cursor used when your computer is in graphics mode). Function 9 doesn't automatically display the cursor. To make the cursor visible, your program must call Function 1 (Show Cursor).

The cursor hot-spot values define one pixel relative to the upper-left corner of the cursor block. Although the values within the cursor block can range from −128 through 127, they usually range from 0 through 15.

Function 9 uses the values found in the screen mask and the cursor mask to build the cursor shape and color. To pass the screen and cursor masks, you assign their values to an integer array (packed 2 bytes per integer). You then use the first element of the array as the *M4%* parameter in the function call.

For more information about the screen mask, the cursor mask, and the graphics cursor hot spot, see Chapter 6, "Mouse Programming Interface."

Examples Each of the following program fragments creates a graphics-mode mouse cursor shaped like a hand. The hot spot is at the tip of the extended index finger.

Interpreted BASIC

```
110 ' Set Graphics Cursor Block
120 '
130 DIM CURSOR(15, 1)
140 '
141 ' Screen mask
150 CURSOR(0, 0)  = &HE1FF          '1110000111111111
160 CURSOR(1, 0)  = &HE1FF          '1110000111111111
170 CURSOR(2, 0)  = &HE1FF          '1110000111111111
180 CURSOR(3, 0)  = &HE1FF          '1110000111111111
190 CURSOR(4, 0)  = &HE1FF          '1110000111111111
200 CURSOR(5, 0)  = &HE000          '1110000000000000
210 CURSOR(6, 0)  = &HE000          '1110000000000000
220 CURSOR(7, 0)  = &HE000          '1110000000000000
230 CURSOR(8, 0)  = &H0             '0000000000000000
240 CURSOR(9, 0)  = &H0             '0000000000000000
250 CURSOR(10, 0) = &H0             '0000000000000000
260 CURSOR(11, 0) = &H0             '0000000000000000
270 CURSOR(12, 0) = &H0             '0000000000000000
280 CURSOR(13, 0) = &H0             '0000000000000000
290 CURSOR(14, 0) = &H0             '0000000000000000
300 CURSOR(15, 0) = &H0             '0000000000000000
310 '
312 ' Cursor mask
320 CURSOR(0, 1)  = &H1E00          '0001111000000000
330 CURSOR(1, 1)  = &H1200          '0001001000000000
340 CURSOR(2, 1)  = &H1200          '0001001000000000
350 CURSOR(3, 1)  = &H1200          '0001001000000000
360 CURSOR(4, 1)  = &H1200          '0001001000000000
370 CURSOR(5, 1)  = &H13FF          '0001001111111111
380 CURSOR(6, 1)  = &H1249          '0001001001001001
390 CURSOR(7, 1)  = &H1249          '0001001001001001
400 CURSOR(8, 1)  = &HF249          '1111001001001001
410 CURSOR(9, 1)  = &H9001          '1001000000000001
420 CURSOR(10, 1) = &H9001          '1001000000000001
430 CURSOR(11, 1) = &H9001          '1001000000000001
440 CURSOR(12, 1) = &H8001          '1000000000000001
450 CURSOR(13, 1) = &H8001          '1000000000000001
460 CURSOR(14, 1) = &H8001          '1000000000000001
470 CURSOR(15, 1) = &HFFFF          '1111111111111111
480 '
490 M1% = 9
500 M2% = 5                'Horizontal hot spot
510 M3% = 0                'Vertical hot spot
520 M4% = VARPOINTER(CURSOR(0,0))        'Versions 6.25 and later
530 CALL MOUSE(M1%, M2%, M3%, M4%)
```

QuickBASIC

```
' Set Graphics Cursor Block

' Build the masks
FOR i = 1 TO 32
    READ wrd%
    mask$ = mask$ + MKI$(wrd%)
NEXT i

' Set Graphics Cursor Block
iReg.ax = 9
iReg.bx = 5                 'Horizontal hot spot
iReg.cx = 0                 'Vertical hot spot
iReg.dx = SADD(mask$)       'Pointer to screen and cursor masks
Interrupt &H33, iReg, oReg

DATA  &HE1FF : REM     1110000111111111
DATA  &HE1FF : REM     1110000111111111
DATA  &HE1FF : REM     1110000111111111
DATA  &HE1FF : REM     1110000111111111
DATA  &HE1FF : REM     1110000111111111
DATA  &HE000 : REM     1110000000000000
DATA  &HE000 : REM     1110000000000000
DATA  &HE000 : REM     1110000000000000
DATA  &H0000 : REM     0000000000000000
DATA  &H0000 : REM     0000000000000000
DATA  &H0000 : REM     0000000000000000
DATA  &H0000 : REM     0000000000000000
DATA  &H0000 : REM     0000000000000000
DATA  &H0000 : REM     0000000000000000
DATA  &H0000 : REM     0000000000000000
DATA  &H0000 : REM     0000000000000000

DATA  &H1E00 : REM     0001111000000000
DATA  &H1200 : REM     0001001000000000
DATA  &H1200 : REM     0001001000000000
DATA  &H1200 : REM     0001001000000000
DATA  &H1200 : REM     0001001000000000
DATA  &H13FF : REM     0001001111111111
DATA  &H1249 : REM     0001001001001001
DATA  &H1249 : REM     0001001001001001
DATA  &HF249 : REM     1111001001001001
DATA  &H9001 : REM     1001000000000001
DATA  &H9001 : REM     1001000000000001
```

(continued)

continued

```
DATA  &H9001 : REM     1001000000000001
DATA  &H8001 : REM     1000000000000001
DATA  &H8001 : REM     1000000000000001
DATA  &H8001 : REM     1000000000000001
DATA  &HFFFF : REM     1111111111111111
```

C/QuickC

```
/* Set Graphics Cursor Block */

static int masks_hand[] =
    {
    /*  screen mask  */

    0xE1FF,    /* 1110000111111111 */
    0xE1FF,    /* 1110000111111111 */
    0xE1FF,    /* 1110000111111111 */
    0xE1FF,    /* 1110000111111111 */
    0xE1FF,    /* 1110000111111111 */
    0xE000,    /* 1110000000000000 */
    0xE000,    /* 1110000000000000 */
    0xE000,    /* 1110000000000000 */
    0x0000,    /* 0000000000000000 */
    0x0000,    /* 0000000000000000 */
    0x0000,    /* 0000000000000000 */
    0x0000,    /* 0000000000000000 */
    0x0000,    /* 0000000000000000 */
    0x0000,    /* 0000000000000000 */
    0x0000,    /* 0000000000000000 */
    0x0000,    /* 0000000000000000 */

    /*  cursor mask  */

    0x1E00,    /* 0001111000000000 */
    0x1200,    /* 0001001000000000 */
    0x1200,    /* 0001001000000000 */
    0x1200,    /* 0001001000000000 */
    0x1200,    /* 0001001000000000 */
    0x13FF,    /* 0001001111111111 */
    0x1249,    /* 0001001001001001 */
    0x1249,    /* 0001001001001001 */
```

(continued)

144

continued

```
    0xF249,   /* 1111001001001001 */
    0x9001,   /* 1001000000000001 */
    0x9001,   /* 1001000000000001 */
    0x9001,   /* 1001000000000001 */
    0x8001,   /* 1000000000000001 */
    0x8001,   /* 1000000000000001 */
    0x8001,   /* 1000000000000001 */
    0xFFFF    /* 1111111111111111 */
    };

/* Set Graphics Cursor Block */
iReg.x.ax = 9;
iReg.x.bx = 5;                    /* Horizontal hot spot */
iReg.x.cx = 0;                    /* Vertical hot spot */
iReg.x.dx = (int) masks_hand;    /* Table offset into DX */
segread(&segregs);
segregs.es = segregs.ds;         /* Table segment into ES */
int86x(0x33, &iReg, &oReg, &segregs);
```

MASM

```
; Set Graphics Cursor Block

hand    dw    0E1FFh  ;  1110000111111111
        dw    0E1FFh  ;  1110000111111111
        dw    0E1FFh  ;  1110000111111111
        dw    0E1FFh  ;  1110000111111111
        dw    0E1FFh  ;  1110000111111111
        dw    0E000h  ;  1110000000000000
        dw    0E000h  ;  1110000000000000
        dw    0E000h  ;  1110000000000000
        dw    00000h  ;  0000000000000000
        dw    00000h  ;  0000000000000000
        dw    00000h  ;  0000000000000000
        dw    00000h  ;  0000000000000000
        dw    00000h  ;  0000000000000000
        dw    00000h  ;  0000000000000000
        dw    00000h  ;  0000000000000000
        dw    00000h  ;  0000000000000000
```

(continued)

continued

```
dw   01E00h   ;   0001111000000000
dw   01200h   ;   0001001000000000
dw   01200h   ;   0001001000000000
dw   01200h   ;   0001001000000000
dw   01200h   ;   0001001000000000
dw   013FFh   ;   0001001111111111
dw   01249h   ;   0001001001001001
dw   01249h   ;   0001001001001001
dw   0F249h   ;   1111001001001001
dw   09001h   ;   1001000000000001
dw   09001h   ;   1001000000000001
dw   09001h   ;   1001000000000001
dw   08001h   ;   1000000000000001
dw   08001h   ;   1000000000000001
dw   08001h   ;   1000000000000001
dw   0FFFFh   ;   1111111111111111


        .
        .
        .


; Set Graphics Cursor Block
mov ax,9
mov bx,5                    ; Hot spot, x
xor cx,cx                   ; Hot spot, y
mov dx,ds                   ; Be sure ES is
mov es,dx                   ; set same as DS
mov dx,OFFSET hand          ; Address of bit pattern
int 33h
```

MOUSE FUNCTION 10: SET TEXT CURSOR

Call with   M1% = 10
M2% = cursor select
M3% = screen mask value or scan line start
M4% = cursor mask value or scan line stop

Returns   Nothing

Description Mouse Function 10 selects the software text cursor or the hardware text cursor. Before your program can call Function 10, it must call Function 1 (Show Cursor) to display the cursor.

The value of the *M2%* parameter specifies which cursor you want to select. If *M2%* is 0, Function 10 selects the software text cursor. If *M2%* is 1, Function 10 selects the hardware text cursor.

If Function 10 selects the software text cursor, the *M3%* and *M4%* parameters must specify the screen mask and the cursor mask. These masks define the attributes of a character when the cursor is over it. The mask values depend on the display adapter in the computer.

If Function 10 selects the hardware text cursor, the *M3%* and *M4%* parameters must specify the line numbers of the first and last scan lines in the cursor. These line numbers depend on the display adapter in the computer.

NOTE: For more information on the software text cursor and the hardware text cursor, see Chapter 6, "Mouse Programming Interface."

Examples Each of the following program fragments sets the software text cursor, which inverts the foreground and background colors:

Interpreted BASIC

```
110 ' Set Text Cursor
120 M1% = 10
130 M2% = 0                    'Select software text cursor
140 M3% = &HFFFF               'Screen mask
150 M4% = &H7700               'Cursor mask
160 CALL MOUSE(M1%, M2%, M3%, M4%)
```

QuickBASIC

```
' Set Text Cursor
iReg.ax = 10
iReg.bx = 0                    'Select software text cursor
iReg.cx = &HFFFF               'Screen mask
iReg.dx = &H7700               'Cursor mask
Interrupt &H33, iReg, oReg
```

C/QuickC

```
/* Set Text Cursor */
iReg.x.ax = 10;
iReg.x.bx = 0;                 /* Select software text cursor */
iReg.x.cx = 0xFFFF;            /* Screen mask */
iReg.x.dx = 0x7700;            /* Cursor mask */
int86(0x33, &iReg, &oReg);
```

MASM

```
; Set Text Cursor
mov ax,10
xor bx,bx                      ; Select software text cursor
mov cx,0FFFFh                  ; Screen mask
mov dx,7700h                   ; Cursor mask
int 33h
```

MOUSE FUNCTION 11: READ MOUSE MOTION COUNTERS

Call with   M1% = 11

Returns   M3% = horizontal mickey count
M4% = vertical mickey count

Description   Mouse Function 11 returns the horizontal and vertical mickey count since your program last called this function. The mickey count is the distance that the mouse has moved, in $1/200$-inch increments. For more information on the mickey, see Chapter 6, ''Mouse Programming Interface.''

The mickey count always ranges from −32768 through 32767. A positive horizontal count indicates motion to the right, whereas a negative horizontal count indicates motion to the left. A positive vertical count indicates motion to the bottom of the screen, whereas a negative vertical count indicates motion to the top of the screen.

Function 11 ignores overflow, and it sets the mickey count to 0 after the call is completed.

Examples   Each of the following program fragments returns the horizontal and vertical mickey counts since your program last called this function:

Interpreted BASIC

```
100 '   Read Mouse Motion Counters
110 '
120 M1% = 11
130 CALL MOUSE(M1%, M2%, M3%, M4%)
140 '
150 PRINT "Horizontal mickey count: "; M3%
160 PRINT "Vertical mickey count:   "; M4%
```

QuickBASIC

```
' Read Mouse Motion Counters
iReg.ax = 11
Interrupt &H33, iReg, oReg

PRINT "Horizontal mickey count: "; oReg.cx
PRINT "Vertical mickey count:   "; oReg.dx
```

C/QuickC

```
/* Read Mouse Motion Counters */
iReg.x.ax = 11;
int86(0x33, &iReg, &oReg);

printf("Horizontal mickey count: %d\n", oReg.x.cx);
printf("Vertical mickey count:   %d\n", oReg.x.dx);
```

MASM

```
; Read Mouse Motion Counters
mov ax,11                      ; M1% = 11
int 33h

mov mickey_x,cx                ; Horizontal mickeys
mov mickey_y,dx                ; Vertical mickeys
```

MOUSE FUNCTION 12:
SET INTERRUPT SUBROUTINE CALL MASK AND ADDRESS

Call with   M1% = 12
M3% = call mask
M4% = subroutine address

Returns   Nothing

Description Mouse Function 12 sets the call mask and the subroutine address for
mouse hardware interrupts.

A mouse hardware interrupt stops your program's execution and
calls the specified subroutine whenever one or more of the conditions
defined by the call mask occurs. When the subroutine ends, your program continues execution at the point of interruption.

The call mask is a single-integer value that defines which conditions cause an interrupt. Each bit in the call mask corresponds to a
specific condition, as shown in the following table:

Mask Bit	Condition
0	Cursor position changed
1	Left button pressed
2	Left button released
3	Right button pressed
4	Right button released
5–15	Not used

To enable the subroutine for a given condition, set the corresponding call mask bit to 1 and pass the mask as the *M3%* parameter.

To disable the subroutine for a given condition, set the corresponding bit to 0 and pass the mask as the *M3%* parameter.

Your program can set any combination of one or more bits in the
call mask. When any one of the indicated conditions is detected, the
mouse hardware interrupt calls the subroutine. The subroutine determines which condition occurred by inspecting the bits passed in the
CX register. The indicated conditions are ignored when you set the
value of the call mask bits to 0.

A call to Function 0 sets the call mask to 0.

Before your program ends, be sure it sets the interrupt call mask to 0. (This is handled automatically if your program calls Mouse Function 0.) If the call mask and subroutine remain defined when the program is no longer running, the subroutine will still execute if one of the conditions defined by the call mask occurs.

When the mouse software makes a call to the subroutine, it loads the following information into the microprocessor's registers:

Register	Information
AX	Condition mask (similar to the call mask except that a bit is set only if the condition occurs)
BX	Button state
CX	Horizontal cursor coordinate
DX	Vertical cursor coordinate
SI	Horizontal mouse counts (mickeys)
DI	Vertical mouse counts (mickeys)

NOTE: The DS register, which contains the mouse driver data segment, is missing from this list. The interrupt subroutine is responsible for setting the DS register as needed. Because the mouse driver loads the hardware registers directly, we recommend that you use assembly language to create your Function 12 routine so that registers can be manipulated easily.

Using Function 12 from Within Programs

To Use Function 12 with interpreted BASIC programs,

1. Load an assembly-language subroutine into the BASIC interpreter's data segment. All exits from the subroutine must use a FAR return instruction.

2. Pass the subroutine's entry address to Function 12 as the fourth parameter (*M4%*).

To use Function 12 with QuickBASIC programs,

1. Load an assembly-language subroutine into QuickBASIC's data segment. You can load the subroutine into a string or into a COMMON array.

2. Pass the subroutine's address to Function 12 as the fourth parameter (*M4%*). The VARPTR function returns the address of an array.

To use Function 12 with C or QuickC programs,

1. Use the appropriate mouse call for the memory model of your program. Use *cmouses* for small-model programs, use *cmousec* for compact-model programs, use *cmousem* for medium-model programs, and use *cmousel* for large-model and huge-model programs.

2. Pass the offset part of the subroutine's address in the fourth parameter (*M4%*). If you want to directly call the mouse interrupt, place the segment part of the address in the ES register.

To use Function 12 with MASM programs,

1. Move the segment of the subroutine into the ES register, the offset into the DX register, the call mask into the CX register, and the mouse function number (12) into the AX register.

Examples   Each of the following short programs calls Function 12 to activate an interrupt-driven subroutine for the mouse. When you press the right mouse button, the mouse cursor moves to the upper-left corner of the screen.

Interpreted BASIC

```
100 ' Set Interrupt Subroutine Call Mask and Address
110 '
120 ' Determine mouse interrupt address
130 DEF SEG = 0
140 MOUSEG = 256 * PEEK(207) + PEEK(206)
150 MOUSE = 256 * PEEK(205) + PEEK(204) + 2
160 DEF SEG = MOUSEG
170 '
180 ' Mouse Reset and Status
190 M1% = 0
200 CALL MOUSE(M1%, M2%, M3%, M4%)
210 '
220 ' Show Cursor
230 M1% = 1
240 CALL MOUSE(M1%, M2%, M3%, M4%)
250 '
260 ' Build interrupt-driven subroutine to activate Function 12
270 DIM MSUB%(5)
280 MSUB%(0) = &H4B8          ' Subroutine is from this code...
```

(continued)

continued

```
290 MSUB%(1) = &HB900       '   MOV AX,4   ; Function 4, Set Mouse Cursor
300 MSUB%(2) = &H0          '   MOV CX,0   ; Left edge of screen
310 MSUB%(3) = &HBA         '   MOV DX,0   ; Top edge of screen
320 MSUB%(4) = &HCD00       '   INT 33h    ; Mouse interrupt
330 MSUB%(5) = &HCB33       '   RETF       ; Return to BASIC
340 '
350 ' Set Interrupt Subroutine Call Mask and Address
360 M1% = 12                      ' Mouse Function 12
370 M3% = 8                       ' Interrupt when right button pressed
380 CALL MOUSE(M1%, M2%, M3%, MSUB%(0))     ' Mouse driver versions before 6.25
390 ' M4% = VARPTR(MSUB%(0))               ' Mouse driver versions 6.25 and later
400 ' CALL MOUSE(M1%, M2%, M3%, M4%)       ' Mouse driver versions 6.25 and later
410 '
420 ' Loop until key press, allowing mouse testing
430 IF INKEY$="" THEN GOTO 410
440 '
450 ' Reset the mouse to deactivate the interrupt
460 M1% = 0
470 CALL MOUSE(M1%, M2%, M3%, M4%)
480 '
490 END
```

QuickBASIC

```
' Set Interrupt Subroutine Call Mask and Address

DEFINT A-Z

TYPE RegType
     ax    AS INTEGER
     bx    AS INTEGER
     cx    AS INTEGER
     dx    AS INTEGER
     bp    AS INTEGER
     si    AS INTEGER
     di    AS INTEGER
     flags AS INTEGER
END TYPE

DECLARE SUB Interrupt (intnum%, iReg AS RegType, oReg AS RegType)

DIM iReg AS RegType
DIM oReg AS RegType
```

(continued)

continued

```
' Build interrupt-driven subroutine to activate Function 12
DIM msub%(5)
COMMON msub%()
msub%(0) = &H4B8          ' Subroutine is from this code...
msub%(1) = &HB900         '   MOV AX,4  ; Function 4, Set Mouse Cursor
msub%(2) = &H0            '   MOV CX,0  ; Left edge of screen
msub%(3) = &HBA           '   MOV DX,0  ; Top edge of screen
msub%(4) = &HCD00         '   INT 33h   ; Mouse interrupt
msub%(5) = &HCB33         '   RETF      ; Return to QuickBASIC

' Mouse Reset and Status
iReg.ax = 0
Interrupt &H33, iReg, oReg

' Show Cursor
iReg.ax = 1
Interrupt &H33, iReg, oReg

' Set Interrupt Subroutine Call Mask and Address
iReg.ax = 12
iReg.cx = 8              ' Interrupt when right button pressed
iReg.dx = VARPTR(msub%(0))
Interrupt &H33, iReg, oReg

' Wait until any key is pressed
DO
LOOP WHILE INKEY$ = ""

' Reset mouse to deactivate the interrupt
iReg.ax = 0
Interrupt &H33, iReg, oReg

END
```

C/QuickC

```
/* Set Interrupt Subroutine Call Mask and Address */

#include <dos.h>
#include <conio.h>

union REGS iReg,oReg;
struct SREGS segregs;
```

(continued)

continued

```c
/* This is the sub to be activated with the right mouse button */
void msub()
{
    iReg.x.ax = 4;                 /* Function 4: Set Mouse Cursor */
    iReg.x.cx = 0;                 /* Left edge of screen */
    iReg.x.dx = 0;                 /* Top edge of screen */
    int86(0x33, &iReg, &oReg);     /* Moves cursor to upper-left corner */
}

main()
{
    printf("\n\n\nDemonstration of mouse Function 12...\n");
    printf("Press any key to quit\n");

    /* Mouse Reset and Status */
    iReg.x.ax = 0;
    int86(0x33, &iReg, &oReg);

    /* Show Cursor */
    iReg.x.ax = 1;
    int86(0x33, &iReg, &oReg);

    /* Set Interrupt Subroutine Call Mask and Address */
    iReg.x.ax = 12;                    /* Mouse Function 12 is called */
    iReg.x.cx = 8;                     /* when right button is pressed */
    iReg.x.dx = (int) msub;            /* Offset of msub() into DX */
    segregs.es = ((long) msub) >> 16;  /* Segment of msub() into ES */
    int86x(0x33, &iReg, &oReg, &segregs);

    /* Wait for a key press */
    getch();

    /* Reset the mouse to deactivate the interrupt */
    iReg.x.ax = 0;
    int86(0x33, &iReg, &oReg);
}
```

MASM

```
;  Set Interrupt Subroutine Call Mask and Address

.MODEL  LARGE
.STACK  100h
.CODE
```

(continued)

continued

```
; This is the subroutine activated by the right mouse button
msub    PROC
        mov ax,4                     ; Function 4, Set Mouse Cursor
        xor cx,cx                    ; Left edge of screen
        mov dx,cx                    ; Top edge of screen
        int 33h                      ; Move the cursor
        ret
msub    ENDP

        ; Set up DS for the data segment
start:  mov ax,@DATA
        mov ds,ax

        ; Mouse Reset and Status
        xor ax,ax
        int 33h

        ; Show Cursor
        mov ax,1
        int 33h

        ; Set Interrupt Subroutine Call Mask and Address
        mov ax,SEG msub
        mov es,ax                    ; Offset of sub into ES
        mov ax,12                    ; Mouse Function 12
        mov cx,8                     ; Interrupt when right button released
        mov dx,OFFSET msub           ; Segment of sub into DX
        int 33h

        ; Wait for a key press, allowing testing of mouse
        mov ah,8
        int 21h

        ; Reset the mouse to deactivate the interrupt
        xor ax,ax
        int 33h

        ; Exit to MS-DOS
        mov ax,4C00H                 ; Exit no error
        int 21h

END     start
```

MOUSE FUNCTION 13: LIGHT PEN EMULATION MODE ON

Call with   M1% = 13

Returns   Nothing

Description Mouse Function 13 lets the mouse emulate a light pen. After your program calls Function 13, calls to the PEN function return the cursor position at the last *pen down*.

The mouse buttons control the *pen down* and *pen off the screen* states. The pen is down when you press both mouse buttons. The pen is off the screen when you release either mouse button.

The mouse software enables the light pen emulation mode after each reset (Function 0).

Examples Each of the following program fragments enables the light pen emulation mode:

Interpreted BASIC

```
110 ' Light Pen Emulation Mode On
120 M1% = 13
130 CALL MOUSE(M1%, M2%, M3%, M4%)
```

QuickBASIC

```
' Light Pen Emulation Mode On
iReg.ax = 13
Interrupt &H33, iReg, oReg
```

C/QuickC

```
/* Light Pen Emulation Mode On */
iReg.x.ax = 13;
int86(0x33, &iReg, &oReg);
```

MASM

```
; Light Pen Emulation Mode On
mov ax,13
int 33h
```

MOUSE FUNCTION 14: LIGHT PEN EMULATION MODE OFF

Call with   M1% = 14

Returns   Nothing

Description Mouse Function 14 disables light pen emulation. After your program calls Function 14, calls to the PEN function return information about the light pen only.

     If a program uses both a light pen and a mouse, the program must disable the mouse light pen emulation mode to work correctly.

Examples   Each of the following program fragments disables the light pen emulation mode:

Interpreted BASIC

```
110 ' Light Pen Emulation Mode Off
120 M1% = 14
130 CALL MOUSE(M1%, M2%, M3%, M4%)
```

QuickBASIC

```
' Light Pen Emulation Mode Off
iReg.ax = 14
Interrupt &H33, iReg, oReg
```

C/QuickC

```
/* Light Pen Emulation Mode Off */
iReg.x.ax = 14;
int86(0x33, &iReg, &oReg);
```

MASM

```
; Light Pen Emulation Mode Off
mov ax,14
int 33h
```

MOUSE FUNCTION 15: SET MICKEY/PIXEL RATIO

Call with   M1% = 15
M3% = horizontal mickey/pixel ratio
M4% = vertical mickey/pixel ratio

Returns   Nothing

Description   Mouse Function 15 sets the mickey-to-pixel ratio for horizontal and vertical mouse motion. The ratios specify the number of mickeys for every 8 virtual-screen pixels. The values must range from 1 through 32767. For more information on the mickey, see Chapter 6, "Mouse Programming Interface."

The default value for the horizontal ratio is 8 mickeys to 8 virtual-screen pixels. The default value for the vertical ratio is 16 mickeys to 8 virtual-screen pixels.

Later in this chapter, you'll see that Mouse Function 26 (Set Mouse Sensitivity) combines Function 15 and Function 19 (Set Double-Speed Threshold) so that you can set the mouse-sensitivity parameters in one function call instead of two.

Examples   Each of the following program fragments sets the mickey-to-pixel horizontal ratio to 16 to 8 and the vertical ratio to 32 to 8. This sets the cursor at half speed.

Interpreted BASIC

```
110 ' Set Mickey/Pixel Ratio
120 M1% = 15
130 M3% = 16                    'Horizontal ratio
140 M4% = 32                    'Vertical ratio
150 CALL MOUSE(M1%, M2%, M3%, M4%)
```

QuickBASIC

```
' Set Mickey/Pixel Ratio
iReg.ax = 15
iReg.cx = 16                    'Horizontal ratio
iReg.dx = 32                    'Vertical ratio
Interrupt &H33, iReg, oReg
```

C/QuickC

```
/* Set Mickey/Pixel Ratio */
iReg.x.ax = 15;
iReg.x.cx = 16;                     /* Horizontal ratio */
iReg.x.dx = 32;                     /* Vertical ratio */
int86(0x33, &iReg, &oReg);
```

MASM

```
; Set Mickey/Pixel Ratio
mov ax,15
mov cx,16                       ;Horizontal ratio
mov dx,32                       ;Vertical ratio
int 33h
```

MOUSE FUNCTION 16: CONDITIONAL OFF

Call with   M1% = 16

M4% = address of the region array

Returns   Nothing

Description   Mouse Function 16 defines a region on the screen that you want to update. If the mouse cursor is in the defined region or moves into it, Function 16 hides the cursor during the updating process. When Function 16 ends, your program must call Function 1 (Show Cursor) to redisplay the cursor.

Function 16 defines a region by placing the screen-coordinate values in a four-element array. The following table defines the elements of the array:

Array Offset	Value
1	Left *x*-screen coordinate
2	Top *y*-screen coordinate
3	Right *x*-screen coordinate
4	Bottom *y*-screen coordinate

Function 16 is similar to Function 2 (Hide Cursor), but you can use Function 16 for advanced applications that require faster screen updates.

Examples   Each of the following program fragments hides the cursor if it moves into the upper-left corner of the screen.

In the QuickBASIC, C/QuickC, and MASM examples, notice that the register parameters are set directly when you use Interrupt 33H. Compare this with the interpreted BASIC example, which passes the address of an integer array that defines the region.

Interpreted BASIC

```
200 ' Conditional Off
210 '
220 DIM REGION%(4)
230 REGION%(0) = 0
240 REGION%(1) = 0
250 REGION%(2) = 64
260 REGION%(3) = 20
270 M1% = 16
280 M4% = VARPOINTER (REGION%(0))    'Versions 6.25 and later
290 CALL MOUSE(M1%, M2%, M3%, M4%)
```

QuickBASIC

```
' Conditional Off
iReg.ax = 16
iReg.cx = 0                    ' Left x
iReg.dx = 0                    ' Upper y
iReg.si = 64                   ' Right x
iReg.di = 20                   ' Lower y
Interrupt &H33, iReg, oReg
```

C/QuickC

```
/* Conditional Off */
iReg.x.ax = 16;
iReg.x.cx = 0;                 /* Left x */
iReg.x.dx = 0;                 /* Upper y */
iReg.x.si = 64;                /* Right x */
iReg.x.di = 20;                /* Lower y */
int86(0x33, &iReg, &oReg);
```

MASM

```
; Conditional Off
mov ax,16
xor cx,cx       ; Left x
mov dx,cx       ; Upper y
mov si,64       ; Right x
mov di,20       ; Lower y
int 33h
```

MOUSE FUNCTION 19:
SET DOUBLE-SPEED THRESHOLD

Call with   M1% = 19
M4% = threshold speed in mickeys per second

Returns   Nothing

Description   Mouse Function 19 sets the threshold speed for doubling the cursor's motion on the screen. This function makes it easier for you to point the cursor at images that are far apart on the screen.

The *M4%* parameter defines the mouse's threshold speed. If you specify a value of 0 or if your program calls Function 0 (Mouse Reset and Status) or Function 33 (Software Reset) to reset the mouse, Function 19 assigns a default value of 64 mickeys per second. If you move the mouse faster than the value of the *M4%* parameter, cursor motion doubles in speed. The threshold speed remains set until your program calls Function 19 again or until Function 0 resets the mouse.

Once your program turns on the speed-doubling feature, this feature is always on, but your program can effectively turn off this feature by calling Function 19 again and setting the *M4%* parameter to a speed faster than the mouse can physically move (for example, 10000 mickeys per second).

Later in this chapter, you'll see that Mouse Function 26 (Set Mouse Sensitivity) combines Function 15 (Set Mickey/Pixel Ratio) and Function 19 so that you can set the mouse-sensitivity parameters in one function call instead of two.

Examples   Each of the following program fragments sets the double-speed threshold to 32 mickeys per second. Later, it sets the threshold to a value that effectively turns off speed doubling.

Interpreted BASIC

```
110 ' Set Double-Speed Threshold
120 M1% = 19
130 M4% = 32
140 CALL MOUSE(M1%, M2%, M3%, M4%)
  .

  .

220 M1% = 19
230 M4% = 10000
240 CALL MOUSE(M1%, M2%, M3%, M4%)
```

QuickBASIC

```
' Set Double-Speed Threshold
iReg.ax = 19
iReg.dx = 32
Interrupt &H33, iReg, oReg
  .

  .

iReg.ax = 19
iReg.dx = 10000
Interrupt &H33, iReg, oReg
```

C/QuickC

```
/* Set Double-Speed Threshold */
iReg.x.ax = 19;
iReg.x.dx = 32;
int86(0x33, &iReg, &oReg);
  .

  .

iReg.x.ax = 19;
iReg.x.dx = 10000;
int86(0x33, &iReg, &oReg);
```

MASM

```
; Set Double-Speed Threshold
mov ax,19
mov dx,32
int 33h
.
.
.
mov ax,19
mov dx,10000
int 33h
```

MOUSE FUNCTION 20: SWAP INTERRUPT SUBROUTINES

Call with   M1% = 20
M2% = segment of new subroutine
M3% = new call mask
M4% = offset of new subroutine

Returns   M2% = segment of old subroutine
M3% = old call mask
M4% = offset of old subroutine

Description   Mouse Function 20 sets new values for the call mask and the subroutine address for mouse hardware interrupts. It also returns the values that you previously specified.

A mouse hardware interrupt stops your program's execution and calls the specified subroutine whenever one or more of the conditions defined by the call mask occurs. When the subroutine ends, your program continues execution at the point of interruption.

The call mask is an integer value that defines which conditions cause an interrupt. Each bit in the call mask corresponds to a specific condition, as shown in the following table:

Mask Bit	Condition
0	Cursor position changed
1	Left button pressed
2	Left button released
3	Right button pressed
4	Right button released
5–15	Not used

To enable the subroutine for a given condition, set the corresponding call mask bit to 1 and pass the mask as the *M3%* parameter.

To disable the subroutine for a given condition, set the corresponding bit to 0 and pass the mask as the *M3%* parameter.

Your program can set any combination of one or more bits in the call mask. When any one of the indicated conditions is detected, the mouse hardware interrupt calls the subroutine. The subroutine determines which condition occurred by inspecting the bits passed in the CX register. The indicated conditions are ignored when you set the value of the call mask bits to 0.

Before your program ends, be sure to restore the initial values of the call mask and the subroutine address by calling Function 0.

When the mouse software makes a call to the subroutine, it loads the following information into the central processing unit's registers:

Register	Information
AX	Condition mask (similar to the call mask except that a bit is set only if the condition occurs)
BX	Button state
CX	Horizontal cursor coordinate
DX	Vertical cursor coordinate
SI	Horizontal mouse counts (mickeys)
DI	Vertical mouse counts (mickeys)

NOTE: The DS register, which contains the mouse driver data segments, is missing from this list. The interrupt subroutine is responsible for setting the DS register as needed. Because the mouse driver loads the hardware directly, we recommend that you use assembly language to create your Function 20 routine so that registers can be manipulated easily.

Using Function 20 from Within Programs

To use Function 20 with interpreted BASIC programs,

1. Load an assembly-language subroutine into the BASIC interpreter's data segment. All exits from the subroutine must use a FAR return instruction.

2. Pass the subroutine's entry address to Function 20 as the fourth parameter (*M4%*).

3. Pass 0 in the second parameter (*M2%*). This is a signal to the mouse driver that the subroutine is in BASIC's data segment.

To use Function 20 with QuickBASIC programs,

1. Load an assembly-language subroutine into QuickBASIC's data segment. You can load the subroutine into a string or into a COMMON array.

2. Pass the subroutine's address to Function 20 as the fourth parameter (*M4%*). The VARPTR function returns the address of an array.

3. Pass the segment of the subroutine in the second parameter (*M2%*). The VARSEG function returns the segment of any Quick-BASIC variable.

To use Function 20 with C or QuickC programs,

1. Use the appropriate mouse call for the memory model of your program. Use *cmouses* for small-model programs, use *cmousec* for compact-model programs, use *cmousem* for medium-model programs, or use *cmousel* for large-model and huge-model programs.

2. Pass the offset part of the subroutine's address in the fourth parameter (*M4%*).

3. Pass the segment part of the subroutine's address in the second parameter (*M2%*).

To use Function 20 with MASM programs,

1. Move the segment of the subroutine into the BX register, the offset into the DX register, the call mask into the CX register, and the mouse function number (20) into the AX register.

Examples   Each of the following program fragments swaps a new interrupt subroutine with the current subroutine. The mouse hardware interrupt calls the new subroutine when you release the left mouse button. The subroutine moves the mouse cursor to the middle of the screen.

Interpreted BASIC

```
100 ' Swap Interrupt Subroutines
  .
  .
  .
290 ' Build replacement subroutine to activate Function 20
300 DIM MSUB2%(5)
310 MSUB2%(0) = &H4B8        ' Subroutine is from this code...
320 MSUB2%(1) = &HB900       '    MOV AX,4   ; Function 4, Set Mouse Cursor
330 MSUB2%(2) = &H140        '    MOV CX,320 ; Middle of screen
340 MSUB2%(3) = &H64BA       '    MOV DX,100 ; Middle of screen
```

(continued)

continued

```
350 MSUB2%(4) = &HCD00        '    INT 33h     ; Mouse Interrupt
360 MSUB2%(5) = &HCB33        '    RETF        ; Return to BASIC
 .
 .
 .
540 ' Swap Interrupt Subroutines
550 M1% = 20                      ' Mouse Function 20
560 M2% = 0                       ' Use BASIC data segment
570 M3% = 4                       ' Interrupt when left button released
579 ' Use lines 580-590 for mouse driver versions 6.25 and later
580 M4% = VARPTR(MSUB2%(0))
590 CALL MOUSE(M1%, M2%, M3%, M4%)
599 ' Use lines 600-620 for mouse driver versions before 6.25
600 'MTEMP% = MSUB2%(0)
610 'CALL MOUSE(M1%, M2%, M3%, MSUB2%(0))
620 'MSUB2%(0) = MTEMP%
```

QuickBASIC

```
' Swap Interrupt Subroutines
 .
 .
 .
DIM msub2%(5)
COMMON msub2%()
 .
 .
 .
' Build interrupt driven subroutine to activate Function 20
msub2%(0) = &H4B8        ' Subroutine is from this code...
msub2%(1) = &HB900       '    MOV AX,4   ; Function 4, Set Mouse Cursor
msub2%(2) = &H140        '    MOV CX,320 ; Middle of screen
msub2%(3) = &H64BA       '    MOV DX,100 ; Middle of screen
msub2%(4) = &HCD00       '    INT 33h    ; Mouse Interrupt
msub2%(5) = &HCB33       '    RETF       ; Return to QuickBASIC
 .
 .
 .
' Swap Interrupt Subroutines
iRegx.ax = 20                      ' Mouse Function 20
iRegx.es = VARSEG(msub2%(0))       ' Segment of msub2
iRegx.cx = 4                       ' Interrupt when left button released
iRegx.dx = VARPTR(msub2%(0))       ' Offset of msub2
Interruptx &H33, iRegx, oRegx
```

C/QuickC

```c
/*  Swap Interrupt Subroutines */
.
.
.
/* This is the replacement subroutine for Function 20 */
void msub2()
{
    iReg.x.ax = 4;               /* Function 4: Set Mouse Cursor */
    iReg.x.cx = 320;             /* Middle of screen */
    iReg.x.dx = 100;             /* Middle of screen */
    int86(0x33, &iReg, &oReg);   /* Moves cursor to upper-left corner */
}
.
.
.

    /* Swap Interrupt Subroutine */
    iReg.x.ax = 20;                       /* Mouse Function 20 */
    iReg.x.cx = 4;                        /* When left button is released */
    iReg.x.dx = (int) msub2;              /* Offset of msub2() into DX */
    segregs.es = ((long) msub2) >> 16;    /* Segment of msub2() into ES */
    int86x(0x33, &iReg, &oReg, &segregs);
```

MASM

```asm
; Swap Interrupt Subroutines
.
.
.
; This is the replacement subroutine for Function 20
msub2   PROC
        mov ax,4                 ; Function 4, Set Mouse Cursor
        mov cx,320               ; Middle of screen
        mov dx,100               ; Middle of screen
        int 33h                  ; Move the cursor
        ret
msub2   ENDP
.
.
.
```

(continued)

continued

```
        ; Swap Interrupt Subroutines
        mov ax,20                   ; Mouse Function 20
        mov bx,SEG msub2            ; Segment of sub into BX
        mov es,bx
        assume es:nothing
        mov cx,4                    ; Interrupt when left button released
        mov dx,OFFSET msub2         ; Offset of sub into DX
        int 33h
```

MOUSE FUNCTION 21:
GET MOUSE DRIVER STATE STORAGE REQUIREMENTS

Call with M1% = 21

Returns M2% = buffer size required to save the mouse driver state

Description Mouse Function 21 returns the size of the buffer required to store the current state of the mouse driver. You can use this function with Functions 22 and 23 when you want to temporarily interrupt a program that uses the mouse in order to execute another program that also uses the mouse, such as the Control Panel.

Example Each of the following program fragments returns the buffer size required to save the mouse driver state:

Interpreted BASIC

```
110 ' Get Mouse Driver State Storage Requirements
120 M1% = 21
130 CALL MOUSE(M1%, M2%, M3%, M4%)
140 BUFSIZE% = M2%
```

QuickBASIC

```
' Get Mouse Driver State Storage Requirements
iReg.ax = 21
Interrupt &H33, iReg, oReg
bufSize% = oReg.bx
```

C/QuickC

```
/* Get Mouse Driver State Storage Requirements */
iReg.x.ax = 21;
int86(0x33, &iReg, &oReg);
bufsize = oReg.x.bx
```

MASM

```
; Get Mouse Driver State Storage Requirements
mov ax,21
int 33h
mov bufsize,bx
```

MOUSE FUNCTION 22: SAVE MOUSE DRIVER STATE

Call with   M1% = 22
                  M4% = pointer to the buffer

Returns   Nothing

Description   Mouse Function 22 saves the current mouse driver state in a buffer allocated by your program. You can use this function with Functions 21 and 23 when you want to temporarily interrupt a program that uses the mouse in order to execute another program that also uses the mouse.

Before your program calls Function 22, it should call Function 21 to determine the buffer size required for saving the mouse driver state. It should then allocate the appropriate amount of memory.

Examples   Each of the following program fragments saves the mouse driver state in a buffer:

Interpreted BASIC

```
100 DIM BUF%(1000)
 .
 .
 .
220 '
230 ' Save Mouse Driver State
240 '
250 IF BUFSIZE% > 1000 THEN PRINT "Buffer not big enough" : END
260 M1% = 22
262 M4% = VARPTR(BUF%(0))
270 CALL MOUSE(M1%, M2%, M3%, M4%)
```

QuickBASIC

```
' Save Mouse Driver State
buf$ = SPACE$(bufsiz%)
iReg.ax = 22
iReg.dx = SADD(buf$)
Interrupt &H33, iReg, oReg
```

C/QuickC

```
/* Save Mouse Driver State */
if ((buf = malloc(bufsize)) != NULL)
    {
    iReg.x.ax = 22;
    iReg.x.dx = (int) buf;              /* Buf offset into DX */
    segread(&segregs);
    segregs.es = segregs.ds;            /* Buf segment into ES */
    int86x(0x33, &iReg, &oReg, &segregs);
    }
```

MASM

```
; Save Mouse Driver State
mov ax,22
mov dx,ds
mov es,dx
assume es:data
mov dx,OFFSET buf
int 33h
```

MOUSE FUNCTION 23: RESTORE MOUSE DRIVER STATE

Call with   M1% = 23
                 M4% = pointer to the buffer

Returns   Nothing

Description   Mouse Function 23 restores the last mouse driver state saved by Function 22. You use this function with Functions 21 and 22 when you want to temporarily interrupt a program that uses the mouse in order to execute another program that also uses the mouse. To restore the mouse driver state saved by Function 22, call Function 23 at the end of the interrupt program.

Examples   Each of the following program fragments restores the state of the mouse driver. The buffer variable contains the state previously saved by Function 22.

Interpreted BASIC

```
310 ' Restore Mouse Driver State
320 '
330 M1% = 23
334 M4% = VARPTR(BUF%(0))
340 CALL MOUSE(M1%, M2%, M3%, M4%)
```

QuickBASIC

```
' Restore Mouse Driver State
iReg.ax = 23
iReg.dx = SADD(buf$)
Interrupt &H33, iReg, oReg
```

C/QuickC

```
/* Restore Mouse Driver State */
iReg.x.ax = 23;
iReg.x.dx = (int) buf;          /* Buf offset into DX */
segread(&segregs);
segregs.es = segregs.ds;        /* Buf segment into ES */
int86x(0x33, &iReg, &oReg, &segregs);
```

177

MASM

```
; Restore Mouse Driver State
mov ax,23
mov dx,ds
mov es,dx
assume es:data
mov dx,OFFSET buf
int 33h
```

MOUSE FUNCTION 24:
SET ALTERNATE SUBROUTINE CALL MASK AND ADDRESS

Call with   M1% = 24
M3% = user interrupt call mask
M4% = user subroutine address

Returns   M1% = error status (−1 if error occurred)

Description   Mouse Function 24 sets the call mask and address for up to three alternate user subroutines. Function 24 differs from Function 12 in two ways. Subroutine calls using Function 24 let the called subroutine make its own interrupt calls, and Function 24 uses more call mask bits to provide a wider range of detectable conditions. The new bits allow detection of Alt, Ctrl, and Shift key presses when you move the mouse or press a button.

A mouse hardware interrupt stops your program and calls the specified subroutine whenever one or more of the conditions defined by the call mask occurs. When the subroutine ends, your program continues execution at the point of interruption.

NOTE: When bits 5 through 7 are set, they require the corresponding shift state to be true in order for other mouse events to call the user subroutine. Unless you set bit 5, 6, or 7, or any combination of those bits, the subroutine won't be called.

The call mask is a single-integer value that defines which conditions cause an interrupt to the subroutine. Each of the first 8 bits in the call mask corresponds to a specific mouse or keyboard condition, as shown in the following table:

Mask Bit	Condition
0	Cursor position changed
1	Left button pressed
2	Left button released
3	Right button pressed
4	Right button released
5	Shift key pressed during button press or release
6	Ctrl key pressed during button press or release
7	Alt key pressed during button press or release
8–15	Not used

To call the subroutine for any of the listed conditions, set the corresponding bit(s) in the call mask to 1 and pass the mask as the *M3%* parameter. One or more of the shift-key bits (bits 5, 6, and 7) must be set in combination with one or more of the mouse activity bits (bits 0 through 4) to allow activation of the user subroutine.

To disable the subroutine for any of the listed conditions, set the corresponding bit(s) in the call mask to 0 and pass the mask as the *M3%* parameter. Failure to reset the mask results in the subroutine's execution whenever the last specified mouse or keyboard condition occurs.

NOTE: None of the mouse driver versions clears the call mask when Function 0 or Function 33 is called. (The only way to reset a mask created by using Function 24 is to use another Function 24 call with the mouse activity bits portion of the mask set to all zeros.) To work around this problem, use Function 20 instead of Function 24 to swap your interrupt subroutine into place. Before your program exits, swap the original call address back into place.

Register	Information
AX	Condition mask. (Similar to the call mask except that a bit is set only if the condition has occurred. Also, only mouse action bits 0 through 4 are affected, and shift-key bits 5 through 15 are always set to 0.)
BX	Button state
CX	Horizontal cursor coordinate
DX	Vertical cursor coordinate
SI	Horizontal mouse counts (mickeys)
DI	Vertical mouse counts (mickeys)

NOTE: The DS register, which contains the mouse driver data segment, is missing from this list. The interrupt subroutine is responsible for setting the DS register as needed. Because the mouse driver works directly with the hardware, we recommend that you use assembly language to create your Function 24 routine so that registers can be manipulated easily.

Using Function 24 from Within Programs

To use Function 24 with interpreted BASIC programs,

1. Load an assembly-language subroutine into the BASIC interpreter's data segment. All exits from the subroutine must use a FAR return instruction.

2. Pass the subroutine's entry address to Function 24 as the fourth parameter (*M4%*).

To use Function 24 with QuickBASIC programs,

1. Load an assembly-language subroutine into QuickBASIC's data segment. You can load the subroutine into a string or into a COMMON array.

2. Pass the subroutine's address to Function 24 as the fourth parameter (*M4%*). The VARPTR function returns the address of an array.

To use Function 24 with C or QuickC programs,

1. Use the appropriate mouse call for the memory model of your program. Use *cmouses* for small-model programs, use *cmousec* for compact-model programs, use *cmousem* for medium-model programs, or use *cmousel* for large-model and huge-model programs.

2. Pass the offset part of the subroutine's address in the fourth parameter (*M4%*). If you want to directly call the mouse interrupt, place the segment part of the address in the ES register.

To use Function 24 with MASM programs,

1. Pass the segment of the subroutine in the ES register, the offset in the DX register, the call mask in the CX register, and the mouse function number (24) in the AX register.

Examples   Each of the following programs calls Function 24 to activate an interrupt-driven subroutine for the mouse. When you press a Shift key and the left mouse button simultaneously, the mouse cursor moves to the upper-left corner of the screen.

Interpreted BASIC

```
100 ' Set Alternate Subroutine Call Mask and Address.
 .
 .
 .
210 ' Build interrupt-driven subroutine to activate Function 24
220 DIM MSUB%(5)
230 MSUB%(0) = &H4B8          ' Subroutine is from this code...
240 MSUB%(1) = &HB900         '   MOV AX,4  ; Function 4, Set Mouse Cursor
```

(continued)

continued

```
250 MSUB%(2) = &H0          '   MOV CX,0  ; Left edge of screen
260 MSUB%(3) = &HBA         '   MOV DX,0  ; Top edge of screen
270 MSUB%(4) = &HCD00        '   INT 33h   ; Mouse Interrupt
280 MSUB%(5) = &HCB33        '   RETF      ; Return to BASIC
  .
  .
  .
380 ' Set Alternate Subroutine Call Mask and Address
390 M1% = 24                      ' Mouse Function 24
400 M3% = 34                      ' When Shift key and left button are pressed
402 M4% = VARPTR(MSUB%(0))
410 CALL MOUSE(M1%, M2%, M3%, M4%)
```

QuickBASIC

```
' Set Alternate Subroutine Call Mask Address
  .
  .
  .
DIM msub%(5)
COMMON msub%()
  .
  .
  .
' Build interrupt-driven subroutine to activate Function 24
msub%(0) = &H4B8        ' Subroutine is from this code...
msub%(1) = &HB900       '   MOV AX,4  ; Function 4, Set Mouse Cursor
msub%(2) = &H0          '   MOV CX,0  ; Left edge of screen
msub%(3) = &HBA         '   MOV DX,0  ; Top edge of screen
msub%(4) = &HCD00        '   INT 33h   ; Mouse Interrupt
msub%(5) = &HCB33        '   RETF      ; Return to QuickBASIC
  .
  .
  .
' Set Alternate Subroutine Call Mask and Address
iReg.ax = 24
iReg.cx = 34              ' When Shift key and left button are pressed
iReg.dx = VARPTR(msub%(0))
Interrupt &H33, iReg, oReg
```

C/QuickC

```c
/*  Set Alternate Subroutine Call Mask and Address */
 .
 .
 .
/* This is the subroutine activated by Function 24 */
void msub()
{
    iReg.x.ax = 4;                  /* Function 4: Set Mouse Cursor */
    iReg.x.cx = 0;                  /* Left edge of screen */
    iReg.x.dx = 0;                  /* Top edge of screen */
    int86(0x33, &iReg, &oReg);      /* Moves cursor to upper-left corner */
}
 .
 .
 .
/* Set Alternate Subroutine Call Mask and Address */
    iReg.x.ax = 24;                       /* Mouse Function 24 is called */
    iReg.x.cx = 34;           /* when Shift key and left button are pressed */
    iReg.x.dx = (int) msub;            /* Offset of msub() into DX */
    segregs.es = ((long) msub) >> 16;  /* Segment of msub() into ES */
    int86x(0x33, &iReg, &oReg, &segregs);
```

MASM

```asm
;   Set Alternate Subroutine Call Mask and Address
 .
 .
 .
; This is the subroutine activated by Function 24
msub    PROC
        mov ax,4                 ; Function 4, Set Mouse Cursor
        xor cx,cx                ; Left edge of screen
        mov dx,cx                ; Top edge of screen
        int 33h                  ; Move the cursor
        ret
msub    ENDP
 .
 .
 .
```

(continued)

continued

```
        ; Set Alternate Subroutine Call Mask and Address
        mov ax,SEG msub
        mov es,ax                  ; Segment of sub into ES
        mov ax,24                  ; Mouse Function 24 when
        mov cx,34                  ; Shift key and left button are pressed
        mov dx,OFFSET msub         ; Offset of sub into DX
        int 33h
```

MOUSE FUNCTION 25:
GET USER ALTERNATE INTERRUPT ADDRESS

Call with M1% = 25
M3% = user interrupt call mask

Returns M1% = error status (−1 if no vector/mask, in which case M2%, M3%, and
M4% return 0)
M2% = user subroutine segment
M3% = user interrupt call mask
M4% = user subroutine address

Description Mouse Function 25 returns the interrupt address of the alternate
mouse user subroutine identified by the specified call mask. You can
call this function to retrieve the last alternate interrupt subroutine
address prior to calling Function 24 so that you can restore the subroutine address later.

The call mask is a single-integer value that defines which conditions cause an interrupt to the subroutine. Each of the first 8 bits in the
call mask corresponds to a specific mouse or keyboard condition, as
shown in the following list:

Mask Bit	Condition
0	Cursor position changed
1	Left button pressed
2	Left button released
3	Right button pressed
4	Right button released
5	Shift key pressed during button press or release
6	Ctrl key pressed during button press or release
7	Alt key pressed during button press or release
8–15	Not used

For assembly-language programs, the subroutine address is
returned as BX:DX.

Examples Assume that Function 24 was used to set the alternate interrupt subroutine. Each of the following program fragments returns the interrupt
address of an alternate mouse-user subroutine.

Interpreted BASIC

```
440 ' Get User Alternate Interrupt Address
450 M1% = 25            ' Mouse Function 25
460 M3% = 34            ' Same call mask
470 CALL MOUSE(M1%, M2%, M3%, M4%)
480 CALLMASK% = M3%
490 SUBSEG% = M2%
500 SUBOFFST% = M4%
```

QuickBASIC

```
' Get User Alternate Interrupt Address
iReg.ax = 25
iReg.cx = 34            ' Same call mask
Interrupt &H33, iReg, oReg
callmask% = oReg.cx
subseg% = oReg.bx
suboff% = oReg.dx
```

C/QuickC

```
/* Get User Alternate Interrupt Address */
iReg.x.ax = 25;         /* Mouse Function 25 */
iReg.x.cx = 34;         /* Same call mask */
int86(0x33, &iReg, &oReg);
callmask = oReg.x.cx;
subseg = oReg.x.bx;
suboff = oReg.x.dx;
```

MASM

```
; Get User Alternate Interrupt Address
mov ax,25               ; Mouse Function 25
mov cx,34               ; Same call mask
int 33h
mov callmask,cx
mov subseg,bx
mov suboff,dx
```

MOUSE FUNCTION 26: SET MOUSE SENSITIVITY

Call with   M1% = 26
M2% = horizontal mickey sensitivity number
M3% = vertical mickey sensitivity number
M4% = threshold for double speed

Returns   Nothing

Description Mouse Function 26 sets mouse-to-cursor movement sensitivity by defining a scaling factor for the mouse mickeys and the double-speed threshold. For more information on the mickey, see Chapter 6, ''Mouse Programming Interface.''

The sensitivity numbers range from 1 through 100, where 50 specifies the default mickey factor of 1. These mickey multiplication factors range from about $1/32$ for a parameter of 5, to $14/4$ for a parameter of 100. The mickeys are multiplied by these factors before the mickey-to-pixel ratios (set by Function 15) are applied.

The double-speed ratio is also set to its default value by setting *M4*% to 50.

This function provides a simplified approach to setting the mouse sensitivity and double-speed ratios. The 0 through 100 range provides an intuitive scale for speeding up or slowing down the mouse motion.

Examples Each of the following program fragments sets the mouse sensitivity to 10 and the double-speed threshold to 32:

Interpreted BASIC

```
110 ' Set Mouse Sensitivity
120 M1% = 26
130 M2% = 10
140 M3% = 10
150 M4% = 32
160 CALL MOUSE(M1%, M2%, M3%, M4%)
```

QuickBASIC

```
' Set Mouse Sensitivity
iReg.ax = 26
iReg.bx = 10
iReg.cx = 10
iReg.dx = 32
Interrupt &H33, iReg, oReg
```

C/QuickC

```
/* Set Mouse Sensitivity */
iReg.x.ax = 26;
iReg.x.bx = 10;
iReg.x.cx = 10;
iReg.x.dx = 32;
int86(0x33, &iReg, &oReg);
```

MASM

```
; Set Mouse Sensitivity
mov ax,26
mov bx,10
mov cx,bx
mov dx,32
int 33h
```

MOUSE FUNCTION 27: GET MOUSE SENSITIVITY

Call with   M1% = 27

Returns   M2% = horizontal mickey sensitivity number
M3% = vertical mickey sensitivity number
M4% = threshold for double speed

Description Mouse Function 27 returns mouse-to-cursor movement sensitivity
scaling factors previously set by Function 26.

These factors range from 1 through 100, with default values of 50.
To slow the mouse-cursor speed, use Function 26 to decrease the set-
ting. To increase the speed (i.e., increase the mouse sensitivity), use
Function 26 to increase the setting within the range 1 through 100.

Examples   Each of the following program fragments returns the current horizontal and vertical mouse sensitivity settings and the double-speed
threshold sensitivity setting.

Interpreted BASIC

```
300 ' Get Mouse Sensitivity
310 '
320 M1% = 27
330 CALL MOUSE(M1%, M2%, M3%, M4%)
340 HFACTOR = M2%
350 VFACTOR = M3%
360 DFACTOR = M4%
```

QuickBASIC

```
' Get Mouse Sensitivity
iReg.ax = 27
Interrupt &H33, iReg, oReg
hfactor% = oReg.bx
vfactor% = oReg.cx
dfactor% = oReg.dx
```

C/QuickC

```
/* Get Mouse Sensitivity */
iReg.x.ax = 27;
int86(0x33, &iReg, &oReg);
hfactor = oReg.x.bx;
vfactor = oReg.x.cx;
dfactor = oReg.x.dx;
```

MASM

```
; Get Mouse Sensitivity
mov ax,27
int 33h
mov hfactor,bx
mov vfactor,cx
mov dfactor,dx
```

MOUSE FUNCTION 28: SET MOUSE INTERRUPT RATE

Call with   M1% = 28

M2% = interrupt rate (in interrupts per second)

Returns   Nothing

Description Mouse Function 28 operates only with the InPort mouse. This function sets the rate at which the mouse driver polls the status of the mouse. Faster interrupt rates provide better resolution in graphics applications, but slower interrupt rates might let the applications run faster.

The interrupt rate is a single-integer value that defines the rate (in interrupts per second). Integer values from 0 through 4 correspond to specific maximum interrupt rates, as shown in the following table:

Rate Number	Maximum Interrupt Rate
0	No interrupts allowed
1	30 interrupts per second
2	50 interrupts per second
3	100 interrupts per second
4	200 interrupts per second
>4	Not defined

NOTE: If a value greater than 4 is used, the InPort mouse driver might behave unpredictably.

Examples Each of the following program fragments sets the mouse driver interrupt rate to 100 interrupts per second.

Interpreted BASIC

```
110 ' Set Mouse Interrupt Rate
120 M1% = 28
130 M2% = 3
140 CALL MOUSE(M1%, M2%, M3%, M4%)
```

QuickBASIC

```
' Set Mouse Interrupt Rate
iReg.ax = 28
iReg.bx = 3
Interrupt &H33, iReg, oReg
```

C/QuickC

```
/* Set Mouse Interrupt Rate */
iReg.x.ax = 28;
iReg.x.bx = 3;
int86(0x33, &iReg, &oReg);
```

MASM

```
; Set Mouse Interrupt Rate
mov ax,28
mov bx,3
int 33h
```

MOUSE FUNCTION 29: SET CRT PAGE NUMBER

Call with
M1% = 29
M2% = CRT page for mouse cursor display

Returns   Nothing

Description Mouse Function 29 specifies the number of the CRT page on which the mouse cursor will be displayed.

For information on the number of CRT pages available in each display mode your adapter supports, see the documentation that came with your graphics adapter.

Examples   The following program fragments set the CRT page number to 3.

Interpreted BASIC

```
110 ' Set CRT Page Number
120 M1% = 29
130 M2% = 3                     ' Page 3
140 CALL MOUSE(M1%, M2%, M3%, M4%)
```

QuickBASIC

```
' Set CRT Page Number
iReg.ax = 29
iReg.bx = 3                     ' Page 3
Interrupt &H33, iReg, oReg
```

C/QuickC

```
/* Set CRT Page Number */
iReg.x.ax = 29;
iReg.x.bx = 3;                  /* Page 3 */
int86(0x33, &iReg, &oReg);
```

MASM

```
; Set CRT Page Number
mov ax,29
mov bx,3                        ; Page 3
int 33h
```

MOUSE FUNCTION 30: GET CRT PAGE NUMBER

Call with   M1% = 30

Returns   M2% = CRT page of current mouse cursor display

Description   Mouse Function 30 returns the number of the CRT page on which the mouse cursor is currently displayed.

Examples   The following program fragments return the number of the CRT page on which the mouse cursor is currently displayed.

Interpreted BASIC

```
300 ' Get CRT Page Number
310 '
320 M1% = 30
330 CALL MOUSE(M1%, M2%, M3%, M4%)
340 CRTPAGE% = M2%
```

QuickBASIC

```
' Get CRT Page Number
iReg.ax = 30
Interrupt &H33, iReg, oReg
CRTPage% = oReg.bx
```

C/QuickC

```
/* Get CRT Page Number */
iReg.x.ax = 30;
int86(0x33, &iReg, &oReg);
crtpage = oReg.x.bx;
```

MASM

```
; Get CRT Page Number
mov ax,30
int 33h
mov crtpage,bx
```

MOUSE FUNCTION 31: DISABLE MOUSE DRIVER

Call with   M1% = 31

Returns   M1% = error status (−1 if error occurred)
M2% = offset of old Interrupt 33H vector
M3% = segment of old Interrupt 33H vector

Description You use Mouse Function 31 in the MOUSE OFF portion of your program
to disable the mouse driver, which subsequently disables the mouse.
When your program calls Function 31, you can restore the Interrupt
33H vector to its value before the mouse driver was enabled by using the
M2% and *M3%* parameters. Function 31 removes all other vectors used
by the mouse driver.

If this function can't remove all mouse-driver vectors, excluding
the Interrupt 33H vector, it returns an error of −1 for the *M1%*
parameter.

Examples   Each of the following program fragments disables the mouse driver
and returns the segment and offset of the old Interrupt 33H.

When your program calls Function 31 from an assembly-language
program, use ES:BX for the address of the old Interrupt 33H vector.

Interpreted BASIC

```
290 ' Disable Mouse Driver
300 M1% = 31                    ' Mouse Function 31
310 CALL MOUSE(M1%, M2%, M3%, M4%)
320 ERRORSTAT% = M1%
330 I330FF% = M2%
340 I33SEG% = M3%
```

QuickBASIC

```
' Disable Mouse Driver
TYPE RegTypeX
    ax      AS INTEGER
    bx      AS INTEGER
    cx      AS INTEGER
    dx      AS INTEGER
```

(continued)

continued

```
    bp     AS INTEGER
    si     AS INTEGER
    di     AS INTEGER
    flags  AS INTEGER
    ds     AS INTEGER
    es     AS INTEGER
END TYPE


DECLARE SUB InterruptX (intnum%, iRegX AS RegTypeX, oRegX AS RegTypeX)

DIM iRegX AS RegTypeX
DIM oRegX AS RegTypeX

' Disable Mouse Driver
iRegX.ax = 31
InterruptX &H33, iRegX, oRegX
errorstat% = oRegX.ax
i33off% = oRegX.bx
i33seg% = oRegX.es
```

C/QuickC

```
/* Disable Mouse Driver */
iReg.x.ax = 31;                        /* Mouse Function 31 */
int86(0x33, &iReg, &oReg, &segregs);
error_stat = oReg.x.ax;
i33_off = oReg.x.bx;
i33_seg = segreg.es;
```

MASM

```
; Disable Mouse Driver
mov ax,31
int 33h
mov err_stat,ax
mov i33_off,bx
mov i33_seg,es
```

MOUSE FUNCTION 32: ENABLE MOUSE DRIVER

Call with   M1% = 32

Returns   Nothing

Description You use Mouse Function 32 in the MOUSE ON portion of your program to enable the mouse driver, which subsequently enables the mouse. When your program calls Function 32, the function sets the Interrupt 33H vector to the mouse-interrupt vector and installs all other mouse-driver vectors.

Examples   Each of the following program fragments enables the mouse driver:

Interpreted BASIC

```
110 ' Enable Mouse Driver
120 M1% = 32
130 CALL MOUSE(M1%, M2%, M3%, M4%)
```

QuickBASIC

```
' Enable Mouse Driver
iReg.ax = 32
Interrupt &H33, iReg, oReg
```

C/QuickC

```
/* Enable Mouse Driver */
iReg.x.ax = 32;
int86(0x33, &iReg, &oReg);
```

MASM

```
; Enable Mouse Driver
mov ax,32
int 33h
```

MOUSE FUNCTION 33: SOFTWARE RESET

Call with   M1% = 33

Returns   M1% = −1 (if mouse driver installed; otherwise, 33)
M2% = 2 (provided M1% = −1)

Description   Mouse Function 33 is similar to Function 0 (Mouse Reset and Status)
except that Function 33 neither initializes the mouse hardware nor
resets other variables that are dependent on display hardware. Resets
are confined to software only.

Function 33 indicates a valid software reset by returning both
values. The *M1%* parameter must be −1, and the *M2%* parameter must
be 2 for a valid reset.

Function 33 resets the mouse driver to the following default
values:

Parameter	*Value*
Cursor position	Center of screen
Internal cursor flag	−1 (cursor hidden)
Graphics cursor	Arrow
Text cursor	Reverse video block
Interrupt call mask	All 0 (no interrupt subroutine specified)*
Horizontal mickey-per-pixel ratio	8 to 8
Vertical mickey-per-pixel ratio	16 to 8
Double-speed threshold	64 mickeys per second
Minimum horizontal cursor position	0
Maximum horizontal cursor position	Current display-mode virtual screen *x*-value minus 1
Minimum vertical cursor position	0
Maximum vertical cursor position	Current display-mode virtual screen *y*-value minus 1

*This is true only for interrupt subroutines that weren't installed using Function 24.

Examples   Each of the following program fragments resets the mouse driver:

Interpreted BASIC

```
300 ' Software Reset
310 '
320 M1% = 33
330 CALL MOUSE(M1%, M2%, M3%, M4%)
340 STAT1% = M1%
350 STAT2% = M2%
```

QuickBASIC

```
' Software Reset
iReg.ax = 33
Interrupt &H33, iReg, oReg
stat1% = oReg.ax
stat2% = oReg.bx
```

C/QuickC

```
/* Software Reset */
iReg.x.ax = 33;
int86(0x33, &iReg, &oReg);
stat1 = oReg.x.ax;
stat2 = oReg.x.bx;
```

MASM

```
; Software Reset
mov ax,33
int 33h
mov stat1,ax
mov stat2,bx
```

MOUSE FUNCTION 34: SET LANGUAGE FOR MESSAGES

Call with: M1% = 34

M2% = language number

Returns: Nothing

Description   Mouse Function 34 operates only with the international version of the mouse driver—it has no effect with the domestic version of the driver. This function lets you specify the language in which messages and prompts from the mouse driver are displayed. You can specify the language with a single integer from the Number column of the following table:

Number	Language
0	English
1	French
2	Dutch
3	German
4	Swedish
5	Finnish
6	Spanish
7	Portuguese
8	Italian

Examples   Each of the following program fragments sets the language to Dutch:

Interpreted BASIC

```
110 ' Set Language for Messages
120 M1% = 34
130 M2% = 2
140 CALL MOUSE(M1%, M2%, M3%, M4%)
```

QuickBASIC

```
' Set Language for Messages
iReg.ax = 34
iReg.bx = 2
Interrupt &H33, iReg, oReg
```

C/QuickC

```
/* Set Language for Messages */
iReg.x.ax = 34;
iReg.x.bx = 2;
int86(0x33, &iReg, &oReg);
```

MASM

```
; Set Language for Messages
mov ax,34
mov bx,2
int 33h
```

MOUSE FUNCTION 35: GET LANGUAGE NUMBER

Call with: M1% = 35

Returns: M2% = the current language

Description   Mouse Function 35 operates only with the international version of the mouse driver. This function returns the number of the language currently set in the mouse driver.

   NOTE: The number returned in M2% represents a language (see the language table in the discussion of Function 34). If you don't have an international mouse driver, English (0) will always be returned.

Examples   Each of the following program fragments returns the current language number from the mouse driver:

Interpreted BASIC

```
110 ' Get Language Number
120 M1% = 35
130 CALL MOUSE(M1%, M2%, M3%, M4%)
140 LANGUAGE% = M2%
```

QuickBASIC

```
' Get Language Number
iReg.ax = 35
Interrupt &H33, iReg, oReg
language% = oReg.bx
```

C/QuickC

```
/* Get Language Number */
iReg.x.ax = 35;
int86(0x33, &iReg, &oReg);
language = oReg.x.bx;
```

MASM

```
; Get Language Number
mov ax,35
int 33h
mov language,bx
```

MOUSE FUNCTION 36:
GET DRIVER VERSION, MOUSE TYPE, AND IRQ NUMBER

Call with: M1% = 36

Returns: M2% = mouse driver version number
M3% = mouse type and IRQ number

Description   Mouse Function 36 returns the version number of the mouse driver, the type of mouse the driver requires, and the number of the interrupt request type (IRQ). In the returned value $M2\%$, the high-order 8 bits contain the major version number and the low-order 8 bits contain the minor version number. For example, if you were using mouse driver version 6.10, Function 36 would return an $M2\%$ value of 1552 (decimal), which is equal to 0610 (hexadecimal).

The high-order 8 bits of the returned value $M3\%$ contain the mouse type as follows:

- A value of 1 indicates a bus mouse.

- A value of 2 indicates a serial mouse.

- A value of 3 indicates an InPort mouse.

- A value of 4 indicates a PS/2 mouse.

- A value of 5 indicates a Hewlett-Packard mouse.

The low-order 8 bits of the returned value $M3\%$ contain the value for the interrupt request type as follows:

- A value of 0 indicates PS/2.

- A value ranging from 2 through 5 or the value 7 indicates a mouse interrupt.

Examples   Each of the following program fragments returns the mouse driver version number, the mouse type, and the IRQ number:

Interpreted BASIC

```
110 ' Get Driver Version, Mouse Type, and IRQ Number
120 '
130 M1% = 36
140 CALL MOUSE(M1%, M2%, M3%, M4%)
150 VERSION$ = RIGHT$("000" + HEX$(M2%),4)
160 MAJORVERSION% = VAL(LEFT$(VERSION$,2))    'Decimal notation
170 MINORVERSION% = VAL(RIGHT$(VERSION$,2))   'Decimal notation
180 MOUSETYPE% = M3% \ 256
190 MOUSEIRQ% = M3% AND &HFF
```

QuickBASIC

```
' Get Driver Version, Mouse Type, and IRQ Number
iReg.ax = 36
Interrupt &H33, iReg, oReg
version$ = RIGHT$("000" + HEX$(oReg.bx), 4)
majorVersion% = VAL(LEFT$(version$, 2))   'Decimal notation
minorVersion% = VAL(RIGHT$(version$, 2))  'Decimal notation
mouseType% = oReg.cx \ 256
mouseIRQ% = oReg.cx AND &HFF
```

C/QuickC

```
/* Get Driver Version, Mouse Type, and IRQ Number */
iReg.x.ax = 36;
int86(0x33, &iReg, &oReg);
majorversion = oReg.h.bh;      /* Hexadecimal-digits notation */
minorversion = oReg.h.bl;      /* Hexadecimal-digits notation */
mousetype = oReg.h.ch;
IRQnum = oReg.h.cl;
```

MASM

```
; Get Driver Version, Mouse Type, and IRQ Number
mov ax,36
int 33h
mov majorversion,bh            ; Hexadecimal-digits notation
mov minorversion,bl            ; Hexadecimal-digits notation
mov mousetype,ch
mov IRQnum,cl
```

Chapter 9

Sample Mouse Programming Interface Programs

This chapter presents mouse programming examples using inter-preted BASIC, QuickBASIC, C and QuickC, MASM, FORTRAN, and Pascal. You will see some overlap of functionality among the programs; however, there are significant differences in style and programming techniques that can provide you with insight into the many ways you can program for the mouse.

You can use two basic methods to call the mouse functions. The MOUSE.LIB library provides subroutines for each of the major Microsoft language products. Using this library is straightforward and self-documenting, as shown in many of these programs. A second method is to call the mouse interrupt (Interrupt 33H) directly. Most of the languages mentioned above provide a mechanism for calling system interrupts. Generally, a method is also provided for passing and retrieving register values. Calling mouse functions in this way is slightly faster and more efficient; however, you might sacrifice some program readability and simplicity.

Several of the programs are presented in more than one lan-guage. These programs provide a good opportunity to learn more about how to program in unfamiliar languages. For example, if you're learning C and you already know QuickBASIC, examine the QBTEST.BAS and CTEST.C programs to compare how the programs use the mouse function calls.

NOTE: For information on writing programs in Turbo Pascal, see Appendix E, "Making Calls from Borland Turbo Pascal Programs."

If you look at the companion disks that come with this book, you will find subdirectories for each language. Programming examples for each language are contained in the subdirectories.

NOTE: This chapter contains descriptions of each of the programs listed below; however, the actual code for some of the lengthy programs appears only on disk. You can use your favorite text editor to view the source code for these programs on your screen, or you can print the source code files on your printer.

```
\BAS
    tst1.bas
    batest.bas
    piano.bas

\QB
    qbmou.bas
    qbint.bas
    qbinc.bas
    absolute.bas
    intrrupt.bas
    mouse.bas
    mousedem.bas
    qb12&20.bas
    qb24.bas
    qbtest.bas
    pencil.bas

\QC&C
    cmouse.c
    ctest.c
    lpen.c
    mous_int.c
    mous_lib.c
    mouh_int.c
    mouh_lib.c
    mscexamp.c
    pencil.c
    m20sub.asm
```

(continued)

continued

```
\ASM
    tst1.asm
    atest.asm
    asmexamp.asm
    tst12&20.asm
    tst24.asm

\FOR
    for1.for
    ftest.for
    fdemo.for
    subs.asm

\PAS
    moushgcp.pas
    initpas.asm
    pasexamp.pas
    subs.asm
    pdemo.pas
```

INTERPRETED BASIC PROGRAMS

The programs in this section demonstrate the use of the mouse from interpreted BASIC. The TST1.BAS program shows the minimum steps required for displaying the default graphics mode cursor. The BATEST.BAS program is the interpreted BASIC version of a program that is presented in several languages in this chapter. The most sophisticated program is PIANO.BAS. This program lets you use the mouse to play music on a simulated piano keyboard. This program also demonstrates the steps necessary to change the graphics mode cursor.

To call the mouse functions from interpreted BASIC, you must first determine the vector address of the mouse driver. The first few lines in each of these programs show how this address is determined. The segment of this address is saved in the *MOUSEG* variable, and the offset is saved in the *MOUSE* variable. After the program uses the DEF SEG statement to set the current segment to *MOUSEG*, it can call the mouse functions with the CALL statement.

The CALL statement should have the following form:

```
CALL MOUSE(M1%, M2%, M3%, M4%)
```

where *MOUSE* is the variable that contains the offset of the BASIC entry point into the mouse driver, and *M1%*, *M2%*, *M3%*, and *M4%* are the names of the integer variables you chose for parameters in this call. (Constants and noninteger variables are not allowed.) All parameters must appear in the CALL statement even if no value is assigned to one or more of them. To ensure that the variables are integer variables, use the percent sign (%) as part of all variable names.

See the TST1.BAS program for a straightforward example of the steps required to use the mouse with interpreted BASIC.

The TST1.BAS Program

The TST1.BAS program demonstrates the steps required to activate and display the default graphics mode cursor. To end the program, press any key.

```
100 '*****************************************************************
110 '*   TST1.BAS                                                   *
120 '*                                                              *
130 '*   Displays graphics-mode mouse cursor until a key is pressed *
140 '*   Note: Program assumes both mouse and mouse driver are installed *
145 '*****************************************************************
150 '
160 ' Set and clear the display
170  SCREEN 2
180  CLS
190 '
200 ' Determine mouse interrupt address
210  DEF SEG = 0
220  MOUSEG = 256 * PEEK(207) + PEEK(206)
230  MOUSE = 256 * PEEK(205) + PEEK(204) + 2
240  DEF SEG = MOUSEG
250 '
260 ' Reset mouse
270  M1% = 0
280  CALL MOUSE(M1%, M2%, M3%, M4%)
290 '
300 ' Show cursor
310  M1% = 1
320  CALL MOUSE(M1%, M2%, M3%, M4%)
330 '
340 ' Wait for any key press
350  IF INKEY$ = "" THEN GOTO 350
360 '
370 ' Hide cursor
```

(continued)

208

continued

```
380  M1% = 2
390  CALL MOUSE(M1%, M2%, M3%, M4%)
400  '
410  ' Reset mouse
420  M1% = 0
430  CALL MOUSE(M1%, M2%, M3%, M4%)
440  '
450  END
```

The BATEST.BAS Program

The BATEST.BAS program uses Mouse Function 11 (Read Mouse Motion Counters) to detect vertical mouse motion. The program displays a three-line menu with one option highlighted. When Function 11 detects vertical mouse motion, the program moves the highlight up or down the list.

In addition, this program uses Mouse Function 5 (Get Button Press Information) to detect a button press. To select a highlighted option, you simply press either mouse button. Before the program terminates, it displays a message stating which option you selected and which button you pressed.

This program is presented in several languages in this chapter so that you can compare the mouse function calls in different languages. If you want to compare the programs, see the QBTEST.BAS, CTEST.C, ATEST.ASM, and FTEST.FOR programs.

```
100  '*********************************************************
110  '*  BATEST.BAS                                          *
120  '*                                                      *
130  '*  Demonstrates use of the Microsoft Mouse from BASICA *
140  '*********************************************************
150  '
160  ' Clear the display
170  CLS
180  '
190  ' Determine mouse interrupt address
200  DEF SEG = 0
210  MOUSEG = 256 * PEEK(207) + PEEK(206)
220  MOUSE = 256 * PEEK(205) + PEEK(204) + 2
230  DEF SEG = MOUSEG
```

(continued)

continued

```
232   IF (MOUSEG OR (MOUSE - 2)) AND PEEK(MOUSE - 2) <> 207
      THEN GOTO 260
234   PRINT "Mouse driver not found" : END
240   '
250   ' Display instructions for user
260   PRINT "BATEST - Mouse demonstration using interpreted BASIC"
270   PRINT
280   PRINT "Use mouse to highlight a menu option."
290   PRINT "Press either button to select option. "
300   '
310   ' Reset mouse and verify its existence
320   M1% = 0
330   CALL MOUSE(M1%, M2%, M3%, M4%)
340   '
350   ' Quit if mouse wasn't found
360   IF M1% = 0 THEN PRINT "Error: Mouse not found ": END
370   '
380   ' Initialize menu pointer to first option
390   MENUPTR% = 1
400   '
410   ' Initialize count of accumulated vertical mouse motion
420   MOTION% = 0
430   '
440   ' Set flag to cause the menu to be updated first time through
450   WFLAG% = 1
460   '
470   ' Main loop starts here
480   WHILE 1
490       '
500       ' Update the menu only when necessary
510       WHILE WFLAG% = 1
520           WFLAG% = 0
530           '
540           ' Print first line of the menu, highlighted if selected
550           IF MENUPTR% = 1 THEN COLOR 0,7 ELSE COLOR 7,0
560           LOCATE 10, 29
570           PRINT " 1. First option    "
580           '
590           ' Print second line of the menu, highlighted if selected
600           IF MENUPTR% = 2 THEN COLOR 0,7 ELSE COLOR 7,0
610           LOCATE 11, 29
620           PRINT " 2. Second option   "
630           '
640           ' Print third line of the menu, highlighted if selected
650           IF MENUPTR% = 3 THEN COLOR 0,7 ELSE COLOR 7,0
660           LOCATE 12, 29
```

(continued)

continued

```
670        PRINT " 3. Third option    "
680        '
690        ' Be sure highlighting is turned off
700        COLOR 7, 0
710        '
720        ' End of updating the menu
730     WEND
740     '
750     ' Accumulate vertical mouse motion counts
760     M1% = 11
770     CALL MOUSE(M1%, M2%, M3%, M4%)
780     MOTION% = MOTION% + M4%
790     '
800     ' Move up the menu if enough mouse motion
810     IF MOTION% > -17 THEN GOTO 880
820        MOTION% = 0
830        IF MENUPTR% <= 1 THEN GOTO 880
840           MENUPTR% = MENUPTR% - 1
850           WFLAG% = 1
860     '
870     ' Move down the menu if enough mouse motion
880     IF MOTION% < 17 THEN GOTO 950
890        MOTION% = 0
900        IF MENUPTR% >= 3 THEN GOTO 950
910           MENUPTR% = MENUPTR% + 1
920           WFLAG% = 1
930     '
940     ' Check if left button pressed
950     M1% = 5
960     M2% = 0
970     CALL MOUSE(M1%, M2%, M3%, M4%)
980     IF M2% = 0 THEN GOTO 1030
990        PRINT "Left button used to select option", MENUPTR%
1000        END
1010     '
1020     ' Check if right button pressed
1030     M1% = 5
1040     M2% = 1
1050     CALL MOUSE(M1%, M2%, M3%, M4%)
1060     IF M2% = 0 THEN GOTO 1110
1070        PRINT "Right button used to select option", MENUPTR%
1080        END
1090     '
1100     ' Loop back until one button is pressed
1110 WEND
```

The PIANO.BAS Program

The PIANO.BAS program creates a graphics mode piano keyboard and lets you play the keys by mouse-cursor selection. If you want to play notes in a lower octave, select the keys using the left mouse button. If you want to play notes in a higher octave, select the keys using the right mouse button.

This program demonstrates several mouse function calls. Function 9 (Set Graphics Cursor Block) sets the cursor shape. Function 4 (Set Mouse Cursor Position) sets the cursor position. Function 1 (Show Cursor) makes the cursor visible. Function 3 (Get Button Status and Mouse Position) gets the mouse location and button status information. The program uses the block of DATA statements at the end of the listing to create the Microsoft logo.

NOTE: Because of the length of this program, it is not listed here. The program is included on the disks that come with this book. You can use your favorite text editor to view the source code for the program on your screen, or you can print the source code on your printer.

QUICKBASIC PROGRAMS

You can call mouse functions from QuickBASIC in several ways. The programs that follow call mouse functions using the MOUSE subprogram in MOUSE.LIB and the INTERRUPT and ABSOLUTE subprograms supplied with QuickBASIC.

The simplest programs are QBMOU.BAS, QBINT.BAS, and QBINC.BAS. Each of these programs displays the text mode cursor and then waits for you to press a key before terminating. In these programs, the mouse functions are called using the MOUSE and INTERRUPT subprograms, providing a direct comparison between the two calling methods. The QBINT.BAS and QBINC.BAS programs differ only in the way you make declarations to prepare for using the INTERRUPT subprogram.

ABSOLUTE.BAS, INTRRUPT.BAS, and MOUSE.BAS are larger programs that demonstrate how you can make the same mouse function calls using CALL ABSOLUTE, CALL INTERRUPT, or CALL MOUSE. Two of these programs create a new graphics mode cursor.

The MOUSEDEM.BAS program presents some useful QuickBASIC subprograms in addition to demonstrating several mouse functions.

MOUSEDEM.BAS changes the text mode cursor and displays pop-up windows as it demonstrates each function.

The QB12&20.BAS and QB24.BAS programs present examples of setting and swapping user-interrupt subroutines by using Mouse Functions 12, 20, and 24. These interrupt subroutines are activated quickly while a program is running when they detect mouse motion, mouse button presses, or combinations of Shift key presses and mouse activity.

The QBTEST.BAS program is the three-line menu program that detects vertical mouse motion. It is presented in several other languages in this chapter for comparison purposes.

All these programs require that you load a Quick Library with the QuickBASIC environment. Programs that use INTERRUPT or ABSOLUTE subprograms can use the QB.QLB Quick Library supplied with QuickBASIC. To load this file with QuickBASIC, type the following command at the MS-DOS prompt:

```
QB /L QB.QLB
```

Programs that call the MOUSE subprogram require that the Quick Library loaded in memory include the code found in the MOUSE.LIB library. You can create a new Quick Library named QBMOUSE.QLB that contains the MOUSE.LIB routines in addition to the QB.QLB routines by typing the following command:

```
LINK /QU /NOE MOUSE.LIB + QB.LIB,QBMOUSE.QLB,NUL,BQLB45.LIB;
```

NOTE: To be sure LINK finds each file, copy MOUSE.LIB, QB.LIB, and BQLB45.LIB into your current directory.

The following command also creates a combined library that lets your programs compile and link into stand-alone .EXE programs:

```
LIB QBMOUSE.LIB + MOUSE.LIB + QB.LIB;
```

After you create the QBMOUSE.QLB and QBMOUSE.LIB libraries, start QuickBASIC with the following command:

```
QB /L QBMOUSE.QLB
```

When you load QBMOUSE.QLB into your QuickBASIC environment, all QuickBASIC programs in this section will run, whether they call the mouse functions using CALL ABSOLUTE, CALL INTERRUPT, or CALL MOUSE.

The first three programs in this section, QBMOU.BAS, QBINT.BAS, and QBINC.BAS, demonstrate three variations on calling the mouse functions. Each program clears the screen, displays the text mode mouse cursor, and waits for you to press a key before terminating.

The QBMOU.BAS Program

The QBMOU.BAS program calls the MOUSE subprogram provided in the MOUSE.LIB library. To call this subprogram from the QuickBASIC environment, you must build and load the QBMOUSE.QLB library as described earlier in this section.

```
'*********************************************************
'*   QBMOU.BAS                                           *
'*                                                       *
'*   Calls mouse functions using the MOUSE subprogram    *
'*                                                       *
'*   To load QBMOUSE.QLB into memory with QuickBASIC,    *
'*   type: QB /L QBMOUSE.QLB                             *
'*********************************************************

' Initialization
  DEFINT A-Z
  DECLARE SUB Mouse (m1%, m2%, m3%, m4%)
  CLS
  PRINT "Press any key to quit"

' Mouse Reset and Status
  m1 = 0
  Mouse m1, m2, m3, m4

' Show Cursor
  m1 = 1
  Mouse m1, m2, m3, m4

' Wait until a key is pressed
  DO
  LOOP WHILE INKEY$ = ""

' Reset mouse driver
  m1 = 0
  Mouse m1, m2, m3, m4

  END
```

The QBINT.BAS Program

The QBINT.BAS program calls the mouse functions using the
INTERRUPT subprogram. The INTERRUPT subprogram is part of the
QB.QLB Quick Library that comes with QuickBASIC. Before you load
and run QBINT.BAS, be sure you load the QB.QLB library into the
QuickBASIC environment.

```
'**********************************************************
'*  QBINT.BAS                                            *
'*                                                       *
'*  Calls mouse functions using the INTERRUPT subprogram *
'*                                                       *
'*  To load QB.QLB into memory with QuickBASIC, type:    *
'*  QB /L QB.QLB                                         *
'**********************************************************


  DEFINT A-Z

  TYPE RegType
       ax    AS INTEGER
       bx    AS INTEGER
       cx    AS INTEGER
       dx    AS INTEGER
       bp    AS INTEGER
       si    AS INTEGER
       di    AS INTEGER
       flags AS INTEGER
  END TYPE

  DECLARE SUB Interrupt (intnum%, iReg AS RegType, oReg AS RegType)

  DIM iReg AS RegType
  DIM oReg AS RegType

' Initialization
  CLS
  PRINT "Press any key to quit"

' Mouse Reset and Status
  iReg.ax = 0
  Interrupt &H33, iReg, oReg
```

(continued)

continued

```
' Show Cursor
  iReg.ax = 1
  Interrupt &H33, iReg, oReg

' Wait until any key is pressed
  DO
  LOOP WHILE INKEY$ = ""

' Hide Cursor
  iReg.ax = 2
  Interrupt &H33, iReg, oReg

' Reset mouse
  iReg.ax = 0
  Interrupt &H33, iReg, oReg

  END
```

The QBINC.BAS Program

The QBINC.BAS program is almost identical to the QBINT.BAS program except that you make the declarations necessary to use the INTERRUPT subprogram by including the QB.BI file. To insert the contents of the QB.BI file at the appropriate place in the listing, simply use the $INCLUDE metacommand. Like QBINT.BAS, the QBINC.BAS program requires that you load the QB.QLB library into the QuickBASIC environment.

```
'***************************************************************
'*   QBINC.BAS                                                *
'*                                                            *
'*   Calls mouse functions using the INTERRUPT subprogram    *
'*                                                            *
'*   Declarations for INTERRUPT are loaded from the          *
'*   QB.BI file by the $INCLUDE metacommand.                 *
'*                                                            *
'*   To load QB.QLB into memory with QuickBASIC, type:       *
'*     QB /L QB.QLB                                           *
'***************************************************************

  DEFINT A-Z
```

(continued)

continued

```
'$INCLUDE: 'QB.BI'

  DIM iReg AS RegType
  DIM oReg AS RegType

' Initialization
  CLS
  PRINT "Press any key to quit"

' Mouse Reset and Status
  iReg.ax = 0
  INTERRUPT &H33, iReg, oReg

' Show Cursor
  iReg.ax = 1
  INTERRUPT &H33, iReg, oReg

' Wait until any key is pressed
  DO
  LOOP WHILE INKEY$ = ""

' Hide Cursor
  iReg.ax = 2
  INTERRUPT &H33, iReg, oReg

' Reset mouse
  iReg.ax = 0
  INTERRUPT &H33, iReg, oReg

  END
```

The ABSOLUTE.BAS Program

The ABSOLUTE.BAS program demonstrates working with the mouse from QuickBASIC 4.5 by using the CALL ABSOLUTE command. This program employs several mouse functions. Function 0 (Mouse Reset and Status) resets the mouse, and Function 1 (Show Cursor) makes the cursor visible. Functions 7 (Set Minimum and Maximum Horizontal Cursor Position) and 8 (Set Minimum and Maximum Vertical Cursor Position) limit the cursor motion to the center of the screen. To get the mouse status, the program calls Function 3 (Get Button Status and Mouse Position). Before the program terminates, it calls Function 0 (Reset Mouse and Status) to hide the mouse cursor.

Before you can run the ABSOLUTE.BAS program, you must load QB.QLB into memory by typing the following command:

```
QB /L QB.QLB
```

The CALL ABSOLUTE function won't work if you don't load QB.QLB with QuickBASIC.

You can now load and run the program. Note that the default graphics cursor appears inside a square that marks cursor-movement limits set by Functions 7 and 8. To end the program, press the left mouse button.

The ABSOLUTE.BAS program was written for EGA graphics mode (SCREEN 9). For CGA operation, change the SCREEN and LINE statements. You should also change the horizontal and vertical motion limits set in the calls to Functions 7 and 8 as required for the CGA mode you set.

```
'*********************************************************************
'*  ABSOLUTE.BAS                                                    *
'*  6/24/88 by Dave Tryon, Microsoft Product Support                *
'*                                                                  *
'*  Demonstrates calling mouse functions using CALL ABSOLUTE        *
'*                                                                  *
'*  To load QB.QLB into memory with QuickBASIC, type: QB /L QB.QLB  *
'*  Assumes EGA - For CGA change SCREEN and LINE statements         *
'*********************************************************************

' Initialization
  DEFINT A-Z
  DEF SEG = 0
  CLS

' Get mouse driver vector
  MSEG = 256 * PEEK(51 * 4 + 3) + PEEK(51 * 4 + 2)
  MOUSE = 256 * PEEK(51 * 4 + 1) + PEEK(51 * 4) + 2

' Proceed if driver found
  IF MSEG OR (MOUSE - 2) THEN
      DEF SEG = MSEG
      IF PEEK(MOUSE - 2) <> 207 THEN

          SCREEN 9

          ' Function 0  Mouse Reset and Status
          M1 = 0
          CALL ABSOLUTE(M1, M2, M3, M4, MOUSE)
```

(continued)

continued

```
' Function 7  Limit Horizontal Motion
  M1 = 7: M3 = 100: M4 = 540
  CALL ABSOLUTE(M1, M2, M3, M4, MOUSE)

' Function 8  Limit Vertical Motion
  M1 = 8: M3 = 50: M4 = 300
  CALL ABSOLUTE(M1, M2, M3, M4, MOUSE)

' Draw box to show mouse motion range
  COLOR 1
  LINE (100, 50) - (540, 50)
  LINE (540, 50) - (540, 300)
  LINE (540, 300) - (100, 300)
  LINE (100, 300) - (100, 50)

' Function 1  Show Cursor
  M1 = 1
  CALL ABSOLUTE(M1, M2, M3, M4, MOUSE)

' Loop until button pressed

  COLOR 7
  M2 = 0
  WHILE (M2 = 0)

    ' Function 3  Get Mouse Status and Mouse Position
      M1 = 3
      CALL ABSOLUTE(M1, M2, M3, M4, MOUSE)

    ' Print cursor location
      LOCATE 2, 2
      PRINT M3, M4
  WEND

' Function 0  Reset Mouse and Status
  M1 = 0
  CALL ABSOLUTE(M1, M2, M3, M4, MOUSE)

ELSE PRINT "Mouse Driver Not Found": END
END IF

ELSE PRINT "Mouse Driver Not Found": END
END IF
```

The INTRRUPT.BAS Program

The INTRRUPT.BAS program demonstrates working with the mouse from QuickBASIC 4.5 by using the CALL INTERRUPT subprogram. This program is similar in design and operation to the ABSOLUTE.BAS program. Many of the functions are called by INTRRUPT.BAS. In addition, INTRRUPT.BAS calls Function 9 (Set Graphics Cursor Block) to set a new graphics mode cursor shape.

Before you can run the INTRRUPT.BAS program, you must load QB.QLB into memory by typing the following command:

```
QB /L QB.QLB
```

The CALL INTERRUPT subprogram won't work if you don't load QB.QLB with QuickBASIC.

You can now load and run the program. Note that the new graphics cursor appears inside a square that marks cursor-movement limits set by Functions 7 (Set Minimum and Maximum Horizontal Cursor Position) and 8 (Set Minimum and Maximum Vertical Cursor Position). To end the program, press the left mouse button.

The INTRRUPT.BAS program was written for EGA graphics mode (SCREEN 9). For CGA operation, change the SCREEN and LINE statements. You should also change the horizontal and vertical motion limits set in the calls to Functions 7 and 8 as required for the CGA mode you set.

NOTE: Because of the length of this program, it is not listed here. The program is included on the disks that come with this book. You can use your favorite text editor to view the source code for the program on your screen, or you can print the source code file on your printer.

The MOUSE.BAS Program

The MOUSE.BAS program demonstrates working with the mouse from QuickBASIC 4.5 by using the CALL MOUSE function. This program is similar in design and operation to the ABSOLUTE.BAS and INTRRUPT.BAS programs.

The MOUSE subprogram is found in the MOUSE.LIB library. To call this subprogram from the QuickBASIC environment, you must build and load the QBMOUSE.QLB library as described earlier in this section.

You can now load and run the program. Note that the new graphics cursor appears inside a square that marks the cursor-movement limits set by Functions 7 (Set Minimum and Maximum

Horizontal Cursor Position) and 8 (Set Minimum and Maximum Vertical Cursor Position). To end the program, press the left mouse button.

The MOUSE.BAS program was written for EGA graphics mode (SCREEN 9). For CGA operation, change the SCREEN and LINE statements. You should also change the horizontal and vertical motion limits set in the calls to Functions 7 and 8 as required for the CGA mode you set.

```
'****************************************************************
'*   MOUSE.BAS                                                 *
'*   6/24/88 by Dave Tryon, Microsoft Product Support          *
'*                                                             *
'*   Demonstrates calling mouse functions using CALL MOUSE     *
'*                                                             *
'*   To load QBMOUSE.QLB into memory with QuickBASIC, type:    *
'*   QB /L QBMOUSE.QLB                                         *
'*                                                             *
'*   Assumes EGA - For CGA change SCREEN and LINE statements   *
'****************************************************************

' Initialization
  DIM CURSOR(15, 1) AS INTEGER
  COMMON CURSOR() AS INTEGER
  DECLARE SUB MOUSE (M1%, M2%, M3%, M4%)
  CLS

' Define Cursor Array
  CURSOR(0, 0) = &HE1FF
  CURSOR(1, 0) = &HE1FF
  CURSOR(2, 0) = &HE1FF
  CURSOR(3, 0) = &HE1FF
  CURSOR(4, 0) = &HE1FF
  CURSOR(5, 0) = &HE000
  CURSOR(6, 0) = &HE000
  CURSOR(7, 0) = &HE000
  CURSOR(8, 0) = &H0
  CURSOR(9, 0) = &H0
  CURSOR(10, 0) = &H0
  CURSOR(11, 0) = &H0
  CURSOR(12, 0) = &H0
  CURSOR(13, 0) = &H0
  CURSOR(14, 0) = &H0
  CURSOR(15, 0) = &H0
```

(continued)

continued

```
CURSOR(0, 1) = &H1E00
CURSOR(1, 1) = &H1200
CURSOR(2, 1) = &H1200
CURSOR(3, 1) = &H1200
CURSOR(4, 1) = &H1200
CURSOR(5, 1) = &H13FF
CURSOR(6, 1) = &H1249
CURSOR(7, 1) = &H1249
CURSOR(8, 1) = &HF249
CURSOR(9, 1) = &H9001
CURSOR(10, 1) = &H9001
CURSOR(11, 1) = &H9001
CURSOR(12, 1) = &H8001
CURSOR(13, 1) = &H8001
CURSOR(14, 1) = &H8001
CURSOR(15, 1) = &HFFFF

' Check whether mouse driver installed--exit if not.
DEF SEG = 0
MSEG = 256 * PEEK(51 * 4 + 3) + PEEK(51 * 4 + 2)
MOUSE1 = 256 * PEEK(51 * 4 + 1) + PEEK(51 * 4) + 2
IF MSEG OR (MOUSE1 - 2) THEN
    DEF SEG = MSEG
    IF PEEK(MOUSE1 - 2) <> 207 THEN
        SCREEN 9

        ' Function 0  Mouse Reset and Status
        M1% = 0
        CALL MOUSE(M1%, M2%, M3%, M4%)

        ' Function 7  Limit Horizontal Motion
        M1% = 7: M3% = 100: M4% = 540
        CALL MOUSE(M1%, M2%, M3%, M4%)

        ' Function 8  Limit Vertical Motion
        M1% = 8: M3% = 50: M4% = 300
        CALL MOUSE(M1%, M2%, M3%, M4%)

        ' Draw box to show mouse motion range
        COLOR 1
        LINE (100, 50) - (540, 50)
        LINE (540, 50) - (540, 300)
        LINE (540, 300) - (100, 300)
        LINE (100, 300) - (100, 50)
```

(continued)

continued

```
         ' Function 9  Set Graphics Cursor Block (custom cursor)
            M1% = 9: M2% = 5: M3% = 0
            CALL MOUSE(M1%, M2%, M3%, VARPTR(CURSOR(0, 0)))

         ' Function 1  Show Cursor
            M1% = 1
            CALL MOUSE(M1%, M2%, M3%, M4%)

         ' Loop until button pressed

            COLOR 7
            M2% = 0
            WHILE (M2% = 0)

               ' Function 3  Get Button Status and Mouse Position
                  M1% = 3
                  CALL MOUSE(M1%, M2%, M3%, M4%)

               ' Print cursor location
                  LOCATE 2, 2
                  PRINT M3%, M4%
            WEND

         ' Function 0  Reset Mouse and Status
            M1% = 0
            CALL MOUSE(M1%, M2%, M3%, M4%)

      ELSE PRINT "Mouse Driver Not Found"
      END IF

   ELSE PRINT "Mouse Driver Not Found"
   END IF
```

The MOUSEDEM.BAS Program

The MOUSEDEM.BAS program uses modular QuickBASIC programming techniques to demonstrate several mouse functions. The program makes calls to the mouse driver by calling the MouseDriver subprogram. The MouseDriver subprogram uses one CALL INTERRUPT to access the mouse driver.

This program demonstrates setting the hardware and software text cursors using Mouse Function 10 (Set Text Cursor). The program makes the cursor blink by setting an appropriate hardware cursor and then sets the cursor back to the default software cursor by means of a second call to Function 10. The comments in the program listing explain this process in detail.

In addition to showing the use of several mouse functions, the MOUSEDEM.BAS program presents several creative subprograms that you may find useful. For example, the MoveFromScreen and MoveToScreen subprograms show one way to save and restore a rectangular area of the text mode display.

Before you can run this program, you must load QB.QLB into memory by typing the following command:

```
QB /L QB.QLB
```

The CALL ABSOLUTE command won't work if you don't load QB.QLB with QuickBASIC.

NOTE: Because of the length of this program, it is not listed here. The program is included on the disks that come with this book. You can use your favorite text editor to view the source code for the program on your screen, or you can print the source code on your printer.

The QB12&20.BAS Program

The QB12&20.BAS program demonstrates Mouse Functions 12 (Set Interrupt Subroutine Call Mask and Address) and 20 (Swap Interrupt Subroutines). Function 12 sets a user-interrupt subroutine, and Function 20 swaps this interrupt subroutine with a second subroutine.

The program displays the text mode mouse cursor and waits until you press a key. It lets you move the cursor around the screen, and the cursor moves to the upper-left corner of the screen whenever you press the right mouse button.

When you press a key, Function 20 replaces the first interrupt subroutine with the second interrupt subroutine. Now when you release the left mouse button, the cursor moves to the center of the screen.

To end the program, again press any key.

```
'*****************************************************************
'*   QB12&20.BAS                                                *
'*                                                              *
'*   Demonstrates Mouse Functions 12 and 20                     *
'*                                                              *
'*   To load QB.QLB into memory with QuickBASIC, type:          *
'*   QB /L QB.QLB                                               *
'*****************************************************************
```

(continued)

continued

```
    DEFINT A-Z

    TYPE RegType
        ax    AS INTEGER
        bx    AS INTEGER
        cx    AS INTEGER
        dx    AS INTEGER
        bp    AS INTEGER
        si    AS INTEGER
        di    AS INTEGER
        flags AS INTEGER
    END TYPE

    DECLARE SUB Interrupt (intnum%, iReg AS RegType, oReg AS RegType)

    DIM iReg AS RegType
    DIM oReg AS RegType

    DIM msub%(5), msub2%(5)
    COMMON msub%(), msub2%()

  ' First instructions
    CLS
    PRINT "Test by pressing right mouse button"
    PRINT "Then press enter"

  ' Build interrupt-driven subroutine to activate Function 12
    msub%(0) = &H4B8            ' Subroutine is from this code:
    msub%(1) = &HB900           '    MOV AX,4   ; Function 4, Set
                                '               ; Mouse Cursor Position
    msub%(2) = &H0              '    MOV CX,0   ; Left edge of screen
    msub%(3) = &HBA             '    MOV DX,0   ; Top edge of screen
    msub%(4) = &HCD00           '    INT 33h    ; Mouse Interrupt
    msub%(5) = &HCB33           '    RETF       ; Return to QuickBASIC

  ' Build interrupt-driven subroutine to activate Function 20
    msub2%(0) = &H4B8           ' Subroutine is from this code:
    msub2%(1) = &HB900          '    MOV AX,4   ; Function 4, Set
                                '               ; Mouse Cursor Position
    msub2%(2) = &H140           '    MOV CX,320 ; Middle of screen
    msub2%(3) = &H64BA          '    MOV DX,100 ; Middle of screen
    msub2%(4) = &HCD00          '    INT 33h    ; Mouse Interrupt
    msub2%(5) = &HCB33          '    RETF       ; Return to QuickBASIC
```

(continued)

continued

```
' Mouse Reset and Status
  iReg.ax = 0
  Interrupt &H33, iReg, oReg


' Show Cursor
  iReg.ax = 1
  Interrupt &H33, iReg, oReg


' Set Interrupt Subroutine Call Mask and Address
  iReg.ax = 12                  ' Mouse Function 12
  iReg.cx = 8                   ' Interrupt when right button pressed
  iReg.dx = VARPTR(msub%(0))    ' Offset of msub1
  Interrupt &H33, iReg, oReg


' Wait until any key is pressed
  DO
  LOOP WHILE INKEY$ = ""


' Next instructions
  CLS
  PRINT "Next, test by pressing and releasing left mouse button"
  PRINT "Then press Enter"


' Swap Interrupt Subroutines
  iReg.ax = 20                   ' Mouse Function 20
  iReg.bx = VARSEG(msub2%(0))  ' Segment of msub2
  iReg.cx = 4                   ' Interrupt when left button released
  iReg.dx = VARPTR(msub2%(0))  ' Offset of msub2
  Interrupt &H33, iReg, oReg


' Wait until any key is pressed
  DO
  LOOP WHILE INKEY$ = ""


' Reset mouse to deactivate the interrupt
  iReg.ax = 0
  Interrupt &H33, iReg, oReg


  END
```

The QB24.BAS Program

The QB24.BAS program uses Function 24 (Set Alternate Subroutine Call Mask and Address) to set a user-interrupt subroutine. The bytes that compose the short subroutine are placed in the *msub%()* array, and the address of the first member of that array is passed to Function 24 as the address of the subroutine.

The program builds the subroutine, displays the mouse cursor, and calls Function 24 to activate the subroutine. The call mask is set so that you must press a Shift key and the left mouse button simultaneously to cause the mouse driver to call the subroutine.

The program then enters a loop, waiting for you to press any key before terminating. During this time, you can move the mouse cursor around the screen. If you press a Shift key and the left mouse button, the cursor moves to the upper-left corner of the screen.

WARNING: Shortly before the program terminates, it calls Mouse Function 0 (Mouse Reset and Status) to reset the mouse. Note that Function 0 will not deactivate the user-interrupt subroutine. The subroutine's address remains with the mouse driver even though the subroutine itself is gone. Activation of the subroutine will then most likely cause your system to crash.

```
'*****************************************************************
'*  QB24.BAS                                                    *
'*                                                              *
'*  Demonstrates Mouse Function 24                              *
'*  Set Alternate Subroutine Call Mask and Address              *
'*                                                              *
'*  To load QB.QLB into memory with QuickBASIC, type:           *
'*  QB /L QB.QLB                                                *
'*****************************************************************

    DEFINT A-Z

    TYPE RegType
        ax    AS INTEGER
        bx    AS INTEGER
        cx    AS INTEGER
        dx    AS INTEGER
        bp    AS INTEGER
        si    AS INTEGER
```

(continued)

227

continued

```
      di    AS INTEGER
      flags AS INTEGER
END TYPE

DECLARE SUB Interrupt (intnum%, iReg AS RegType, oReg AS RegType)

DIM iReg AS RegType
DIM oReg AS RegType

DIM msub%(5)
COMMON msub%()

' Build interrupt-driven subroutine to activate Function 24
msub%(0) = &H4B8              ' Subroutine is from this code...
msub%(1) = &HB900            '   MOV AX,4  ; Function 4, Set
                             '             ; Mouse Cursor Position
msub%(2) = &H0              '   MOV CX,0  ; Left edge of screen
msub%(3) = &HBA             '   MOV DX,0  ; Top edge of screen
msub%(4) = &HCD00           '   INT 33h   ; Mouse Interrupt
msub%(5) = &HCB33           '   RETF      ; Return to QuickBASIC

' Display instructions
CLS
PRINT "Test while holding Shift key while pressing
PRINT "and releasing the left mouse button"
PRINT "Then press Enter"

' Mouse Reset and Status
iReg.ax = 0
Interrupt &H33, iReg, oReg

' Show Cursor
iReg.ax = 1
Interrupt &H33, iReg, oReg

' Set Alternate Subroutine Call Mask and Address
iReg.ax = 24
iReg.cx = 36                 ' Left button released and Shift key pressed
iReg.dx = VARPTR(msub%(0))
Interrupt &H33, iReg, oReg

' Wait until any key is pressed
DO
LOOP WHILE INKEY$ = ""
```

(continued)

continued

```
' Deactivate Function 24
   iReg.ax = 24
   iReg.cx = 32
   Interrupt &H33, iReg, oReg

' Reset mouse
   iReg.ax = 0
   Interrupt &H33, iReg, oReg

   END
```

The QBTEST.BAS Program

The QBTEST.BAS program uses Mouse Function 11 (Read Mouse Motion Counters) to detect vertical mouse motion. The program displays a three-line menu with one option highlighted. When Function 11 detects vertical mouse motion, the program moves the highlight up or down the list.

In addition, this program uses Mouse Function 5 (Get Button Press Information) to detect a button press. To select a highlighted option, you simply press either mouse button. Before the program terminates, it displays a message stating which option you selected and which button you pressed.

This program is presented in several languages in this chapter so that you can compare the mouse function calls in different languages. If you want to compare the programs, see the BATEST.BAS, CTEST.C, ATEST.ASM, and FTEST.FOR programs in this chapter.

NOTE: Because of the length of this program, it is not listed here. The program is included on the disks that come with this book. You can use your favorite text editor to view the source code for the program on your screen, or you can print the source code on your printer.

The PENCIL.BAS Program

The PENCIL.BAS program is an enjoyable sketching program that you can expand into a complete graphics editing package. Several mouse functions are well demonstrated in this program, and more than one graphics mode cursor is defined and used. Depending on the state of the program, the cursor appears as an image of the Microsoft Mouse or as a pencil.

This chapter also offers the PENCIL program in C and QuickC. (See the PENCIL.C program later in this chapter.)

NOTE: Because of the length of this program, it is not listed here. The program is included on the disks that come with this book. You can use your favorite text editor to view the source code for the program on your screen, or you can print the source code on your printer.

C AND QUICKC PROGRAMS

This section presents a variety of mouse programming examples using the C and QuickC languages. Most of the following programs were set up for the medium-memory model, which is the default memory model for QuickC. In the header of each program listing, you will find instructions for compiling and linking under C version 5.1 and instructions for the program list requirements under QuickC.

To change these programs for other memory models under C, change all occurrences of *cmousem* to the function call appropriate for the desired model. These calls are listed in several program headers. Notice that the programs that call the mouse functions using *int86x()* rather than the functions supplied in MOUSE.LIB require no change to the function names when compiling for other memory models.

The CMOUSE.C Program

The CMOUSE.C program demonstrates and tests several important mouse functions. It also shows some useful programming techniques to help keep your mouse programs well organized. As the program exercises these mouse functions, it displays a sequence of instructions.

The program also defines constants for the mouse functions, making the program listing easier to follow. In addition, the #define statements near the beginning of the program redefine these function numbers with text labels.

As listed in the program header, the C versions of the mouse calls in the MOUSE.LIB library are provided for all the memory models. To change memory models, you must change all occurrences of the mouse function call to the function name for the desired model. In this program, a #define statement creates a generic mouse function call, requiring changes to be made only in the #define statement to affect all mouse calls. Notice that there is only one occurrence of *cmousem()* in the entire listing.

NOTE: Because of the length of this program, it is not listed here. The program is included on the disks that come with this book. You can use your favorite text editor to view the source code for the program on your screen, or you can print the source code on your printer.

The CTEST.C Program

The CTEST.C program uses Mouse Function 11 (Read Mouse Motion Counters) to detect vertical mouse motion. The program displays a three-line menu with one option highlighted. When Function 11 detects vertical mouse motion, the program moves the highlight up or down the list.

In addition, this program uses Mouse Function 5 (Get Button Press Information) to detect a button press. To select a highlighted option, you simply press either mouse button. Before the program terminates, it displays a message stating which option you selected and which button you pressed.

This program is presented in several languages in this chapter so that you can compare the mouse function calls in different languages. If you want to compare the programs, see the BATEST.BAS, QBTEST.BAS, ATEST.ASM, and FTEST.FOR programs in this chapter.

NOTE: Because of the length of this program, it is not listed here. The program is included on the disks that come with this book. You can use your favorite text editor to view the source code for the program on your screen, or you can print the source code on your printer.

The LPEN.C Program

The LPEN.C program uses Mouse Function 14 (Light Pen Emulation Mode Off) to turn off light pen emulation.

When the mouse is initialized by calling Mouse Function 0 (Mouse Reset and Status), light pen emulation is turned on. This program resets the mouse and enters a loop, displaying the light pen status returned by Function 4 (Set Mouse Cursor Position) of the BIOS video interrupt. The AX, BX, CX, and DX registers are displayed constantly so that you can watch the effects of emulating the light pen by pressing both mouse buttons.

If you press any key, the program exits the first loop. The light pen emulation is then turned off and a second loop is entered. Again, the registers are displayed as the program continuously gets the light pen position information from the BIOS. To end the program, again press any key.

NOTE: The BIOS function that returns the light pen information isn't set up for VGA, but only for CGA and EGA. With VGA, you'll see a difference in the returned value of the AX register when the light pen emulation is on or off; however, the returned position information remains constant.

```
/****************************************************************
*   LPEN.C                                                      *
*                                                               *
*   Demonstrates use of light pen emulation from C 5.1          *
*   and QuickC. First, emulation is on. Press both mouse        *
*   buttons to emulate pen down. Press any key to turn          *
*   off emulation. Registers returned from BIOS Function 4,     *
*   Interrupt 10H, are displayed (Get Light Pen Position).      *
*                                                               *
*   Note: The BIOS Function 4, Interrupt 10H, doesn't           *
*         return the light pen position for VGA. It's           *
*         designed to work with CGA and EGA only.               *
*                                                               *
*   This program uses int86() to call the mouse driver.         *
*                                                               *
*   Microsoft C 5.1:                                            *
*       cl lpen.c                                               *
*                                                               *
*   QuickC:                                                     *
*   .  Program List (not required)                              *
*   Note: Program assumes mouse driver and mouse installed      *
****************************************************************/

#include <stdio.h>
#include <stdlib.h>
#include <dos.h>
#include <graph.h>

main()
{
    union REGS iReg,oReg;
    struct SREGS segregs;

    /* Mouse Reset and Status */
    iReg.x.ax = 0;
    int86(0x33, &iReg, &oReg);

    /* Show Cursor */
    iReg.x.ax = 1;
    int86(0x33, &iReg, &oReg);

    /* Display message */
    printf("\n\nLight Pen Emulation Mode On, Status...\n");
```

(continued)

continued

```
while (!kbhit())
   {
   iReg.h.ah = 4;                        /* Get Light Pen Position */
   int86(0x10, &iReg, &oReg);
   printf("\rAX: %.4X  BX: %.4X  CX: %.4X  DX: %.4X",
          iReg.x.ax,iReg.x.bx,iReg.x.cx,iReg.x.dx);
   }
getch();

/* Light Pen Emulation Mode Off */
iReg.x.ax = 14;
int86(0x33, &iReg, &oReg);

/* Display message */
printf("\n\nLight Pen Emulation Mode Off, Status...\n");

while (!kbhit())
   {
   iReg.h.ah = 4;                        /* Get Light Pen Position */
   int86(0x10, &iReg, &oReg);
   printf("\rAX: %.4X  BX: %.4X  CX: %.4X  DX: %.4X",
          iReg.x.ax,iReg.x.bx,iReg.x.cx,iReg.x.dx);
   }
getch();

/* Mouse Reset and Status */
iReg.x.ax = 0;
int86(0x33, &iReg, &oReg);
}
```

The MOUS_INT.C, MOUS_LIB.C, MOUH_INT.C, and MOUH_LIB.C Programs

The MOUS_INT.C, MOUS_LIB.C, MOUH_INT.C, and MOUH_LIB.C programs demonstrate the differences between calling mouse functions using the *int86x()* function and using the mouse calls provided in the MOUSE.LIB library. MOUH_INT.C and MOUH_LIB.C also show the differences required for using the Hercules Graphics Card. All of these programs produce almost identical results.

Functions 7 (Set Minimum and Maximum Horizontal Cursor Position) and 8 (Set Minimum and Maximum Vertical Cursor Position) limit the cursor motion to the middle of the screen. Function 9 (Set Graphics Cursor Block) sets a new graphics mode cursor, shaped like a pointing hand. As you move the cursor around the middle of the screen, Function 3 (Get Button Status and Mouse Position) continuously gets the mouse position, which is displayed in the upper-left corner of the screen. To end the program, press either mouse button.

NOTE: Because of the length of these programs, they are not listed here. The programs are included on the disks that come with this book. You can use your favorite text editor to view the source code for the programs on your screen, or you can print the source code on your printer.

The MSCEXAMP.C Program

The MSCEXAMP.C program demonstrates several common mouse functions and a subroutine that checks whether the mouse driver is installed. The default graphics mode cursor is displayed, and its motion is limited by calls to Mouse Functions 7 (Set Minimum and Maximum Horizontal Cursor Position) and 8 (Set Minimum and Maximum Vertical Cursor Position). To end the program, press the left mouse button.

This program is set up for a medium-memory model, which is the default for QuickC. To change it to any other model for C version 5.1, globally change all occurrences of *cmousem* to the appropriate call for the desired model. You'll also need to change the /AM option on the CL command line for the new model.

```
/****************************************************************
*  MSCEXAMP.C                                                  *
*                                                              *
*  Demonstrates use of the Microsoft Mouse from C 5.1          *
*  and QuickC. It checks to see that the mouse driver was      *
*  installed, displays a graphics mode cursor, and limits      *
*  mouse cursor motion to the middle of the screen.            *
*                                                              *
*  cmousem() is for medium-memory model (QuickC default).      *
*  For other memory models, replace cmousem() with the         *
*  appropriate function:                                       *
*      cmouses() - C small model                               *
*      cmousec() - C compact model                             *
*      cmousem() - C medium model                              *
*      cmousel() - C large or huge model                       *
*                                                              *
*  Microsoft C 5.1:                                            *
```

(continued)

continued

```
*      cl /AM mscexamp.c -link mouse                        *
*                                                           *
*  QuickC:                                                  *
*      Program List MSCEXAMP.C, MOUSE.LIB                   *
***********************************************************/

#include <stdio.h>
#include <dos.h>
#include <graph.h>

void chkdrv();

main()
{
    int m1, m2, m3, m4;

    chkdrv();                   /* Check for mouse driver   */

    m1 = 0;                     /* Initialize mouse         */
    cmousem( &m1, &m2, &m3, &m4);

    if ( m1 == 0 )
        {
        printf("Microsoft Mouse NOT found");
        exit (-1);              /* Exit, if mouse not found */
        }

    _setvideomode(_HRESBW);

    m1 = 4;                     /* Function call 4          */
    m3 = 200;                   /* Set mouse position at    */
    m4 = 100;                   /* center of the screen     */
    cmousem( &m1, &m2, &m3, &m4);

    m1 = 7;                     /* Function call 7          */
    m3 = 150;                   /* minimum horizontal value */
    m4 = 450;                   /* maximum horizontal value */
    cmousem( &m1, &m2, &m3, &m4);

    m1 = 8;                     /* Function call 8          */
    m3 = 50;                    /* minimum vertical value   */
    m4 = 150;                   /* maximum vertical value   */
    cmousem( &m1, &m2, &m3, &m4);
```

(continued)

continued

```
    printf("Graphics cursor limited to center of the screen.\n");
    printf("Press the left button to EXIT.");

    m1 = 1;                    /* Function 1, Show Cursor  */
    cmousem( &m1, &m2, &m3, &m4);

    m2 = 0;                    /* Loop until left mouse    */
    while ( m2 != 1 )          /* button is pressed        */
        {
        m1 = 3;
        cmousem( &m1, &m2, &m3, &m4 );
        }

    m1 = 2;                    /* Function 2, Hide Cursor  */
    cmousem( &m1, &m2, &m3, &m4);

    _setvideomode(_DEFAULTMODE);
}

void chkdrv ()
{
    unsigned long address;
    unsigned char first_byte;

    union REGS inregs, outregs;    /*  Structures to contain    */
    struct SREGS segregs;          /*  register values for intdosx */

    inregs.x.ax = 0x3533;          /* Get interrupt vector for 0x33 */
    intdosx (&inregs, &outregs, &segregs);
    address = (((long) segregs.es) << 16) + (long) outregs.x.bx ;
    first_byte = (unsigned char) * (long far *) address;

    /* Be sure vector isn't 0 and first instruction isn't iret */
    if ((address == 0L) !! (first_byte == 0xCF))
    {
        printf ("\nThe Mouse Driver must be installed to use this program");
        exit ();
    }
}
```

The PENCIL.C Program

The PENCIL.C program is an enjoyable sketching program that you
can expand into a complete graphics editing package. Several mouse
functions are well demonstrated in this program, and more than one

graphics mode cursor is defined and used. Depending on the state of the program, the cursor appears as an image of the Microsoft Mouse or as a pencil.

This chapter also offers the PENCIL program in QuickBASIC (See the PENCIL.BAS program earlier in this chapter.)

This program uses Mouse Function 20 (Swap Interrupt Subroutines) to set an interrupt-driven user subroutine. Function 20 swaps subroutines, which is acceptable even if the subroutine is the only one being used. Function 24 (Get Alternate Subroutine Call Mask Address) could have been used also.

In the header of the program listing, you will find a list of the mouse functions used in the program, as well as the commands used to build the program under C version 5.1 or QuickC.

NOTE: Because of the length of this program, it is not listed here. The program is included on the disks that come with this book. You can use your favorite text editor to view the source code for the program on your screen, or you can print the source code on your printer.

The M20SUB.ASM Program

The M20SUB.ASM program provides the interrupt-driven subroutine named NewMouseHardwareSub for the PENCIL.C program. This subroutine returns the current status of the mouse in four C variables, each of which is declared EXTRN in this listing.

PENCIL uses Mouse Function 20 (Swap Interrupt Subroutines) to set this subroutine. The call mask passed causes this subroutine to activate when you release the right mouse button.

```
;******************************************************************
;*  M20SUB.ASM                                                   *
;*                                                               *
;*  MASM subroutine for C/QuickC program PENCIL.C                *
;*                                                               *
;*  _NewMouseHardwareSub:                                        *
;*  Description: Passes the mouse variables to the C routine     *
;*               when a mouse interrupt occurs                   *
;*                                                               *
;*  This code is to be linked with PENCIL                        *
;*  Example:                                                     *
;*  masm /Ml m20sub;                                             *
;*  cl /AM pencil.c m20sub.obj -link mouse                       *
;******************************************************************
```

(continued)

continued

```
EXTRN _ButtonState:WORD            ; Mouse button state
EXTRN _HorizCursCoord:WORD         ; Current horizontal cursor position
EXTRN _VertCursCoord:WORD          ; Current vertical cursor position
EXTRN _MouseConditionBits:WORD     ; Condition that occurred resulting in
                                   ; a call to this routine


code SEGMENT para public 'code'
        assume cs:code
        public _NewMouseHardwareSub

_NewMouseHardwareSub PROC far       ; Far procedure
        push DS                     ; Save current data segment
        push AX                     ; Save condition mask
        mov AX,SEG _ButtonState     ; Load data segment
        mov DS,AX
        pop AX                      ; Restore condition mask
        mov _MouseConditionBits,ax  ; Pass condition to C routine
        mov _ButtonState,BX         ; Pass button state to C routine
        mov _HorizCursCoord,CX      ; Pass cursor coordinates to C routine
        mov _VertCursCoord,DX
        pop DS                      ; Restore data segment
        RET                         ; Far return
_NewMouseHardwareSub ENDP

code ENDS
end                                 ; End of NewMouseHardwareSub
```

MASM PROGRAMS

The programs in this section demonstrate calls to several mouse functions from MASM. The TST1.ASM program is a simple program that
shows the basics of activating and displaying the standard default
graphics cursor. Other programs show the use of mouse functions that
provide flexible, creative programming from the MASM environment.
For example, the TST12&20.ASM program demonstrates how you can
use more than one interrupt subroutine in your programs to respond
quickly to mouse activity.

Making mouse function calls from MASM is similar to making
mouse function calls from high-level languages. The most important difference is the use of the AX, BX, CX, and DX registers (instead of the *M1*,
M2, *M3*, and *M4* integer variables) followed by a call to Interrupt 33H.
Parameters passed to and received from the mouse functions use these
registers. They correspond directly with the four integer variables.

In addition to the AX, BX, CX, and DX registers, some mouse function calls use the ES, DI, and SI registers. For example, Function 12 (Set Interrupt Subroutine Call Mask and Address) requires all four registers. (For more information on Function 12, see Chapter 8, "Mouse Function Calls.")

The TST1.ASM Program

The TST1.ASM program resets the mouse, sets the graphics adapter to 640-by-200 black-and-white mode, and displays the standard graphics mode cursor at the center of the screen.

To end this program, press any key. The cursor disappears and the video mode returns to 80-by-25 text mode.

```
;-------------------------------------------------------------
; Program:      TST1.ASM
;
; Description:  Demonstrates the mouse in graphics mode
;
; To Run:       MASM TST1;
;               LINK TST1;
;               TST1
;
; Note: Program assumes mouse and mouse driver are installed.
;
;-------------------------------------------------------------

.MODEL  LARGE
.STACK  100h
.CODE

start:
        ; Set 640 x 200 two-color graphics mode
        xor ax,ax
        int 10h

        ; Mouse Reset and Status
        xor ax,ax
        int 33h
```

(continued)

continued

```
        ; Show Cursor
        mov ax,1
        int 33h

        ; Wait for a key press, allowing testing of mouse
        mov ah,8
        int 21h

        ; Reset the mouse
        xor ax,ax
        int 33h

        ; Set 80 x 25 text mode
        mov ax,3
        int 10h

        ; Exit to MS-DOS
        mov ax,4C00h
        int 21h

END     start
        END
```

The ATEST.ASM Program

The ATEST.ASM program uses Mouse Function 11 (Read Mouse Motion Counters) to detect vertical mouse motion. The program displays a three-line menu with one option highlighted. When Function 11 detects vertical mouse motion, the program moves the highlight up or down the list.

In addition, this program uses Mouse Function 5 (Get Button Press Information) to detect a button press. To select a highlighted option, you simply press either mouse button. Before the program terminates, it displays a message stating which option you selected and which button you pressed.

This program is presented in several languages in this chapter so that you can compare the mouse function calls in different languages. If you want to compare the programs, see the BATEST.BAS, QBTEST.BAS, CTEST.C, and FTEST.FOR programs in this chapter.

NOTE: Because of the length of the ATEST.ASM program, it is not listed here. The program is included on the disks that come with this book. You can use your favorite text editor to view the source code for the program on your screen, or you can print the source code on your printer.

The ASMEXAMP.ASM Program

The ASMEXAMP.ASM program demonstrates several mouse functions and checks carefully for the mouse driver. Functions 7 (Set Minimum and Maximum Horizontal Cursor Position) and 8 (Set Minimum and Maximum Vertical Cursor Position) limit the mouse cursor position to the middle section of the screen. In addition, Function 3 (Get Button Status and Mouse Position) detects when you press the left button, at which time the program terminates.

```
;----------------------------------------------------------------
; Program:      ASMEXAMP.ASM
;
; Description:  Demonstrates Mouse Functions 0, 1, 2, 3, 4, 7,
;               and 8.  Displays graphics mode cursor and
;               checks for installation of the mouse driver.
;
; To Run:       MASM ASMEXAMP;
;               LINK ASMEXAMP;
;               ASMEXAMP
;----------------------------------------------------------------

data    segment public 'data'
        msg0    db   "Mouse driver not installed","$"
        msg1    db   "Mouse not found","$"
        msg2    db   "Graphics cursor limit at center of the screen",0dh,0ah
                db   "Press the left mouse button to EXIT","$"
data    ends

code    segment public 'code'
        assume cs:code, ds:nothing, es:nothing
start:
        mov     ax,seg data             ;Set DS to the
        mov     ds,ax                   ;data segment
        assume  ds:data

        ; Check if mouse driver installed
        mov     ax, 03533h              ;Get Int 33H vector
        int     21h                     ;by calling Int 21H.
        mov     ax, es                  ;Check segment and offset of
        or      ax, bx                  ;Int 33H.  If 0 then driver
        jz      not_installed           ;is not installed.
        cmp byte ptr es:[bx], 0CFh      ;Also, if IRET then driver is
        jne     check_mouse             ;not installed.
```

(continued)

continued

```
not_installed:
        mov     dx, offset msg0         ;Message 0
        mov     ah, 09h                 ;Output message to screen
        int     21h
        mov     ax, 4C01h               ;Exit
        int     21h


check_mouse:
        xor     ax, ax                  ;Initialize mouse
        int     33h
        or      ax, ax                  ;Is mouse installed?
        jnz     mouse_ok                ;Then continue

        ; Mouse not found
        mov     dx, offset msg1         ;Message 1
        mov     ah, 09h                 ;Output message to screen
        int     21h
        mov     ax, 4C01h               ;Exit
        int     21h

mouse_ok:
        mov     ax,0006h                ;Set up for 640 x 200 resolution
        int     10h                     ;graphics mode (CGA mode 6)

        mov     ax, 4                   ;Function 4
        mov     cx, 200                 ;M3 = 200
        mov     dx, 100                 ;M4 = 100
        int     33h                     ;Set Mouse Cursor Position

        mov     ax, 7                   ;Function 7
        mov     cx, 150                 ;M3 = 150
        mov     dx, 450                 ;M4 = 450
        int     33h                     ;Set Minimum and Maximum Horizontal
                                        ;Cursor Position

        mov     ax, 8                   ;Function 8
        mov     cx, 50                  ;M3 = 50
        mov     dx, 150                 ;M4 = 150
        int     33h                     ;Set Minimum and Maximum Vertical
                                        ;Cursor Position

        mov     ax,1                    ;Show cursor
        int     33h
```

(continued)

continued

```
        mov     dx, offset msg2         ;Get exit message
        mov     ah, 09h                 ;Output message to screen
        int     21h

around:
        mov     ax, 3                   ;Function 3
        int     33h                     ;Get Button Status and Mouse Position

        test    bx, 0001h               ;Left button pressed ?
        jz      around                  ;Branch if left button NOT pressed

        xor     ax, ax                  ;Function 0
        int     33h                     ;Mouse Reset and Status

        mov     ax, 0003h               ;Set up 80 x 25 character text mode
        int     10h

        mov     ax,04C00h               ;Normal exit
        int     21h

code    ends
end     start
```

The TST12&20.ASM Program

The TST12&20.ASM program demonstrates Mouse Functions 12 (Set Interrupt Subroutine Call Mask and Address) and 20 (Swap Interrupt Subroutines).

Function 12 sets the first user-interrupt subroutine. This subroutine, which is activated when you press the right mouse button, uses Function 4 to set the cursor position at the upper-left corner of the screen. You can test this action by moving the cursor around the screen and occasionally pressing the right mouse button. To begin testing Function 20, press any key.

Function 20 swaps user-interrupt subroutines. In this program, the second subroutine replaces the first, causing the mouse cursor to act differently. Now when you press the left mouse button, the cursor moves to the middle of the screen. To test this action, move the cursor around the screen and press the left mouse button. To terminate the program, press any key.

```
;------------------------------------------------------------------
; Program:      TST12&20.ASM
;
; Description:  Demonstrates Mouse Functions 12 and 20.
;
; To Run:       MASM TST12&20;
;               LINK TST12&20;
;               TST12&20
;
; Note: Program assumes mouse and mouse driver are installed.
;
;------------------------------------------------------------------

.MODEL  LARGE
.STACK  100h
.CODE

; This is the subroutine activated by Function 12
msub    PROC
        mov ax,4                ; Function 4, Set Mouse Cursor
        xor cx,cx               ; Left edge of screen
        mov dx,cx               ; Top edge of screen
        int 33h                 ; Move the cursor
        ret
msub    ENDP

; This is the replacement subroutine for Function 20
msub2   PROC
        mov ax,4                ; Function 4, Set Mouse Cursor
        mov cx,320              ; Middle of screen
        mov dx,100              ; Middle of screen
        int 33h                 ; Move the cursor
        ret
msub2   ENDP

        ; Set up DS for the data segment
start:  mov ax,@DATA
        mov ds,ax

        ; Mouse Reset and Status
        xor ax,ax
        int 33h

        ; Show Cursor
        mov ax,1
        int 33h
```

(continued)

continued

```
                ; Set Interrupt Subroutine Call Mask and Address
                mov ax,SEG msub
                mov es,ax                ; Segment of sub into ES
                mov ax,12                ; Mouse Function 12
                mov cx,8                 ; Interrupt when right button pressed
                mov dx,OFFSET msub       ; Offset of sub into DX
                int 33h


                ; Wait for a key press, allowing testing of mouse
                mov ah,8
                int 21h


                ; Swap Interrupt Subroutines
                mov ax,20                ; Mouse Function 20
                mov bx,SEG msub2         ; Offset of sub into BX
                mov cx,4                 ; Interrupt when left button released
                mov dx,OFFSET msub2      ; Segment of sub into DX
                int 33h


                ; Wait for a key press, allowing testing of mouse
                mov ah,8
                int 21h


                ; Reset the mouse to deactivate the interrupt
                xor ax,ax
                int 33h


                ; Exit to MS-DOS
                mov ax,4C00h
                int 21h


END     start
        END
```

The TST24.ASM Program

The TST24.ASM program demonstrates Mouse Function 24 (Set Alternate Subroutine Call Mask and Address). Function 24 is similar to Function 12 (Set Interrupt Subroutine Call Mask and Address) in the way it sets a user-interrupt subroutine. However, unlike Function 12, this function allows activation of the subroutine based on Shift key status at the time of the detected mouse activity. In this case, the mouse cursor moves to the upper-left corner of the screen only when you press a Shift key and the left mouse button simultaneously.

```
;--------------------------------------------------------------
; Program:      TST24.ASM
;
; Description:  Demonstrates Mouse Function 24.
;
; To Run:       MASM TST24;
;               LINK TST24;
;               TST24
;
; Note: Program assumes mouse and mouse driver are installed.
;
;--------------------------------------------------------------


.MODEL  LARGE
.STACK  100h
.CODE

; This is the subroutine activated by Function 24
msub    PROC
        mov ax,4                ; Function 4, Set Mouse Cursor
        xor cx,cx               ; Left edge of screen
        mov dx,cx               ; Top edge of screen
        int 33h                 ; Move the cursor
        ret
msub    ENDP

        ; Set up DS for the data segment
start:  mov ax,@DATA
        mov ds,ax

        ; Mouse Reset and Status
        xor ax,ax
        int 33h

        ; Show Cursor
        mov ax,1
        int 33h

        ; Set Interrupt Subroutine Call Mask and Address
        mov ax,SEG msub
        mov es,ax               ; Segment of sub into ES
        mov ax,24               ; Mouse Function 24
        mov cx,34               ; When Shift key and left button pressed
        mov dx,OFFSET msub      ; Offset of sub into DX
        int 33h
```

(continued)

continued

```
        ; Wait for a key press, allowing testing of mouse
        mov ah,8
        int 21h

        ; Deactivate Function 24
        mov ax,24
        mov cx,32
        int 33h

        ; Reset the mouse
        xor ax,ax
        int 33h

        ; Exit to MS-DOS
        mov ax,4C00h
        int 21h

END     start
        END
```

FORTRAN PROGRAMS

The following programs demonstrate calling mouse functions from FORTRAN 4.1. The shortest program is FOR1.FOR, which simply displays the default text mode cursor and waits for you to press either mouse button before the program terminates. The FDEMO.FOR program sets a high-resolution graphics mode and displays a new cursor shaped like a mouse. The FTEST.FOR program is the FORTRAN version of the three-line menu that appears in several languages in this chapter.

The best way to program the mouse from FORTRAN is by calling the MOUSEL subroutine in the MOUSE.LIB library. When you are linking the programs, be sure to link with the MOUSE.LIB file. Each program uses the MOUSEL call.

In the header of each program listing, you will find the compile-and-link command line used to create each executable module.

The FOR1.FOR Program

The FOR1.FOR program resets the mouse, displays the cursor, and waits until you press either mouse button. When the program detects a button press, it hides the cursor and terminates.

This program shows the basic method of programming the mouse from FORTRAN. Each mouse function is called using the MOUSEL subroutine provided in the MOUSE.LIB library. You must link this library file with FOR1.FOR for the program to run.

```
********************************************************************
*   FOR1.FOR                                                      *
*                                                                 *
*   Short example of calling mouse functions from FORTRAN 4.1     *
*                                                                 *
*   Compile using large model (default), and link with MOUSE.LIB *
*   Example:   fl /FPc for1.for -link mouse                       *
********************************************************************

        PROGRAM FOR1

        INTEGER*2 M1, M2, M3, M4

* Display short message for user
        WRITE (*,*) 'Press either mouse button to quit'

* Mouse Reset and Status
        M1 = 0
        CALL MOUSEL (M1, M2, M3, M4)

* Show Cursor
        M1 = 1
        CALL MOUSEL (M1, M2, M3, M4)

100  CONTINUE

* Get Button Status and Mouse Position
        M1 = 3
        CALL MOUSEL (M1, M2, M3, M4)

* Loop until either button is pressed
        M2 = MOD(M2, 4)
        IF (M2 .EQ. 0) GOTO 100

* Mouse Reset and Status
        M1 = 0
        CALL MOUSEL (M1, M2, M3, M4)

        STOP
        END
```

The FTEST.FOR Program

The FTEST.FOR program uses Mouse Function 11 (Read Mouse Motion Counters) to detect vertical mouse motion. The program displays a three-line menu with one option highlighted. When Function 11 detects vertical mouse motion, the program moves the highlight up or down the list.

In addition, this program uses Mouse Function 5 (Get Button Press Information) to detect a button press. To select a highlighted option, you simply press either mouse button. Before the program terminates, it displays a message stating which option you selected and which button you pressed.

This program is presented in several languages in this chapter so that you can compare the mouse function calls in different languages. If you want to compare the programs, see the BATEST.BAS, QBTEST.BAS, CTEST.C, and ATEST.ASM programs in this chapter.

NOTE: This program uses the ANSI.SYS escape-code sequences to clear the screen, locate the cursor, and set the character attributes. You must load the ANSI.SYS file into memory, or these escape-code sequences will display strange-looking characters and the menu won't function correctly. ANSI.SYS is loaded at system boot-up from a command in the CONFIG.SYS file. For more information, see your MS-DOS documentation.

NOTE: Because of the length of the FTEST.FOR program, it is not listed here. The program is included on the disks that come with this book. You can use your favorite text editor to view the source code for the program on your screen, or you can print the source code on your printer.

The FDEMO.FOR Program

The FDEMO.FOR program shows one method of programming graphics mode mouse functions using FORTRAN. The MASM program SUBS.ASM supplies some important subroutines for this program. You must link SUBS.ASM and the MOUSE.LIB library with FDEMO.FOR for proper operation.

The INTEGER*2 array named MCURSOR holds the mask data for redefining the graphics mode mouse cursor. Mouse Function 9 (Set Graphics Cursor Block) sets the new cursor shape, and the mask redefines the cursor to look like a mouse—whiskers, tail, and all.

This program also demonstrates the operation of Mouse Function 16 (Conditional Off), which defines a rectangular region of the display that hides the mouse cursor. The cursor remains visible unless you move it into the defined part of the screen. To see how this works, move the cursor to the upper-left corner of the screen.

NOTE: Because of the length of FDEMO.FOR, it is not listed here. The program is included on the disks that come with this book. You can use your favorite text editor to view the source code for the program on your screen, or you can print the source code on your printer.

PASCAL PROGRAMS

The programs in this section demonstrate how you can program the mouse from Microsoft Pascal. A procedure named *mousel* is provided in the MOUSE.LIB library for making calls from Pascal. Notice that this is the same routine called from FORTRAN. The languages share the same parameter-passing and procedure-calling mechanisms.

All these program examples use assembly-language procedures. In addition, the following routines set the graphics modes and check for mouse driver installation.

The MOUSHGCP.PAS Program

The MOUSHGCP.PAS program demonstrates programming the mouse for the Hercules Graphics Card. You must link this program with the INITPAS.OBJ object module and the MOUSE.LIB library for proper operation.

This program first calls the GRAF assembly routine to set the Hercules graphics mode (720 by 348 pixels). The program calls mouse functions to reset the mouse, show the cursor, and check for button press information. When you press a button, the program resets the mouse driver and sets the Hercules Graphics Card back to text mode.

```
(*
 *   Programmer:
 *   Eric Fogelin
 *       June 1, 1987
 *
 *   Purpose:
 *       Using Microsoft Pascal to program mouse support for the Hercules
 *       Monochrome Graphics Card (HGC).
 *
 *   Arguments:
 *   None
```

(continued)

250

continued

```
*    Limits:
*    Must link with MOUSE.LIB and INITPAS.OBJ to resolve mouse function
*        calls and HGC display routine references.
*
*    Make file:
*
*        moushgcp.obj: moushgcp.pas
*            pas1 moushgcp;
*            pas2;
*
*        initpas.obj: initpas.asm
*            masm initpas.asm;
*
*        moushgcp.exe: moushgcp.obj initpas.obj
*            link moushgcp + initpas,,,mouse.lib;
*
*    History:
*        6/1/87 - Created
*)

program mouse_hgc;

(* External references to mouse library and HGC screen routines *)
procedure mouse1 (vars m1, m2, m3, m4:word);extern;
procedure GMODE;extern;
procedure TMODE;extern;

var
    adsbyte: ads of char;    (* 32-bit pointer, segment and offset *)
    m1, m2, m3, m4: word;    (* Standard mouse parameters *)
    videomode: char;         (* Used to save/restore video mode *)

begin

    (* Point to byte which holds Video BIOS mode *)
    adsbyte.s := 16#0000;
    adsbyte.r := 16#0449;

    (* Save current screen mode value *)
    videomode := adsbyte^;

    (* Put HGC into graphics mode using modified Hercules INIT.ASM routine *)
    GMODE;
```

(continued)

continued

```
      (* Put byte value of 6 to direct graphics mouse cursor to HGC page 0 *)
      adsbyte^ := chr(6);

      (* Reset mouse driver. HGC 720 x 348 resolution is recognized *)
      m1 := 0;
      mousel (m1, m2, m3, m4);

      (* Turn on default graphics mouse cursor *)
      m1 := 1;
      mousel (m1, m2, m3, m4);

      (* Loop until either mouse button pressed *)
      repeat
        m1 := 3;
        mousel (m1, m2, m3, m4);
      until (m2 <> 0);

      (* Reset mouse driver *)
      m1 := 0;
      mousel (m1, m2, m3, m4);

      (* Set HGC back to text mode *)
      TMODE;

      (* Restore state of Video BIOS mode value *)
      adsbyte^ := videomode;

  end.
```

The INITPAS.ASM Program

The INITPAS.ASM module provides support code for the MOUSHGCP.PAS program. The *gmode* procedure sets the 6845 CRT controller for the 720-by-348 graphics mode of the Hercules Graphics Card. The *tmode* procedure sets Hercules text mode.

NOTE: Because of the length of this program, it is not listed here. The program is included on the disks that come with this book. You can use your favorite text editor to view the source code for the program on your screen, or you can print the source code on your printer.

The PASEXAMP.PAS Program

The PASEXAMP.PAS program demonstrates several mouse functions. It also checks that you installed the mouse driver before it tries to reset the driver. Mouse Functions 0 (Mouse Reset and Status) and 1 (Show

Cursor) reset the mouse and show the cursor. Function 4 (Set Mouse
Cursor Position) is used to set the cursor position. In addition, Functions 7 (Set Minimum and Maximum Horizontal Cursor Position) and
8 (Set Minimum and Maximum Vertical Cursor Position) limit cursor
motion to the middle part of the screen.

The program enters a loop, using Mouse Function 3 (Get Button
Status and Mouse Position) to check continuously for a press of the left
mouse button. To end the program, press the left mouse button.

*NOTE: You must assemble and link the SUBS.ASM assembly-language
module with this program for proper operation. You must also link the MOUSE.LIB
library to satisfy the mouse function calls.*

```
{---------------------------------------------------------}
{   PASEXAMP.PAS - Mouse functions and Microsoft Pascal   }
{                                                         }
{   Program enters graphics mode, displays default        }
{   cursor, limits its range of motion, and quits when    }
{   the left mouse button is pressed.                     }
{                                                         }
{   Make File:                                            }
{                                                         }
{        pasexamp.obj:   pasexamp.pas                     }
{              pas1 pasexamp;                             }
{              pas2                                       }
{                                                         }
{        pasexamp.exe:   pasexamp.obj subs.obj            }
{              link pasexamp subs,,,..\mouse;             }
{                                                         }
{---------------------------------------------------------}

program mtest (output);

procedure mousel(vars m1, m2, m3, m4:word);extern;
procedure chkdrv;extern;
procedure graf;extern;

var
   m1, m2, m3, m4: word;

begin {demo}
   chkdrv;                {Check mouse driver. If not }
                          {installed, exit.          }
   m1: = 0;               {Installed, initialize mouse}
   mousel( m1, m2, m3, m4);
```

(continued)

continued

```
  if ( m1 = 0 ) then
    writeln('Microsoft Mouse NOT found')
  else
    begin

      m1 := 4;          {Function call 4, set mouse }
      m3 := 200;        {horizontal position        }
      m4 := 100;        {vertical position          }
      mouse1( m1, m2, m3, m4 );

      m1 := 7;          {Function call 7, set mouse }
      m3 := 150;        {minimum horizontal position}
      m4 := 450;        {maximum horizontal position}
      mouse1( m1, m2, m3, m4 );

      m1 := 8;          {Function call 8, set mouse }
      m3 := 50;         {minimum vertical position  }
      m4 := 150;        {maximum vertical position  }
      mouse1( m1, m2, m3, m4 );

      graf;             {Change into graphics mode  }

      writeln('Graphics cursor limited to center of the screen.');
      writeln('Press the left mouse button to EXIT.');

      m1 := 1;          {Function call 1            }
      mouse1( m1, m2, m3, m4 ); {show mouse cursor }

      m2 := 999;        {Dummy value for loop       }
      repeat            {until left button pressed  }
        m1 := 3;        {Function call 3            }
        mouse1( m1, m2, m3, m4 ); {get current mouse status }
      until m2 := 1;    {Left mouse button pressed  }

      m1 := 0;          {Reset mouse driver         }
      mouse1( m1, m2, m3, m4 );
    end

end. {demo}
```

The SUBS.ASM Program

The SUBS.ASM program module provides the *graf* and *chkdrv* subroutines for the PASEXAMP.PAS program. The *graf* subroutine sets a high-resolution graphics mode (640-by-200 pixels, 2-color), and *chkdrv* checks that you installed the mouse driver.

The code in this module is identical to that in the SUBS.ASM module for the FORTRAN examples. Also, the parameter-passing conventions for Microsoft Pascal and Microsoft FORTRAN are the same. This explains why both languages call the same procedure (*mousel*) from the MOUSE.LIB library.

```
;*******************************************************************
;*  SUBS.ASM                                                      *
;*                                                                *
;*  MASM subroutines for PASCAL program PASEXAMP.PAS              *
;*                                                                *
;*  graf - Set 640 x 200, 2-color graphics mode                  *
;*  chkdrv - Check that mouse driver is installed                *
;*                                                                *
;*  See PASEXAMP.PAS program for information on linking.          *
;*                                                                *
;*******************************************************************

mdata           segment byte public 'data'

                msg     db    "Mouse Driver NOT installed","$"

mdata           ends

mcode           segment para public 'CODE'
                assume  cs:mcode

                public  graf

; graf - Set 640 x 200, 2-color graphics mode

graf            proc    far
                push    bp
                mov     ax, 06h                 ;Change to graphics
                int     10h                     ;mode by calling
                pop     bp                      ;Int 10H service
                ret
graf            endp

; chkdrv - Check that mouse driver is installed

                public  chkdrv
```

(continued)

continued

```
chkdrv         proc    far
               push    bp
               push    es

               mov     ax, 03533h              ;Get Int 33H
               int     21h                     ;by calling Int 21H
               mov     ax, es                  ;Check segment and
               or      ax, bx                  ;offset of Int 33H
               jnz     NotInstalled            ;vector if 0 or IRET
               cmp     byte ptr es:[bx],0cfh   ;mouse driver not installed
               jne     back                    ;Exit

NotInstalled:
               mov     ax,seg mdata            ;Set up DS to
               mov     ds,ax                   ;point to data segment
               mov     dx, offset msg          ;Get message
               mov     ah, 09h                 ;out to screen
               int     21h
               pop     es
               pop     bp
               mov     ax,04c01h               ;Function code for
               int     21h                     ;end process

back:
               pop     es
               pop     bp
               ret
chkdrv         endp

mcode          ends
               end
```

The PDEMO.PAS Program

The PDEMO.PAS program demonstrates several mouse functions. Mouse Function 0 (Mouse Reset and Status) initializes the mouse. Function 9 (Set Graphics Cursor Block) sets a new graphics mode cursor shape. In addition, Function 16 (Conditional Off) defines an area of the screen that hides the mouse. If you move the cursor to the upper-left part of the screen, Function 16 causes the mouse cursor to disappear. Mouse Function 3 (Get Button Status and Mouse Position) waits for you to press the left mouse button. When the left button is pressed, the program terminates.

```
{------------------------------------------------------------}
{    PDEMO.PAS - Mouse functions and Microsoft Pascal        }
{                                                            }
{    Program checks that mouse driver was installed,         }
{    displays a graphics cursor, and hides the cursor        }
{    if it moves into the upper-left part of the screen.     }
{    Program ends when left mouse button is pressed.         }
{                                                            }
{    Make File:                                              }
{                                                            }
{        pdemo.obj:    pdemo.pas                             }
{                pas1 pdemo;                                 }
{                pas2                                        }
{                                                            }
{        pdemo.exe:    pdemo.obj subs.obj                    }
{                link pdemo subs,,,..\mouse;                 }
{                                                            }
{------------------------------------------------------------}

program mtest(output);

procedure mouse1(vars m1,m2,m3,m4:word);extern;
procedure chkdrv;extern;
procedure graf;extern;

var
    m1,m2,m3,m4:word;
    Cursor : array [0..31]of word;
    bound  : array [0..3] of word;
    ptradd : array [1..2] of word;
    i, j : integer;

begin

    for i := 0 to 15  do cursor[i] := 16#ffff;
    Cursor[16] := 16#8000;
    Cursor[17] := 16#E000;
    Cursor[18] := 16#F800;
    Cursor[19] := 16#FE00;      {Initialize cursor array}
    Cursor[20] := 16#D800;
    Cursor[21] := 16#0C00;
    Cursor[22] := 16#0600;
    Cursor[23] := 16#0300;
    for j := 24 to 31 do Cursor[j] := 16#0000;
```

(continued)

257

continued

```
    chkdrv;                   {Check for mouse      }
                              {driver installation  }
    m1 := 0;                  {Function call 0      }
    mousel(m1,m2,m3,m4);      {Initialize mouse     }
    if ( m1 = 0 ) then        {No, output message   }
       writeln('Microsoft Mouse NOT found')
    else
       begin                  {Yes, demo Function 9}
                              { and Function 16     }
        graf;                 {set to graphics mode}

        m1:=9;                {Function call 9      }
        m2:=1;                { set graphics cursor}
        m3:=1;
        ptradd[1] := (ads Cursor).r; {offset  of the array}
        ptradd[2] := (ads Cursor).s; {segment of the array}
        mousel(m1,m2,m3,ptradd[1]);

        writeln('Mouse cursor will disappear within this area.');
        writeln('Press the right mouse button to EXIT.........');

        m1 := 1;                  {Function call 1    }
        mousel(m1,m2,m3,m4);      { show mouse cursor  }

        m1 := 16;             {Function call 16      }
        bound[0] := 0;        {Left  x coordinate    }
        bound[1] := 0;        {Upper y coordinate    }
        bound[2] := 390;      {Right x coordinate    }
        bound[3] := 25;       {Lower y coordinate    }
        ptradd[1] := (ads bound).r;  {offset  of the array}
        ptradd[2] := (ads bound).s;  {segment of the array}
        mousel(m1,m2,m3,ptradd[1]);

        m2 := 999;            {Dummy value for loop}
        repeat                {until...            }
           m1 := 3;                  {Function call 3, get}
           mousel( m1, m2, m3, m4 ); {current mouse status}
        until m2 := 2;        {Left button pressed }

      m1 := 0;            {Reset mouse driver       }
      mousel( m1, m2, m3, m4 );

      end
  end.
```

Chapter 10

Writing Mouse Programs for IBM EGA Modes

If your application program includes mouse support for IBM enhanced graphics modes D, E, F, and 10, your program must interact with the IBM Enhanced Graphics Adapter (EGA) through the new video interrupt functions provided in the mouse driver. You can simplify this programming by using a special library, the Microsoft EGA Register Interface library (EGA.LIB), which is included on the disks that come with this book. Or, if you are programming in a language that can call interrupts, the language can call the video interrupt functions directly.

To prevent unnecessary problems when using EGA graphics, follow this rule: If your program will modify the EGA registers and if it uses the mouse, then use the EGA Register Interface library. If your program will not modify the EGA hardware directly, you won't need to use the EGA.LIB library.

The EGA hardware uses several write-only registers to control the many EGA display attributes. However, without the new video interrupt functions, the mouse driver would be unable to keep track of the contents of these special registers, and it would be impossible to correctly update the mouse cursor position and shape when these registers were altered.

The EGA Register Interface lets your program write to and read from write-only registers on the EGA by keeping *shadow maps,* or working copies, of the registers. This capability is required for interrupt-driven graphics such as the cursor update code in the mouse driver.

THE EGA REGISTER INTERFACE LIBRARY

The Microsoft EGA Register Interface library consists of nine functions that you can call from MASM programs or from programs written in high-level languages such as Microsoft QuickBASIC, C, QuickC, FORTRAN, and Pascal. These functions do the following:

- Read from or write to one or more of the EGA write-only registers.

- Define default values for EGA write-only registers or reset the registers to these default values.

- Check whether the EGA Register Interface is present and if so, return its version number.

How the Interface Library Works

Current versions of the mouse driver install the EGA Register Interface library if the driver detects an EGA installed in the system. The interface maintains shadow maps of the EGA write-only registers, which lets application programs read these registers. The shadow maps are updated whenever your program calls one of the interface functions to set a register; therefore, the shadow maps always contain the last values written to the registers. When your program calls one of the interface functions to read a register, the function call returns the value stored in the shadow map.

The code in the interface intercepts mode-change calls to the ROM BIOS (Interrupt 10H with AH = 0) and updates the shadow maps and default register tables accordingly.

Calling the Library from MASM Programs

To call EGA Register Interface functions from a MASM program, do the following:

1. Load the AX, BX, CX, DX, and ES registers (as required) with the parameter values.

2. Execute software Interrupt 10H.

Values returned by the EGA Register Interface functions are placed in the registers.

NOTE: When called from MASM programs, Functions F2, F3, F4, F5, and F7 expect ES:BX to be a table pointer. These functions are discussed in detail later in this chapter.

MASM Example

Use the following instructions to set the palette registers to the values in the *mytable* array:

```
mytable db 00h,01h,02h,03h,04h,05h,14h,07h
        db 38h,39h,3ah,3bh,3ch,3dh,3eh,3fh
        .
        .
        .
        mov ax, ds
        mov es, ax              ;Set ES to the data segment
        mov bx, offset mytable  ;Now ES:BX --> mytable
        mov cx, 0010h           ;Starting at reg 0 for 16
        mov dx, 18h             ;18H = attribute chip
        mov ah, 0f3h            ;F3H = write register range
        int 10h                 ;Execute the interrupt
        .
        .
        .
```

Calling the Library from High-Level Language Programs

You can call EGA Register Interface functions from QuickBASIC, C, QuickC, FORTRAN, and Pascal programs by linking the programs with the EGA.LIB library. This library provides several calls that match the parameter passing and memory-model requirements of each language.

For all these languages, the EGA Register Interface call requires four integer parameters: *E1, E2, E3,* and *E4.* The following table shows how these parameters correspond to the registers listed in the function descriptions later in this chapter:

Parameter	Register
E1	AH
E2	BX
E3	CX
E4	DX

When your program calls the EGA Register Interface, the register copies the parameters into the corresponding registers, calls the video interrupt, and copies the returned register values back into the parameters.

For Function FA, the value returned in the ES register is placed in the *E4* parameter. The way the parameters are passed to the EGA Register Interface determines how the ES register is loaded. Those calls that use short parameter addresses (EGAS, *cegas*, and *cegam*) copy the DS register into ES. Those calls that use long parameter addresses (EGAL, *cegac*, and *cegal*) copy the segment part of the address pointed to by *E2* into the ES register.

Calling from QuickBASIC

To call the EGA Register Interface library from QuickBASIC programs, use the EGAS subprogram. For functions requiring a table, pass the first element of an integer array or pass the address of a string using the SADD function.

To access EGA.LIB from within the QuickBASIC environment, create a Quick Library that contains EGA.LIB. For example, the following command combines the QB.QLB, MOUSE.LIB, and EGA.LIB libraries into a composite Quick Library named QBNEW.QLB:

```
LINK /QU /NOE MOUSE.LIB+EGA.LIB+QB.LIB,QBNEW.QLB,NUL,BQLB45.LIB;
```

To load this new Quick Library with QuickBASIC, enter the following command:

```
QB /L QBNEW.QLB
```

Alternately, you can create the equivalent library file QBNEW.LIB by entering,

```
LIB QBNEW.LIB+MOUSE.LIB+EGA.LIB+QB.LIB;
```

This lets your programs compile and link into .EXE programs, which you can run from the MS-DOS prompt.

QuickBASIC example The following example prints the version number of the EGA Register Interface:

```
' Get version number of EGA Register Interface

DEFINT A-Z
```

(continued)

continued

```
e1 = &HFA       'Interrogate driver
e2 = 0

CALL egas(e1, e2, e3, e4)

IF e2 <> 0 THEN
    PRINT "EGA Register Interface found, version";
    DEF SEG = e4
    majorVersion = PEEK(e2)
    minorVersion = PEEK(e2 + 1)
    DEF SEG
    PRINT USING "##_.##"; majorVersion; minorVersion
ELSE
    PRINT "EGA Register Interface not found"
END IF
```

Calling from C and QuickC

To call the EGA Register Interface library from C programs, use the *cegas* function for small-model programs, the *cegam* function for medium-model programs, the *cegac* function for compact-model programs, or the *cegal* function for large-model programs. For functions requiring a table, pass a pointer to the name of a character array or a pointer to the array pointer.

To call the EGA Register Interface library from the QuickC programming environment, use the *cegam* function (the C function for medium-model programs) and add EGA.LIB to the program list. For functions requiring a table, pass a pointer to the name of a character array or a pointer to the array pointer.

C example In a small-model C program (versions 3.0 and later), the following example restores the default settings for the EGA registers:

```
int ah, bx, cx, dx;

ah = 0xF6;                /* Restore default settings */
cegas(&ah, &bx, &cx, &dx);
```

Calling from FORTRAN

To call the EGA Register Interface library from FORTRAN programs, use the EGAL subprogram. For functions requiring a table, pass the first element of an integer array (packed 2 bytes per integer).

FORTRAN example The EGA.FOR program calls EGAL to access the EGA Register Interface and uses Function FA to interrogate the driver. If the EGA Register Interface is present, its version number is displayed.

You must link this program with EGA.LIB so that you can use the EGAL call, and you must link this program with IPEEK.OBJ so that you can use the IPEEK function.

```
***************************************************************
*  EGA.FOR                                                    *
*                                                             *
*  Example of calling the EGA Register Interface from         *
*  FORTRAN                                                    *
*                                                             *
*  Compile using large model (default), and link with         *
*  IPEEK.OBJ and EGA.LIB                                       *
*                                                             *
*  Example:   fl /FPc ega.for ipeek.obj -link ega             *
***************************************************************

       PROGRAM EGA

       INTEGER*2 E1, E2, E3, E4
       INTEGER*2 MAJVER, MINVER

* Interrogate Driver
       E1 = #FA
       E2 = 0
       CALL EGAL (E1, E2, E3, E4)

* Check results
       IF (E2 .EQ. 0) GOTO 100

* Get the version numbers
       MAJVER = IPEEK(E4, E2)
       E2 = E2 + 1
       MINVER = IPEEK(E4, E2)

* Print the returned version number
       WRITE(*,10) MAJVER, MINVER
    10 FORMAT(1X,'EGA Register Interface found. Version ',I2,'.',I2)
```

(continued)

continued

```
* We're done
      GOTO 900

  100 CONTINUE

* EGA Register Interface wasn't found
      WRITE(*,*) 'EGA Register Interface not found.'

  900 CONTINUE
      END
```

You must assemble and link the IPEEK.ASM file with the EGA.FOR program. The IPEEK function lets a FORTRAN program get a byte from any location in memory.

```
;----------------------------------------------------------
; Function:      IPEEK
;
; Description:   Called from EGA.FOR to get a byte from
;                any location in memory.
;
; Example:       BYTVAL = IPEEK(SEG, OFS)
;
; To assemble:   MASM IPEEK;
;
;----------------------------------------------------------

.MODEL  LARGE
.CODE

        public  IPEEK

IPEEK   proc

; Standard entry
        PUSH  BP
        MOV   BP,SP
        PUSH  ES

; Load address, then load contents of first parameter into AX
        LES   BX,DWORD PTR[BP + 10]
        MOV   AX,ES:[BX]
```

(continued)

continued

```
; Save first parameter on stack (the segment for IPEEK)
        PUSH   AX

; Load address, then load contents of second parameter into AX
        LES    BX,DWORD PTR[BP + 6]

; Load the registers with the parameters
        MOV    BX,ES:[BX]   ; Offset into BX
        POP    ES           ; Segment into ES

; Peek at the byte
        MOV    AL,ES:[BX]

; Zero the high byte of AX
        XOR    AH,AH

; Clean up and exit
        POP    ES
        POP    BP
        RET    8

; All done
        IPEEK endp
        END
```

Calling from Pascal

To call the EGA Register Interface library from Pascal programs, use
the EGAS procedure if the argument addresses are in the program's
data segment (short addresses). If the arguments are in another segment (long addresses), use the EGAL procedure. For functions requiring a table, pass a pointer to the first element of an integer array
(packed 2 bytes per integer).

Pascal example In a Pascal program with long argument addresses,
include the following statement to declare EGAL as an external
procedure:

```
PROCEDURE EGAL
(VARS E1, E2, E3, E4:INTEGER);
EXTRN;
```

Once the procedure is declared, include the following statements to restore the default settings for the EGA registers:

```
E1  :=  246  (*Function number is 246 = F6 (hexadecimal)*)
EGAL (E1, E2, E3, E4)
```

Considerations When Calling ROM BIOS Video Routines

You need to be aware of certain considerations when your program uses the EGA Register Interface library. The EGA Register Interface library intercepts only those calls to the ROM BIOS video routines that change the screen mode (Interrupt 10H, AH = 0, AL = 13h or less). It does not intercept any other ROM BIOS video routine calls. However, any other ROM BIOS video routine calls should restore all registers, so using them is no problem.

A call to Interrupt 10H to set the color palette (AH = 0Bh) is an exception to this rule. You should use EGA Register Interface Function F5 (Write Register Set) to set the color palette. For more information about Function F5, see "EGA Register Interface Functions" later in this chapter.

Attribute Controller Registers

Before your application program uses the Attribute Controller registers (input/output address 3C0h) in one of the new Interrupt 10H calls, the program must set the Address or Data register flip-flop to the Address register. It does this by performing an input from input/output port 3BAh or C3DAh. The flip-flop is always reset to this state when the program returns from the Interrupt 10H call. (Note: The version of EGA.LIB included with this book sets the Address or Data register flip-flop to the Address register automatically.)

An interrupt routine that accesses the attribute chip always leaves the flip-flop set to the Address register when the program returns from the interrupt call. Therefore, if your application program sets the flip-flop to the Data register and expects the flip-flop to remain in this state, the program must disable interrupts between the time it sets the flip-flop to the Data register state and the last time the flip-flop is assumed to be in this state.

Sequencer Memory Mode Register

When the Sequencer Memory Mode register (input/output address 3C5h, Data register 4) is accessed, the sequencer produces a glitch on the CAS lines that can cause problems with video random-access memory (VRAM). As a result, your application program cannot use the EGA Register Interface to read from or write to this register. Instead, use the following procedure to alter this register:

1. Disable the interrupts.

2. Set Synchronous Reset (bit 1) in the Sequencer Reset register to 0.

3. Read from, write to, or modify the Sequencer Memory Mode register.

4. Set Synchronous Reset (bit 1) in the Sequencer Reset register to 1.

5. Enable the interrupts.

Input Status Registers

Your application program cannot use the EGA Register Interface to read Input Status registers 0 (input/output address 3C2h) and 1 (input/output address 3BAh or 3DAh). If the program must read these registers, it should do so directly.

Graphics Controller Miscellaneous Register

When the Graphics Controller Miscellaneous register (input/output address 3CFh, Data register 6) is accessed, a glitch on the CAS lines occurs that can cause problems with video random-access memory (VRAM). As a result, your application program should not use the EGA Register Interface to read from or write to this register.

EGA Register Interface Function F6 (Revert to Default Registers) doesn't alter the state of the Graphics Controller Miscellaneous register. Use the following procedure to alter this register:

1. Disable the interrupts.

2. Set Synchronous Reset (bit 1) in the Sequencer Reset register to 0.

3. Read from, write to, or modify the Graphics Controller Miscellaneous register.

4. Set Synchronous Reset (bit 1) in the Sequencer Reset register to 1.

5. Enable the interrupts.

EGA Register Interface Functions

The following table shows the number and the name of each function described in detail in this chapter:

Function Number (Hex)	Function Name
F0	Read One Register
F1	Write One Register
F2	Read Register Range
F3	Write Register Range
F4	Read Register Set
F5	Write Register Set
F6	Revert to Default Registers
F7	Define Default Register Table
FA	Interrogate Driver

NOTE: Function calls F8H, F9H, and FBH through FFH are reserved.
Each function description includes the following:

- The parameters required to make the call (input) and the expected return values (output)

- Any special considerations regarding the function

If the function description doesn't specify an input value for a parameter, you don't need to supply a value for that parameter before making the call. If the function description doesn't specify an output value for a parameter, the parameter's value is the same before and after the call.

NOTE: The EGA Register Interface doesn't check input values, so be sure that the values you load into the registers are correct before making a call.

FUNCTION F0: READ ONE REGISTER

Function F0 reads data from a specified register on the EGA.

Call with AH = F0h

BX = Pointer for pointer/data chips:

BH = 0

BL = pointer

Ignored for single registers

DX = Port number:

Pointer/data chips

00h: CRT Controller (3B4h for monochrome modes;
3D4h for color modes)

08h: Sequencer (3C4h)

10h: Graphics Controller (3CEh)

18h: Attribute Controller (3C0h)

Single registers

20h: Miscellaneous Output register (3C2h)

28h: Feature Control register (3B4h for monochrome
modes; 3D4h for color modes)

30h: Graphics 1 Position register (3CCh)

38h: Graphics 2 Position register (3CAh)

Returns AX: Restored

BH: Restored

BL: Data

DX: Restored

All other registers restored

Examples The following example saves the contents of the Sequencer Map Mask
register in *myvalue*:

```
myvalue db  ?

        mov ah, 0f0h        ;F0 = read one register
        mov bx, 0002h       ;BH = 0 / BL = map mask index
        mov dx, 0008h       ;DX = sequencer
        int 10h             ;Call the interrupt
        mov myvalue, bl     ;Save the value
```

The following example saves the contents of the Miscellaneous Output register in *myvalue*:

```
myvalue db  ?

        mov ah, 0f0h       ;F0 = read one register
        mov dx, 0020h      ;DX = miscellaneous output register
        int 10h            ;Call the interrupt
        mov myvalue, bl    ;Save the value
```

FUNCTION F1: WRITE ONE REGISTER

Function F1 writes data to a specified register on the EGA.

When your application program returns from a call to Function F1, the contents of the BH and DX registers are not restored. If you want to save and restore these registers, you must instruct your application program to do so.

Call with
AH = F1h
BL = Pointer for pointer/data chips
   or
   Data for single registers
BH = Data for pointer/data chips (ignored for single registers)
DX = Port number:
   Pointer/data chips
      00h: CRT Controller (3B4h for monochrome modes; 3D4h for color modes)
      08h: Sequencer (3C4h)
      10h: Graphics Controller (3CEh)
      18h: Attribute Controller (3C0h)
   Single registers
      20h: Miscellaneous Output register (3C2h)
      28h: Feature Control register (3B4h for monochrome modes; 3D4h for color modes)
      30h: Graphics 1 Position register (3CCh)
      38h: Graphics 2 Position register (3CAh)

Returns
AX: Restored
BL: Restored
BH: Not restored
DX: Not restored
All other registers restored

Examples The following example writes the contents of *myvalue* into the CRT Controller Cursor Start register:

```
myvalue db  3h

        mov ah, 0f1h    ; F1 = write one register
        mov bh, myvalue ; BH = data from myvalue
        mov bl, 000ah   ; BL = cursor start index
        xor dx, dx      ; DX = crt controller
        int 10h         ; Call the interrupt
```

The following example writes the contents of *myvalue* into the Feature Control register:

```
myvalue db  2h

        mov ah, 0f1h     ; F1 = write one register
        mov bl, myvalue  ; BL = data from myvalue
        mov dx, 0028h    ; DX = feature control register
        int 10h          ; Call the interrupt
```

FUNCTION F2: READ REGISTER RANGE

Function F2 reads data from a specified range of registers on the EGA. (A range of registers is several registers on a single chip that have consecutive indexes.) This call makes sense only for the pointer/data chips.

Call with

AH = F2h
CH = Starting pointer value
CL = Number of registers (must be > 1)
DX = Port number:
    00h: CRT Controller (3B4h for monochrome modes; 3D4h for color modes)
    08h: Sequencer (3C4h)
    10h: Graphics Controller (3CEh)
    18h: Attribute Controller (3C0h)
ES:BX = Points to a table of one-byte entries (length = value in CL). On return, each entry is set to the contents of the corresponding register.

Returns

AX: Restored
BX: Restored
CX: Not restored
DX: Restored
ES: Restored
All other registers restored

Example

The following example saves the contents of the Attribute Controller Palette registers in *paltable*:

```
paltable db  16 dup (?)

        mov ax, ds            ; Assume paltable in
                              ; data segment
        mov es, ax            ; ES = data segment
        mov bx, offset paltable ; ES:BX = paltable address
        mov ah, 0f2h          ; F2 = read register range
        mov cx, 0010h         ; CH = start index of 0
                              ; CL = 16 registers
                              ; to read
        mov dx, 0018h         ; DX = attribute
                              ; controller
        int 10h               ; Call the interrupt
```

FUNCTION F3: WRITE REGISTER RANGE

Function F3 writes data to a specified range of registers on the EGA. (A range of registers is several registers on a single chip that have consecutive indexes.) This call makes sense only for the pointer/data chips.

Call with AH = F3h
CH = Starting pointer value
CL = Number of registers (must be > 1)
DX = Port number
00h: CRT Controller (3B4h for monochrome modes; 3D4h for color modes)
08h: Sequencer (3C4h)
10h: Graphics Controller (3CEh)
18h: Attribute Controller (3C0h)
ES:BX = Points to a table of one-byte entries (length = value in CL). Each entry contains the value to be written to the corresponding register.

Returns AX: Restored
BX: Not restored
CX: Not restored
DX: Not restored
ES: Restored
All other registers restored

Example The following example writes the contents of *cursloc* into the CRT Controller Cursor Location High and Cursor Location Low registers.

```
cursloc db  01h, 00h         ; Cursor at page
                             ; offset 0100h

        mov ax, ds           ; Assume cursloc in
                             ; data segment
        mov es, ax           ; ES = data segment
        mov bx, offset cursloc ; ES:BX = cursloc address
        mov ah, 0f3h         ; F3 = write register
                             ; range
        mov cx, 0e02h        ; CH = start index of 14
                             ; CL = 2 registers to
                             ; write
        xor dx, dx           ; DX = crt controller
        int 10h              ; Call the interrupt
```

FUNCTION F4: READ REGISTER SET

Function F4 reads data from a set of registers on the EGA. (A set of registers is several registers that might or might not have consecutive indexes and that might or might not be on the same chip.)

Call with   AH   = F4h

CX   = Number of registers (must be > 1)

ES:BX   = Points to table of records with each entry in the following format:

Byte 0: Port number

Pointer/data chips

00h: CRT Controller (3B4h for monochrome modes; 3D4h for color modes)

08h: Sequencer (3C4h)

10h: Graphics Controller (3CEh)

18h: Attribute Controller (3C0h)

Single registers

20h: Miscellaneous Output register (3C2h)

28h: Feature Control register (3B4h for monochrome modes; 3D4h for color modes)

30h: Graphics 1 Position register (3CCh)

38h: Graphics 2 Position register (3CAh)

Byte 1: Must be zero

Byte 2: Pointer value (0 for single registers)

Byte 3: EGA Register Interface fills in data read from register specified in bytes 0 through 2

Returns   AX: Restored

BX: Restored

CX: Not restored

ES: Restored

All other registers restored

Example   The following example saves the contents of the Miscellaneous Output register, Sequencer Memory Mode register, and CRT Controller Mode Control register in *results*:

```
outvals dw  0020h ; Miscellaneous Output register
        db  0     ; 0 for single registers
        db  ?     ; Returned value

        dw  0008h ; Sequencer
        db  04h   ; Memory Mode register index
        db  ?     ; Returned value

        dw  0000h ; CRT Controller
        db  17h   ; Mode Control register index
        db  ?     ; Returned value

results db  3 dup (?)

        mov ax, ds            ; Assume outvals in
                              ; data segment
        mov es, ax            ; ES = data segment
        mov bx, offset outvals ; ES:BX = outvals address
        mov ah, 0f4h          ; F4 = read register set
        mov cx, 3             ; Number of entries in
                              ; outvals
        int 10h               ; Get values into outvals
        mov si, offset outvals +3  ; Move the returned
                                   ; values from outvals
        mov di, offset results ; to results
        mov cx, 3             ; 3 values to move
        cld                   ; Make moves forward

movloop: movsb                ; Move one value from outvals
                              ; to results
        add si, 3             ; Skip to next source byte
        loop movloop          ; Get next byte
```

FUNCTION F5: WRITE REGISTER SET

Function F5 writes data to a set of registers on the EGA. (A set of registers is several registers that might or might not have consecutive indexes and that might or might not be on the same chip.)

Call with
AH = F5h
CX = Number of registers (must be > 1)
ES:BX = Points to table of values with each entry in the following format:

Byte 0: Port number

Pointer/data chips

00h: CRT Controller (3B4h for monochrome modes; 3D4h for color modes)

08h: Sequencer (3C4h)

10h: Graphics Controller (3CEh)

18h: Attribute Controller (3C0h)

Single registers

20h: Miscellaneous Output register (3C2h)

28h: Feature Control register (3B4h for monochrome modes; 3D4h for color modes)

30h: Graphics 1 Position register (3CCh)

38h: Graphics 2 Position register (3CAh)

Byte 1: Must be zero

Byte 2: Pointer value (0 for single registers)

Byte 3: Data to be written to register specified in bytes 0 through 2

Returns
AX: Restored
BX: Restored
CX: Not restored
ES: Restored

All other registers restored

Example   The following example writes the contents of *outvals* to the Miscellaneous Output register, Sequencer Memory Mode register, and CRT
Controller Mode Control register:

```
outvals dw   0020h ; Miscellaneous Output register
        db   0     ; 0 for single registers
        db   0a7h  ; Output value

        dw   0008h ; Sequencer
        db   04h   ; Memory Mode register index
        db   03h   ; Output value

        dw   0000h ; CRT Controller
        db   17h   ; Mode Control register index
        db   0a3h  ; Output value

        mov ax, ds              ; Assume outvals in
                                ; data segment
        mov es, ax              ; ES = data segment
        mov bx, offset outvals  ; ES:BX = outvals address
        mov ah, 0f5h            ; F5 = write register set
        mov cx, 3               ; Number of entries in
                                ; outvals
        int 10h                 ; Call the interrupt
```

FUNCTION F6: REVERT TO DEFAULT REGISTERS

Function F6 restores the default settings of any registers your application program changed through the EGA Register Interface. The default settings are defined in a call to Function F7.

Call with   AH   = F6h

Returns   All registers restored

> *NOTE: If your program makes a call to Interrupt 10H, Function 0, to set the display mode, the default register values change to the BIOS values for the selected mode.*

Example   The following example restores the default settings of the EGA registers:

```
mov ah, 0f6h  ; F6 = revert to default registers
int 10h       ; Call the interrupt
```

FUNCTION F7: DEFINE DEFAULT REGISTER TABLE

Function F7 defines a table that contains default values for any pointer/ data chip or single register. If you define default values for a pointer/ data chip, you must define them for all registers within that chip.

WARNING: Function F7 sets the default values for all registers within a chip. You must know what to set in all affected registers to prevent unwanted results. Some combinations of register settings might cause physical damage to the EGA adapter or the monitor.

Call with
AH = F7h
CX = VGA Color Select Flag:
5448h: Allows the EGA Register Interface to recognize byte off-set 14h of the table pointed to by ES:BX as the value for the VGA color select register.
DX = Port number:
Pointer/data chips
00h: CRT Controller (3B4h for monochrome modes; 3D4h for color modes)
08h: Sequencer (3C4h)
10h: Graphics Controller (3CEh)
18h: Attribute Controller (3C0h)
Single registers
20h: Miscellaneous Output register (3C2h)
28h: Feature Control register (3B4h for monochrome modes; 3D4h for color modes)
30h: Graphics 1 Position register (3CCh)
38h: Graphics 2 Position register (3CAh)
ES:BX = Points to a table of one-byte entries. Each entry contains the default value for the corresponding register. The table must contain entries for all registers.

Returns
AX: Restored
BX: Not restored
DX: Not restored
ES: Restored
All other registers restored

Examples   The following example defines default values for the Attribute
Controller:

```
attrdflt db   00h, 01h, 02h, 03h, 04h, 05h, 06h, 07h
         db   10h, 11h, 12h, 13h, 14h, 15h, 16h, 17h
         db   08h, 00h, 0fh, 00h, 00h

         mov ax, ds               ; Assume attrdflt in
                                  ; data segment
         mov es, ax               ; ES = data segment
         mov bx, offset attrdflt  ; ES:BX = attrdflt
                                  ; address
         mov ah, 0f7h             ; F7 = define default
                                  ; register table
         xor cx,cx                ; No VGA color select register
         mov dx, 0018h            ; DX = attribute
                                  ; controller
         int 10h                  ; Call the interrupt
```

The following example defines a default value for the Feature
Control register:

```
featdflt db   00h

         mov ax, ds               ; Assume featdflt in
                                  ; data segment
         mov es, ax               ; ES = data segment
         mov bx, offset featdflt  ; ES:BX = featdflt
                                  ; address
         mov ah, 0f7h             ; F7 = define default
                                  ; register table
         mov dx, 0028h            ; DX = feature control
                                  ; register
         int 10h                  ; Call the interrupt
```

FUNCTION FA: INTERROGATE DRIVER

Function FA interrogates the mouse driver and returns a value that specifies whether the mouse driver is present.

Call with   AH = FAh

                 BX = 0

Returns   AX   = Restored

             BX   = 0 if mouse driver is not present

             ES:BX = Points to EGA Register Interface version number, if present:

                          Byte 0: Major release number

                          Byte 1: Minor release number (in $1/100$ths)

Example   The following example interrogates the mouse driver and displays the result:

```
gotmsg db  "EGA Register Interface found", 0dh, 0ah, "$"
nopmsh db  "EGA Register Interface not found", 0dh, 0ah, "$"
revmsg db  "Revision $"
crlf   db  0dh, 0ah, "$"


ten    db  10

           xor bx, bx              ; Must be 0 for this call
           mov ah, 0fah            ; FA = interrogate driver
           int 10h                 ; Interrogate!
           or  bx, bx              ; BX = 0 ?
           jnz found               ; Branch if driver present
           mov dx, offset nopmsg   ; Assume nopmsg in data
                                   ; segment
           mov ah, 09h             ; 9 = print string
           int 21h                 ; Output not found message
           jmp continue            ; That's all for now

found: mov dx, offset gotmsg   ; Assume gotmsg in data
                                   ; segment
           mov ah, 09h             ; 9 = print string
           int 21h                 ; Output found message
           mov dx, offset revmsg   ; Assume revmsg in data
                                   ; segment
```

(continued)

283

continued

```
        mov ah, 09h              ; 9 = print string
        int 21h                  ; Output "revision"
        mov dl, es:[bx]          ; DL = major release number
        add dl, "0"              ; Convert to ASCII
        mov ah, 2                ; 2 = display character
        int 21h                  ; Output major release
                                 ; number
        mov dl, "."              ; DL = "."
        mov ah, 2                ; 2 = display character
        int 21h                  ; Output a period
        mov al, es:[bx + 1]      ; AL = minor release number
        xor ah, ah               ; AH = 0
        idiv ten                 ; AL = 10ths, AH = 100ths
        mov bx, ax               ; Save AX in BX
        mov dl, al               ; DL = 10ths
        add dl, "0"              ; Convert to ASCII
        mov ah, 2                ; 2 = display character
        int 21h                  ; Output minor release 10ths
        mov dl, bh               ; DL = 100ths
        add dl, "0"              ; Convert to ASCII
        mov ah, 2                ; 2 = display character
        int 21h                  ; Output minor release
                                 ; 100ths
        mov dx, offset crlf      ; Assume crlf in data
                                 ; segment
        mov ah, 09h              ; 9 = print string
        int 21h                  ; Output end of line
continue:                        ; The end
```

PART IV

Appendixes

Appendix A

Mouse Command Line Switches

This appendix describes the mouse command line switches you can use to customize the operation of the Control Panel and the mouse driver.

CONTROL PANEL SWITCHES

The Control Panel (CPANEL.EXE), which is included with the Microsoft Mouse, is a memory-resident program that lets you adjust the mouse sensitivity level—the ratio of cursor movement to actual mouse movement. (For information on using the Control Panel, see Chapter 4, "Moving the Mouse," in your Microsoft Mouse User's Guide.)

Whenever you invoke the Control Panel, the CPANEL program reserves memory for the area of the screen the Control Panel overlays. The amount of memory required depends on the type of display adapter you use and the complexity of the image the Control Panel overlays. You can change the Control Panel's default size for the overlay buffer by using a command line switch to change the amount of memory reserved by the Control Panel. If your system beeps when you activate the Control Panel, however, the screen buffer is too small and you must increase the size of the buffer.

Use one of the following command line switches to change the size of the buffer, depending on the type of display adapter installed in your system:

Use This Switch	For This Display Adapter
/Cn	IBM Color/Graphics Adapter
/En	IBM Enhanced Graphics Adapter
/Hn	Hercules Graphics Card
/Mn	IBM Monochrome Adapter
/An	AT&T 6300 Display Adapter

The n placeholder is a number ranging from 0 through 9. The larger the number, the larger the screen overlay buffer. If you do not specify a switch and a number, the default switch and number (/E7) are used.

The size of the buffer required depends on the screen mode that the Control Panel overlays. For example, screens displayed in the enhanced graphics modes require a larger Control Panel overlay buffer than screens displayed in the text modes do.

In general, you should specify a value ranging from 0 through 4 if the Control Panel will overlay only text screens. If the Control Panel will overlay graphics screens, you should specify a value ranging from 5 through 9.

The following table shows how many bytes of memory are occupied by the Control Panel and buffer for each switch setting:

			Switch		
Setting	/M	/H	/A	/C	/E
0	9712	14240	14992	9360	9360
1	9760	14288	15040	9456	9456
2	9808	14336	15088	9552	9552
3	9856	14384	15136	9744	9744
4	9904	14432	15184	10128	10128
5	9952	14480	15232	11872	19088
6	10000	14528	15280	12128	19344
7	10048	14576	15328	14768	29168
8	10096	14624	15376	15024	29424
9	10144	14672	15424	15280	29680

Using a Control Panel Switch

You use a Control Panel switch to specify the size of the overlay buffer when you load the Control Panel into memory. If the Control Panel is already in memory, you must first remove it from memory.

To remove the Control Panel from memory, type **cpanel off**.

To specify the size of a screen buffer when you load the Control Panel, type **cpanel** followed by the appropriate switch.

For example, to specify the largest possible screen buffer for the area the Control Panel overlays on a CGA system, you would type **cpanel/C9**.

MOUSE DRIVER SWITCHES

You use mouse driver command line switches to do the following:

- Specify the mouse sensitivity.

- Set the interrupt rate (for the InPort mouse only).

- Tell the mouse driver the type and location of the Microsoft Mouse installed in your system so that the driver can bypass its usual procedure for determining mouse hardware configuration.

- Disable the mouse driver or remove it from memory.

Using a Mouse Driver Switch

You can add mouse driver command line switches to the mouse command lines in the AUTOEXEC.BAT or CONFIG.SYS file, or you can type **mouse** and the command line switches at the MS-DOS prompt. If you type one or more switches at the MS-DOS prompt, you must leave a space between **mouse** and each switch.

The following sections describe how to use the mouse driver command line switches.

Specifying Mouse Sensitivity

Use the following command line switches to set mouse sensitivity levels:

Use This Switch	*To Set*
/S*nnn*	Horizontal and vertical sensitivity
/H*nnn*	Horizontal sensitivity only
/V*nnn*	Vertical sensitivity only
/D*nnn*	Double-speed threshold

The *nnn* placeholder is a number ranging from 0 through 100.

The switches for horizontal and vertical sensitivity are interpreted in the same manner as a Control Panel setting is interpreted. The double-speed-threshold switch determines the threshold speed for doubling the cursor's motion on the screen. Setting a double-speed threshold makes it easier to move the cursor to widely separated images on the screen. For example, the following command sets the vertical sensitivity to 20 and the double-speed threshold to 32:

```
MOUSE /V20 /D32
```

You can also use Mouse Function 19 to build this feature into an application program. For more information on Function 19, see Chapter 8, "Mouse Function Calls."

Setting the Interrupt Rate for the InPort Mouse

If you use an InPort mouse, you can use one of the following command line switch settings to specify the interrupt rate for the mouse:

Switch Setting	Interrupt Rate
/R0	Disabled
/R1	30 Hz (default)
/R2	50 Hz
/R3	100 Hz
/R4	200 Hz

Specifying the Type and Location of the Mouse

The command line switches described in this section do the following:

- They direct the mouse driver to bypass its usual search to determine the mouse hardware configuration.

- They look for a specific type of Microsoft mouse at a specific input/output port.

You will find this feature useful if:

- The mouse driver has trouble determining which port the mouse is connected to, given your system's configuration.

- More than one InPort device is connected to your computer.

- You want to decrease the time required to load the mouse driver.

The following table lists each switch you can use to tell the mouse driver to look for a specific mouse hardware configuration:

Use This Switch	To Look For
/B	Bus or InPort mouse at primary InPort address
/I1	InPort mouse at primary InPort address
/I2	InPort mouse at secondary InPort address
/C1	Serial mouse on COM1
/C2	Serial mouse on COM2

NOTE: At this time, the PS/2 mouse port doesn't have a switch.

Disabling or Removing the Mouse Driver

If necessary, you can disable the mouse driver or remove it from memory. However, before you disable or remove the mouse driver, you must remove the Control Panel from memory and you must also end any mouse menu program you are using in addition to any other TSR program you loaded after you loaded the mouse menu.

To remove the Control Panel from memory, type **cpanel off**.

To end a Microsoft Expert mouse menu program, type *filename* **off**. (*Filename* is the name of the Expert mouse menu program.)

To end a mouse menu program that you wrote yourself, type **menu off**.

To disable or remove the mouse driver from memory, type **mouse off**.

When you type **mouse off**, one of the following actions occurs:

- If your mouse driver is MOUSE.SYS, it is disabled.

- If your mouse driver is MOUSE.COM, it is removed from memory.

Appendix B

Domestic Mouse Driver Messages

This appendix lists the messages that the domestic mouse driver might display. It also describes possible causes of the messages and the actions you can take in response to them.

Invalid parameter

You typed an invalid parameter in a command line switch. For more information on command line switches, see Appendix A, "Mouse Command Line Switches."

Driver not installed—Internal Error 1

Insufficient space was found to load the interrupt service routine. If you receive this message, please call Microsoft Product Support.

Driver not installed—Microsoft Mouse not found

The mouse hardware was not found on the system in which the mouse driver attempted to install itself. A hardware component in your computer might be defective.

Driver not installed—interrupt jumper missing

A jumper on the bus card of a bus or InPort mouse is missing. You need to verify that the jumper has been installed. You might also need to select another interrupt position.

Driver not installed—multiple interrupt jumpers found

The mouse driver detected multiple interrupt jumpers on an InPort mouse. You need to verify that only one jumper block is present on the interrupt select jumper.

MSX Mouse driver installed

The driver for an MSX mouse on an MSX system was installed. No action is required.

Mouse driver installed

The installation of the mouse driver was successful. No action is required.

Switch values passed to existing mouse driver

Command-line switch values were passed to the existing driver when you reran MOUSE.COM from the MS-DOS prompt. No action is required.

Existing mouse driver enabled

The previously loaded mouse driver was enabled when you reran MOUSE.COM from the command line while a mouse driver was present. No action is required.

Existing mouse driver removed from memory

An existing mouse driver was removed from memory. No action is required.

Existing mouse driver disabled

An existing mouse driver was disabled, but the driver was not unloaded from memory. No action is required.

Mouse driver not installed

You used the *mouse off* command line, but no mouse driver was installed.

Mouse driver installed, cannot change port (/i, /c, and /b invalid)

The mouse driver was successfully installed to use either an InPort port, a serial port, or a bus port. Once the driver has been successfully installed, you can't use the command-line switch to change the port.

Mouse driver already installed

You are trying to install another copy of MOUSE.SYS on top of an existing one. Check your CONFIG.SYS file and modify it to load only one copy of the driver.

Unable to disable Mouse driver—Control Panel is active

You can't disable the mouse driver when Control Panel is active. Disable Control Panel by entering **cpanel off** with the appropriate pathname at the MS-DOS prompt. You can now unload the mouse driver.

Unable to disable Mouse driver—Mouse Menu is active

You can't unload the mouse driver while a mouse menu is active in the system. Type **menu off** to disable the mouse menu.

Appendix C:

Mouse Menu Messages

This appendix lists the messages that the MENU program and the MAKEMENU utility might display, along with descriptions of possible causes and the actions you can take in response to them.

nnnn error(s) detected

This message informs you how many errors MAKEMENU detected while attempting to process the .DEF file.

nnnn symbol(s) used

After successfully converting the .DEF file, MAKEMENU presents this message telling you how many symbols were used in the .DEF file.

xxxxxx before BEGIN

The first statement in your .DEF file must be a BEGIN statement. Correct the .DEF file and run MAKEMENU again.

Cannot use system reserved label: *xxxxxx*

One of the labels in the .DEF file is reserved for use by MAKEMENU. Change each occurrence of the specified label in the .DEF file and run MAKEMENU again.

Cannot use system reserved parameter: *xxxxxx*

One of the parameters in the .DEF file is reserved for use by MAKEMENU. Change each occurrence of the specified parameter in the .DEF file and run MAKEMENU again.

Close quote missing

A statement in the .DEF file contained an item missing a closing quotation mark. Correct the .DEF file and run MAKEMENU again.

Conversion completed

The MAKEMENU utility has finished creating a loadable menu file. No action is required. The MS-DOS system prompt appears after MAKEMENU displays this message.

Error—Invalid statement: *xxxxx*

The statement didn't have a label, the statement's label didn't end with a colon (:), the statement had an invalid parameter, or a syntax error occurred. Be sure that all statements (except the BEGIN statement and statements within menu and pop-up subroutines) are labeled. Also, be sure that each label is followed by a colon. Check the statement syntax for correct use of commas and spaces.

Error—Label already used: *xxxxx*

The same label was used to name more than one statement. Be sure that the labels are unique for each statement.

Error—Label not found: *xxxxx*

A label specified for a parameter did not exist. Be sure that the statements have labels and that the labels are correct.

Extra colon after label: *xxxxx*

MAKEMENU detected an extra colon after one of the labels. You can use only one colon after a label. Correct the .DEF file and run MAKEMENU again.

Illegal function call at address *nnnn*

A TYPE or an EXECUTE statement had too many parameters, a SELECT statement defined the item-selection area outside the menu, or a SELECT or an OPTION statement had quotation marks placed incorrectly. Use the correct number of parameters, redefine the item-selection area, or ensure that double-quotation marks are used correctly to designate text strings.

Invalid statement

MAKEMENU detected an invalid statement in the .DEF file. Correct the .DEF file and run MAKEMENU again.

Keyboard emulation off

The mouse menu program is no longer running. No action is required.

Keyboard emulation on

The mouse menu program is running. No action is required.

xxxxxx — Label pointer not found

One of the statement parameters refers to a label that does not exist in the file. Correct the .DEF file and run MAKEMENU again.

Label previously used

You used the same label twice in the same program. Correct the .DEF file and run MAKEMENU again.

Menu installed

You started up a mouse menu program, and it is running. No action is required. Use the mouse menu as usual.

Must run under DOS 2.00 or later

You cannot use MAKEMENU with a version of MS-DOS earlier than 2.00.

Name of file to convert:

You typed **makemenu** to create a loadable mouse menu file. Type in a mouse menu filename without the .DEF extension.

OPTION statement before MENU statement

You can use OPTION statements only within a MENU/MEND subroutine. Correct the .DEF file and run MAKEMENU again.

Program too large

The size of the mouse menu .DEF file will cause the resulting .MNU file to be larger than the maximum size of 57 KB. Reduce the size of the .DEF file.

Too many symbols (user-defined labels)

Your .DEF file used more than 967 symbols. (MAKEMENU allows 1,000 symbols. However, MAKEMENU uses 33, so only 967 are available to the user.) Correct the .DEF file and run MAKEMENU again.

Appendix D

Linking Existing Mouse Programs with MOUSE.LIB

If you have a high-level language program that links with an earlier version of the Microsoft Mouse library, you might need to modify the program to link it with the new MOUSE.LIB library on the disks that come with this book.

The new MOUSE.LIB library works in the same way as did previous mouse libraries except that the new library has the following new features:

- New Mouse Functions 24, 25, 26, 27, 28, 29, 30, 31, 32, 33, 34, 35, and 36.

- You must pass the fourth parameter (*M4%*) of Mouse Function 9 by reference instead of by value.

- Mouse Function 16 requires four parameters instead of five.

If your program doesn't call Functions 9 or 16, you can link it with the new MOUSE.LIB library without modification.

If your program calls Functions 9 or 16, you must modify the program so that it conforms with the new interface definitions before you can link it with the new MOUSE.LIB.

Appendix E

Making Calls from Borland Turbo Pascal Programs

To call mouse functions from a program in Borland Turbo Pascal, use the following procedure, which passes the correct parameters to the mouse driver. Include this procedure in your code, and then call the mouse functions by passing values into this procedure.

```
Procedure Mouse ( Var m1, m2, m3, m4, m5 : integer );

Var
   CpuReg: record of
              AX, BX, CX, DX, BP,
              SI, DI, DS, ES, FLAGS: integer;
           end;

begin {mouse}

   if m1 >= 0 then
      begin
         CpuReg.AX := m1;          {Load parameters  }
         CpuReg.BX := m2;          { into appropriate}
         CpuReg.CX := m3;          { registers       }
```

(continued)

continued

```
        if (m1 = 9) or (m1 = 12) or (m1 = 20)
          or (m1 = 22) or (m1 = 23) or (m1 = 24) then
          begin
            CpuReg.DX := ofs (m4); {m4 = pointer of }
            CpuReg.ES := seg (m4); { the address of }
          end;                       { the user array }
                                     { or subroutine  }


        else if m1 = 16
          begin
            CpuReg.CX := m2; {Left  x coordinate}
            CpuReg.DX := m3; {Upper y coordinate}
            CpuReg.SI := m4; {Right x coordinate}
            CpuReg.DI := m5; {Lower y coordinate}
          end;
        else
            CpuReg.DX := m4;

        intr ($33, CpuReg);    {Call mouse driver }
                               { at Interrupt 33H }

        m1 := CpuReg.AX;       {Return values back}
        m2 := CpuReg.BX;       { to parameters    }
        m3 := CpuReg.CX;
        m4 := CpuReg.DX;

        if (m1 = 20) then      {Special returns   }
          m2:= CpuReg.ES;

      end;

end; {mouse}
```

Appendix F

Using the Mouse with the Hercules Graphics Card

Before you use the Hercules Monochrome Graphics Card with a program that has built-in mouse support, you must do the following:

1. Put the Hercules card into graphics mode. (If necessary, see the documentation that came with your Hercules card).

2. If the Hercules card is using CRT page 0, store a *6* in memory location 40H:49H. If the Hercules card is using CRT page 1, store a *5* in memory location 40H:49H.

3. Call Mouse Function 0 to set the mouse cursor boundaries and CRT page number to the appropriate values.

If you are using Microsoft C and MSHERC.COM or Microsoft QuickBASIC and QBHERC.COM, you should follow the steps in this order:

1. If the Hercules card is using CRT page 0, store a *6* in memory location 40H:49H. If the Hercules card is using CRT page 1, store a *5* in memory location 40H:49H.

2. Call Mouse Function 0 to set the mouse cursor boundaries and CRT page number to the appropriate values.

3. Put the Hercules card into graphics mode. (If necessary, see the documentation that came with your Hercules card).

Appendix G

ASCII Character Set

This appendix provides tables for the ASCII standard character set, the IBM extended character set, and the line-drawing characters in the extended character set. In addition, the section at the end of this appendix discusses how you can use ASCII characters and extended-keyboard-scan codes with the TYPE statement.

ASCII TABLES

Figures G-1 and G-2 show all 256 characters of the IBM extended character set supported by most computers that run MS-DOS. The figures show the characters in four columns; each character is followed by its corresponding code in decimal and hexadecimal. Many compatible printers print the full character set; if you're not sure about your printer, check its manual.

The ASCII Standard Character Set

Figure G-1 shows the first 128 characters (codes 0 through 127) of the ASCII standard character set.

ASCII	Dec	Hex	ASCII	Dec	Hex	ASCII	Dec	Hex	ASCII	Dec	Hex
	0	00	\<space\>	32	20	@	64	40		96	60
☺	1	01	!	33	21	A	65	41	a	97	61
☻	2	02	"	34	22	B	66	42	b	98	62
♥	3	03	#	35	23	C	67	43	c	99	63
♦	4	04	$	36	24	D	68	44	d	100	64
♣	5	05	%	37	25	E	69	45	e	101	65
♠	6	06	&	38	26	F	70	46	f	102	66
•	7	07	'	39	27	G	71	47	g	103	67
◘	8	08	(	40	28	H	72	48	h	104	68
○	9	09	)	41	29	I	73	49	i	105	69
◎	10	0A	*	42	2A	J	74	4A	j	106	6A
♂	11	0B	+	43	2B	K	75	4B	k	107	6B
♀	12	0C	,	44	2C	L	76	4C	l	108	6C
♪	13	0D	−	45	2D	M	77	4D	m	109	6D
♫	14	0E	.	46	2E	N	78	4E	n	110	6E
☼	15	0F	/	47	2F	O	79	4F	o	111	6F
►	16	10	0	48	30	P	80	50	p	112	70
◄	17	11	1	49	31	Q	81	51	q	113	71
↕	18	12	2	50	32	R	82	52	r	114	72
‼	19	13	3	51	33	S	83	53	s	115	73
¶	20	14	4	52	34	T	84	54	t	116	74
§	21	15	5	53	35	U	85	55	u	117	75
▬	22	16	6	54	36	V	86	56	v	118	76
↨	23	17	7	55	37	W	87	57	w	119	77
↑	24	18	8	56	38	X	88	58	x	120	78
↓	25	19	9	57	39	Y	89	59	y	121	79
→	26	1A	:	58	3A	Z	90	5A	z	122	7A
←	27	1B	;	59	3B	[	91	5B	{	123	7B
∟	28	1C	<	60	3C	\	92	5C	|	124	7C
↔	29	1D	=	61	3D	]	93	5D	}	125	7D
▲	30	1E	>	62	3E	^	94	5E	~	126	7E
▼	31	1F	?	63	3F	_	95	5F	⌂	127	7F

Figure G-1. *The ASCII standard character set.*

The IBM Extended Character Set

Figure G-2 shows the IBM extended character set (codes 128 through 255).

ASCII	Dec	Hex	ASCII	Dec	Hex	ASCII	Dec	Hex	ASCII	Dec	Hex
Ç	128	80	á	160	A0	└	192	C0	α	224	E0
ü	129	81	í	161	A1	┴	193	C1	β	225	E1
é	130	82	ó	162	A2	┬	194	C2	Γ	226	E2
â	131	83	ú	163	A3	├	195	C3	π	227	E3
ä	132	84	ñ	164	A4	─	196	C4	Σ	228	E4
à	133	85	Ñ	165	A5	┼	197	C5	σ	229	E5
å	134	86	ª	166	A6	╞	198	C6	µ	230	E6
ç	135	87	º	167	A7	╟	199	C7	τ	231	E7
ê	136	88	¿	168	A8	╚	200	C8	Φ	232	E8
ë	137	89	⌐	169	A9	╔	201	C9	Θ	233	E9
è	138	8A	¬	170	AA	╩	202	CA	Ω	234	EA
ï	139	8B	½	171	AB	╦	203	CB	δ	235	EB
î	140	8C	¼	172	AC	╠	204	CC	∞	236	EC
ì	141	8D	¡	173	AD	═	205	CD	φ	237	ED
Ä	142	8E	«	174	AE	╬	206	CE	ε	238	EE
Å	143	8F	»	175	AF	╧	207	CF	∩	239	EF
É	144	90	░	176	B0	╨	208	D0	≡	240	F0
æ	145	91	▒	177	B1	╤	209	D1	±	241	F1
Æ	146	92	▓	178	B2	╥	210	D2	≥	242	F2
ô	147	93	│	179	B3	╙	211	D3	≤	243	F3
ö	148	94	┤	180	B4	╘	212	D4	⌠	244	F4
ò	149	95	╡	181	B5	╒	213	D5	⌡	245	F5
û	150	96	╢	182	B6	╓	214	D6	÷	246	F6
ù	151	97	╖	183	B7	╫	215	D7	≈	247	F7
ÿ	152	98	╕	184	B8	╪	216	D8	°	248	F8
Ö	153	99	╣	185	B9	┘	217	D9	∙	249	F9
Ü	154	9A	║	186	BA	┌	218	DA	·	250	FA
¢	155	9B	╗	187	BB	█	219	DB	√	251	FB
£	156	9C	╝	188	BC	▄	220	DC	η	252	FC
¥	157	9D	╜	189	BD	▌	221	DD	²	253	FD
₧	158	9E	╛	190	BE	▐	222	DE	∙	254	FE
ƒ	159	9F	┐	191	BF	▀	223	DF		255	FF

Figure G-2. *The IBM extended character set.*

Line-drawing Characters

Figure G-3 shows the four sets of line-drawing characters in the IBM extended character set.

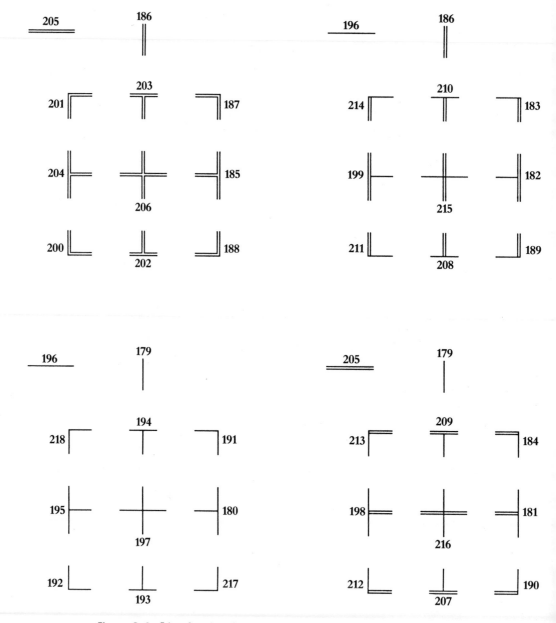

Figure G-3. *Line-drawing characters in the extended character set.*

USING THE TYPE STATEMENT

The remaining sections list the following:

- The functions of the ASCII control characters and the extended-keyboard-scan codes when you use them with the TYPE statement

- The key sequences that can't be simulated by using the TYPE statement

NOTE: The output characteristics listed for particular key functions are for mouse menus running at the MS-DOS level. Therefore, standard applications might not interpret all keyboard operations in the same way. Applications that reprogram or directly access the keyboard or applications that bypass the MS-DOS system facilities for keyboard input might not function correctly with mouse menus.

Using ASCII Control Characters with the TYPE Statement

The following table lists the function of each ASCII control character when you use it with the TYPE statement:

ASCII Code	Key Equivalent	ASCII Code	Key Equivalent
0	none	16	Ctrl-P
1	Ctrl-A	17	Ctrl-Q
2	Ctrl-B	18	Ctrl-R
3	Ctrl-C	19	Ctrl-S
4	Ctrl-D	20	Ctrl-T
5	Ctrl-E	21	Ctrl-U
6	Ctrl-F	22	Ctrl-V
7	Ctrl-G	23	Ctrl-W
8	Backspace	24	Ctrl-X
9	Tab	25	Ctrl-Y
10	Line Feed	26	Ctrl-Z
11	Ctrl-K	27	Esc
12	Ctrl-L	28	Ctrl-\
13	Enter/Return	29	Ctrl-]
14	Ctrl-N	30	Ctrl-^
15	Ctrl-O	31	Ctrl-_

Using Extended-Keyboard-Scan Codes with the TYPE Statement

Extended-keyboard-scan codes have two components: a character code (which is always 0) and a scan code (for example, 0,75). The following tables list the scan codes you can use with the TYPE statement and the character code 0 to simulate specific keys. (You can't use standard or extended ASCII characters as extended-keyboard-scan codes.)

Simulating Direction and Editing Keys

The following table lists the scan codes you can use with the TYPE statement to simulate direction and editing keys:

Keys	*Scan Code*
Ctrl-End	117
Ctrl-Home	119
Ctrl-left-arrow key	115
Ctrl-PgDn	118
Ctrl-PgUp	132
Ctrl-PrtSc	114
Ctrl-right-arrow key	116
Delete	83
End	79
Down-arrow key	80
Home	71
Insert	82
Left-arrow key	75
PgDn	81
PgUp	73
Right-arrow key	77
Shift-Tab	15
Up-arrow key	72

NOTE: Your computer might offer additional codes. Refer to the technical documentation for your particular computer.

Simulating Function Keys and Set Key Combinations

The following table lists the scan codes you can use with the TYPE statement to simulate the function keys and set key combinations:

Keys	Scan Code	Keys	Scan Code
F1	59	Alt-0	129
F2	60	Alt-1	120
F3	61	Alt-2	121
F4	62	Alt-3	122
F5	63	Alt-4	123
F6	64	Alt-5	124
F7	65	Alt-6	125
F8	66	Alt-7	126
F9	67	Alt-8	127
F10	68	Alt-9	128
Shift-F1 (F11)	84	Alt--	130
Shift-F2 (F12)	85	Alt-=	131
Shift-F3 (F13)	86	Alt-A	30
Shift-F4 (F14)	87	Alt-B	48
Shift-F5 (F15)	88	Alt-C	46
Shift-F6 (F16)	89	Alt-D	32
Shift-F7 (F17)	90	Alt-E	18
Shift-F8 (F18)	91	Alt-F	33
Shift-F9 (F19)	92	Alt-G	34
Shift-F10 (F20)	93	Alt-H	35
Ctrl-F1 (F21)	94	Alt-I	23
Ctrl-F2 (F22)	95	Alt-J	36
Ctrl-F3 (F23)	96	Alt-K	37
Ctrl-F4 (F24)	97	Alt-L	38
Ctrl-F5 (F25)	98	Alt-M	50
Ctrl-F6 (F26)	99	Alt-N	49
Ctrl-F7 (F27)	100	Alt-O	24
Ctrl-F8 (F28)	101	Alt-P	25
Ctrl-F9 (F29)	102	Alt-Q	16
Ctrl-F10 (F30)	103	Alt-R	19
Alt-F1 (F31)	104	Alt-S	31
Alt-F2 (F32)	105	Alt-T	20
Alt-F3 (F33)	106	Alt-U	22
Alt-F4 (F34)	107	Alt-V	47
Alt-F5 (F35)	108	Alt-W	17
Alt-F6 (F36)	109	Alt-X	45
Alt-F7 (F37)	110	Alt-Y	21
Alt-F8 (F38)	111	Alt-Z	44
Alt-F9 (F39)	112		
Alt-F10 (F40)	113		

Index

Special Characters

The manuscript for this book was prepared and submitted to Microsoft Press in electronic form. Text files were processed and formatted using Microsoft Word.

Cover design by Greg Hickman
Cover photography by Ed Lowe
Interior text design by Darcie S. Furlan
Principal typography by Lisa G. Iversen

Text composition by Microsoft Press in New Baskerville with display in Avant Garde Demi, using the Magna composition system and the Linotronic 300 laser imagesetter.